WEBSTER'S
BOOK OF
QUOTATIONS

WEBSTER'S
BOOK OF
QUOTATIONS

PMC Publishing Company, Inc.

ISBN: 1-881275-17-5

ABILITY

There may be luck in getting a good job
—but there's no luck in keeping it.
Jonathan Ogden Armour

The winds and the waves are always on
the side of the ablest navigators.
Edward Gibbon

Faith in the ability of a leader is of slight
service unless it be united with faith in
his justice.
George Washington Goethals

There is something that is much more
scarce, something finer far, something
rarer than ability. It is the ability to recognize ability.
Elbert Green Hubbard

A few highly endowed men will rescue
the world for centuries to come.
John Henry Newman

Ability hits the mark where presumption overshoots and diffidence falls
short.
Nicholas of Cusa

Without the assistance of natural capacity,
rules and precepts are of no efficacy.
Quintilian

The ability to deal with people is as pur-
chasable a commodity as sugar or cof-
fee. And I pay more for that ability than
for any other under the sun.
John Davison Rockefeller

A dwarf is small, even if he stands on a
mountain; a colossus keeps his height,
even if he stands in a well.
Seneca

As long as a man imagines that he
cannot do a certain tiding, so long . . . is
it impossible for him to do it.
Baruch (Benedict) Spinoza

A man likes his wife to be just clever
enough to comprehend his cleverness,
and just stupid enough to admire it.
Israel Zangwill

See also: **Action, Character, Genius,
Power, Strength**

ABORTION

A woman who intentionally destroys a
fetus is guilty of murder. And we do not
even talk about the fine distinction as to
its being completely formed or un-
formed.
Basil the Great

It is a capital crime to destroy an embryo
in the womb.
Ishmael

Mature women, as mature human beings with all the respect and dignity to
be accorded mature human beings,
should have the right to decide whether
or not they carry a specific pregnancy to
term.
Harold Rosen

See also: **Birth Control, Mother**

ABSENCE

Absence makes the heart grow fonder:
Isle of Beauty, fare thee well!
Thomas Haynes Bayly

Wives in their husbands' absences grow
subtler, and daughters sometimes run
off with the butler.
George Gordon Byron (Lord Byron)

The absent are never without fault. Nor the present without excuse.

Benjamin Franklin

When a man is out of sight, it is not too long before he is out of mind.

Thomas à Kempis

Absence lessens weak and increases violent passions, as wind extinguishes tapers and lights up a fire.

Duc François de La Rochefoucauld

The absent are like children, helpless to defend themselves.

Charles Reade

The joy of meeting pays the pangs of absence; else who could bear it?

Nicholas Rowe

See also: **Farewell, Loneliness, Memory**

ABSOLUTION

The sunshine dreaming upon Salmon's height
Is not so sweet and white
As the most heretofore sin-spotted Soul
That darts to its delight
Straight from the absolution of a faithful fight.

Coventry Kersey Dighton Patmore

He's half absolv'd who has confess'd.

Matthew Prior

Absolve the sins of your people, we beseech you, O Lord, and may we be delivered by your goodness from the bonds of our sins which, in our weakness, we have committed.

Roman Missal

See also: **Clemency, Forgiveness**

ABSTINENCE

Complete abstinence is easier than perfect moderation.

Augustine of Hippo

It is continued temperance which sustains the body for the longest period of time, and which most surely preserves it free from sickness.

Wilhelm von Humboldt

To set the mind above the appetites is the end of abstinence, which if not a virtue, is the groundwork of a virtue.

Samuel Johnson

Always rise from the table with an appetite, and you will never sit down without one.

William Penn

See also: **Moderation**

ABSURDITY

The privilege of absurdity; to which no living creature is subject but man only.

Thomas Hobbes

There are people whose whole merit consists in speaking and acting absurdly, though with good results, and who would spoil all if they changed their conduct.

Duc François de La Rochefoucauld

To pardon those absurdities in ourselves which we condemn in others, is neither better nor worse than to be more willing to be fools ourselves than to have others so.

Alexander Pope

See also: **Ridicule, Sarcasm**

ABUSE

It is the wit and policy of sin to hate those we have abused.
Sir William Davenant

Abuse of any one generally shows that he has marked traits of character. The stupid and indifferent are passed by in silence.
Tryon Edwards

The difference between coarse and refined abuse is the difference between being bruised by a club and wounded by a poisoned arrow.
Samuel Johnson

Almost nobody is worth the hurt one causes oneself when one wounds him.
Jean Rostand

There are none more abusive to others than they that lie most open to it themselves; but the humor goes round, and he that laughs at me today will have somebody to laugh at him tomorrow.
Seneca

See also: ***Cruelty, Injury, Insult, Slander***

ACCENT

I once knew a fellow who spoke a dialect with an accent.
Irvin Shrewsbury Cobb

The twentieth century is only the nineteenth speaking with a slightly American accent.
Philip Guedalla

Accent is the soul of language; it gives to it both feeling and truth.
Jean Jacques Rousseau

See also: ***Language, Speech, Talking***

ACCIDENT

Accident counts for much in companionship as in marriage.
Henry Brooks Adams

What men call accident is the doing of God's providence.
Gamaliel Bailey

At first laying down, as a fact fundamental, That nothing with God can be accidental.
Henry Wadsworth Longfellow

What reason, like the careful ant, draws laboriously together, the wind of accident sometimes collects in a moment.
Johann Christoph Friedrich von Schiller

See also: ***Chance, Fate, Fortune, Luck***

ACCURACY

Accuracy of statement is one of the first elements of truth; inaccuracy is a near kin to falsehood.
Tryon Edwards

Insanity is often the logic of an accurate mind overtaxed.
Oliver Wendell Holmes

In all pointed sentences, some degree of accuracy must be sacrificed to conciseness.
Samuel Johnson

Accuracy is the twin brother of honesty; inaccuracy, of dishonesty.
Charles Simmons

See also: ***Facts, Science***

ACHIEVEMENT

Every man who is high up loves to think
that he has done it all himself; and the
wife smiles, and lets it go at that.
Sir James Matthew Barrie

Death comes to all
But great achievements build a monument
Which shall endure until the sun grows cold.
Georg Fabricius

The mode by which the inevitable comes
to pass is effort.
Oliver Wendell Holmes

About all some men accomplish in life is
to send a son to Harvard.
Edgar Watson Howe

Nothing will ever be attempted if all
possible objections must be first overcome.
Samuel Johnson

I feel that the greatest reward for doing
is the opportunity to do more.
Jonas Edward Salk

*See Also: Aim, Ambition, Labor,
        Purpose, Success, Work*

ACQUAINTANCE

It is a good discretion not to make too
much of any man at the first; because
one cannot hold out that proportion.
Francis Bacon

If a man does not make new acquain-
tances as he advances through life, he
will soon find himself left alone; one
should keep his friendships in constant
repair.
Samuel Johnson

Never say you know a man till you have
divided an inheritance with him.
Johann Kaspar Lavater

The wisest man I have ever known once
said to me: "Nine out of every ten people improve on acquaintance"; and I
have found his words true.
Frank Arthur Swinnerton

See also: Familiarity, Friendship

ACTION

Good thoughts, though God accept
them, yet toward men are little better
than good dreams except they be put in
action.
Francis Bacon

What man knows should find expression in what he does. The chief value of
superior knowledge is that it leads to a
performing manhood.
Christian Nestell Bovee

A good action is never lost; it is a treasure laid up and guarded for the doer's
need.
Pedro Calderón de la Barca

The end of man is action, and not
thought, though it be of the noblest.
Thomas Carlyle

Nothing ever happens but once in this
world. What I do now I do once for all.
It is over and gone, with all its eternity
of solemn meaning.
Thomas Carlyle

Our grand business is not to see what
lies dimly at a distance, but to do what
lies clearly at hand.
Thomas Carlyle

Every action of our lives touches on
some chord that will vibrate in eternity.
Edwin Hubbel Chapin

We should not be so taken up in the search for truth, as to neglect the needful duties of active life; for it is only action that gives a true value and commendation to virtue.

Cicero

Deliberate with caution, but act with decision; and yield with graciousness, or oppose with firmness.

Charles Caleb Colton

Action may not always bring happiness; but there is no happiness without action.

Benjamin Disraeli

Every noble activity makes room for itself.

Ralph Waldo Emerson

It is by acts and not by ideas that people live.

Anatole France

Mark this well, you proud men of action! you are, after all nothing but unconscious instruments of the men of thought.

Heinrich Heine

See also: **Deed, Labor, Work**

ADAPTABILITY

If you are at Rome live in the Roman style; if you are elsewhere live as they live elsewhere.

Ambrose of Milan

One learns to itch where one can scratch.
Ernest Bramah (Smith)

Adaptability is not imitation. It means power of resistance and assimilation.
Mohandas Karamchand (Mahatma) Gandhi

See also: **Adjustment, Custom**

ADJUSTMENT

Every new adjustment is a crisis in self-esteem.

Eric Hoffer

Adjustment as an educational goal is a pricked balloon. To adjust to the twentieth century is to come to terms with madness. What is needed is the adjustment of our environment to ourselves, or rather to what we would like ourselves to be.

Max Rafferty

See also: **Adaptability, Conformity**

ADVANCEMENT

I have found some of the best reasons I ever had for remaining at the bottom simply by looking at the men at the top.
Frank Moore Colby

The man who makes an appearance in the business world, the man who creates personal interest, is the man who gets ahead. Be liked and you will never want.

Arthur Miller

Speak softly and carry a big stick; you will go far.

Theodore Roosevelt

See also: **Ambition, Improvement, Progress, Reform, Success, Work**

ADVERSITY

No man is more unhappy than the one who is never in adversity; the greatest affliction of life is never to be afflicted.

Anonymous

Heaven often smites in mercy, even when the blow is severest.

Joanna Baillie

Adversity is the first path to truth.

George Gordon Byron (Lord Byron)

Friendship, of itself a holy tie,
Is made more sacred by adversity.

John Dryden

Adversity is the trial of principle. Without it a man hardly knows whether he is honest or not.

Henry Fielding

Prosperity is a great teacher; adversity is a greater. Possession pampers the mind; privation trains and strengthens it.

William Hazlitt

Adversity has the effect of eliciting talents which in prosperous circumstances would have lain dormant.

Horace

Adversity has ever been considered the state in which a man most easily becomes acquainted with himself, then especially, being free from flatterers.

Samuel Johnson

Prosperity is too apt to prevent us from examining our conduct; but adversity leads us to think properly of our state, and so is most beneficial to us.

Samuel Johnson

The flower that follows the sun does so even in cloudy days.

Robert Leighton

Who hath not known ill fortune, never knew himself, or his own virtue.

David Mallet

Prosperity is no just scale; adversity is the only balance to weigh friends.

Plutarch

See also: **Affliction, Calamity, Difficulty, Disappointment, Failure, Sorrow, Suffering, Trouble**

ADVERTISING

Great designers seldom make great advertising men, because they get overcome by the beauty of the picture—and forget that merchandise must be sold.

James Randolph Adams

The business that considers itself immune to the necessity for advertising sooner or later finds itself immune to business.

Derby Brown

Advertising promotes that divine discontent which makes people strive to improve their economic status.

Ralph Starr Butler

Sanely applied advertising could remake the world.

Stuart Chase

The advertising man is a liaison between the products of business and the mind of the nation. He must know both before he can serve either.

Glenn Frank

Honesty in advertising and selling will do the job, and this will be found to be the best policy when science has replaced guesswork in gauging consumer demands.

Elizabeth Hawes

The advertisement is one of the most interesting and difficult of modern literary forms.

Aldous Leonard Huxley

Advertising is the key to world prosperity; without it today modern business would be paralyzed.

Julius Klein

Advertising may be described as the science of arresting the human intelligence long enough to get money from it.

Stephen Butler Leacock

See also: **Business**

ADVICE

When a man has been guilty of any vice of folly, the best atonement he can make for it is to warn others not to fall into the like.

Joseph Addison

It is easy when we are in prosperity to give advice to the afflicted.

Aeschylus

We give advice by the bucket, but take it by the grain.

William Rounseville Alger

Never give advice in a crowd.

Arabian Proverb

The worst men often give the best advice.

Philip James Bailey

Let no man value at a little price a virtuous woman's counsel.

George Chapman

Advice is like snow; the softer it falls the longer it dwells upon, and the deeper it sinks into the mind.

Samuel Taylor Coleridge

To profit from good advice requires more wisdom than to give it.

John Churton Collins

Giving advice is sometimes only showing our wisdom at the expense of another.

Anthony Ashley Cooper (Lord Shaftesbury)

An empty stomach is not a good political adviser.

Albert Einstein

They that will not be counselled, cannot be helped. If you do not hear reason she will rap you on the knuckles.

Benjamin Franklin

Good counsels observed are chains of grace.

Thomas Fuller

To accept good advice is but to increase one's own ability.

Johann Wolfgang von Goethe

Unasked advice is a trespass on sacred privacy.

Henry Stanley Haskins

A good scare is worth more to a man than good advice.

Edgar Watson (Ed) Howe

A bad cold wouldn't be so annoying if it weren't for the advice of our friends.

Frank McKinney (Kin) Hubbard

Advice is seldom welcome. Those who need it most, like it least.

Samuel Johnson

See also: **Guidance, Instruction**

AFFECTION

Of all earthly music that which reaches farthest into heaven is the beating of a truly loving heart.

Henry Ward Beecher

Our affections are our life. We live by them; they supply our warmth.

William Ellery Channing

The affections are like lightning: you cannot tell where they will strike till they have fallen.

Jean Baptiste Henri Lacordaire

See also: **Esteem, Friendship, Kiss, Love**

AFFLICTION

As threshing separates the chaff, so does affliction purify virtue.

Richard Eugene Burton

I have learned more of experimental religion since my little boy died than in all my life before.

Horace Bushnell

The gem cannot be polished without friction, nor man perfected without trials.

Chinese Proverb

It is not until we have passed through the furnace that we are made to know how much dross there is in our composition.

Charles Caleb Colton

I thank God for my handicaps, for through them, I have found myself, my work and my God.

Helen Adams Keller

It may serve as a comfort to us, in all our calamities and afflictions, that he that loses anything and gets wisdom by it is a gainer by the loss.

Sir Roger L'Estrange

See also: **Adversity, Calamity, Disease, Suffering, Trouble**

AGE

Age acquires no value save through thought and discipline.

James Truslow Adams

Age—that period of life in which we compound for the vices that we still cherish by reviling those that we no longer have the enterprise to commit.

Ambrose Gwinnett Bierce

Eclipses of the sun and moon happen far too often to suit me.

Edward Bluestone

Old age has deformities enough of its own. It should never add to them the deformity of vice.

Cato the Younger

Age does not depend upon years, but upon temperament and health. Some men are born old, and some never grow so.

Tryon Edwards

I don't believe one grows older. I think that what happens early on in life is that at a certain age one stands still and stagnates.

Thomas Stearns Eliot

Age that lessens the enjoyment of life, increases our desire of living.

Oliver Goldsmith

Age is rarely despised but when it is contemptible.

Samuel Johnson

Cautious age suspects the flattering form, and only credits what experience tells.

Samuel Johnson

At sixty a man has passed most of the reefs and whirlpools. Excepting only death, he has no enemies left to meet....... That man has awakened to a new youth....... Ergo, he is young.

George Benjamin Luks

Years do not make sages; they only make old men.

Anne Sophie Swetchine

See also: *Age, Antiquity*

AGGRESSION

The truth is often a terrible weapon of aggression. It is possible to lie, and even to murder, with the truth.

Alfred Adler

It is the habit of every aggressor notion to claim that it is acting on the defensive.

Jawaharlal Nehru

See also: *Anger, Communism, Enemy, War*

AGITATION

The purely agitational attitude is not good enough for a detailed consideration of a subject.

Jawaharlal Nehru

Agitation is the marshalling of the conscience of a nation to mould its laws.

Sir Robert Peel

Agitation is the method that plants the school by the side of the ballot-box.

Wendell Phillips

Agitation prevents rebellion, keeps the peace, and secures progress. Every step she gains is gained forever. Muskets are the weapons of animals. Agitation is the atmosphere of the brains.

Wendell Phillips

See also; *Argument, Discussion, Reform*

AGNOSTICISM

Agnosticism is the philosophical, ethical, and religious dry-rot of the modern world.

Francis Ellingwood Abbot

The mystery of the beginning of all things is insoluble by us; and I for one must be content to remain an agnostic.

Charles Robert Darwin

It is wrong for a man to say that he is certain of the objective truth of any proposition unless he can produce evidence which logically justifies that certainty. This is what agnosticism asserts.

Thomas Henry Huxley

I do not see much difference between avowing that there is no God, and implying that nothing definite can for certain be known about Hun.

John Henry Newman

See also: *Atheism, God, Unbelief*

AGREEMENT

I do not want people to be very agreeable, as it saves me the trouble of liking them a great deal.

Jane Austen

He that complies against his will
Is of his own opinion still.

Samuel Butler

"My idea of an agreeable person," said
Hugo Bohun, "is a person who agrees
with me."

Benjamin Disraeli

We hardly find any persons of good
sense save those who agree with us.

Duc François de La Rochefoucauld

When people agree with me I always
feel that I must be wrong.

Oscar Wilde

See also: **Unity**

AIM

Have a purpose in life, and having it,
throw into your work such strength of
mind and muscle as God has given you.

Thomas Carlyle

Resolve to live with all my might while I
do live, and as I shall wish I had done
ten thousand ages hence.

Jonathan Edwards

High aims form high characters, and
great objects bring out great minds.

Tryon Edwards

Aim at the sun, and you may not reach
it; but your arrow will fly far higher
than if aimed at an object on a level with
yourself.

Joel Hawes

What are the aims which at the same
time duties?—they are the perfecting of
ourselves, and the happiness of others.

Immanuel Kant

In great attempts it is glorious even to
fail.

Dionysius Cassius Longinus

Not failure, but low aim, is crime.

James Russell Lowell

See also: **Desire, Ideal, Objective,
Purpose**

AMBIGUITY

Clearly spoken, Mr. Fogg; you explain
English by Greek.

Benjamin Franklin

I fear explanations explanatory of things
explained.

Abraham Lincoln

That must be wonderful; I have no idea
of what it means.

Molière (Jean Baptiste Poquelin)

See also: **Accuracy, Certainty, Obscurity**

AMBITION

He who surpasses or subdues mankind,
must look down on the hate of those
below.

George Gordon Byron (Lord Byron)

The noblest spirit is most strongly at-
tracted by the love of glory.

Cicero

It is attempting to reach the top at a
single leap, that so much misery is
caused in the world.

William Cobbett

Ambition is the avarice of power; and
happiness herself is soon sacrificed to
that very lust of dominion which was
first encouraged only as the best means
of obtaining it.

Charles Caleb Colton

All ambitions are lawful except those which climb upward on the miseries or credulities of mankind.

> *Joseph Conrad*

Ambition is like love, impatient both of delays and rivals.

> *Sir John Denham*

Ambition is the germ from which all growth of nobleness proceeds.

> *Thomas Dunn English*

A strategy that uses up its strength in the defensive, gradually paralyzes a people's initiative and activity.

> *Joseph Paul Goebbels*

Ambition is not a weakness unless it be disproportioned to the capacity. To have more ambition than ability is to be at once weak and unhappy.

> *George Stillman Hillard*

Nothing is too high for the daring of mortals: we storm heaven itself in our folly.

> *Horace*

Some folks can look so busy doing nothin' that they seem indispensable.

> *Frank McKinney (Kin) Hubbard*

Where ambition can cover its enterprises, even to the person himself, under the appearance of principle, it is the most incurable and inflexible of passions.

> *David Hume*

Ambition has one heel nailed in well, though she stretch her fingers to touch the heavens.

> *William Lilly*

Most people would succeed in small things if they were not troubled by great ambitions.

> *Henry Wadsworth Longfellow*

Ambition is not a vice of little people.

> *Michel Eyquem de Montaigne*

See also: *Aim, Ideal, Purpose, Success, Work*

AMERICA

If there is anything this nation has to give the world beyond its technological and organizational skill, it is surely that sense of expectancy which has possessed us and which, up to this time, we have never completely lost.

> *James Donald Adams*

We can prate as we like about the idealism of America, but it is only money success which really counts.

> *James Truslow Adams*

America, thou half-brother of the world; With something good and bad of every land.

> *Philip James Bailey*

America is the country where you buy a lifetime supply of aspirin for one dollar and use it up in two weeks.

> *John Barrymore*

America has never forgotten and will never forget—the nobler things that brought her into being and that light her path—the path that was entered upon only one hundred and fifty years ago. . . . How young she is! It will be centuries before she will adopt that maturity of custom—the clothing of the grave—that some people believe she is already fitted for.

> *Bernard Mannes Baruch*

America has been the intellectual battle-ground of the nations.

Randolph Silliman Bourne

America has believed that in differentiation, not in uniformity, lies the path of progress. It acted on this belief; it has advanced human happiness, and it has prospered.

Louis Dembitz Brandeis

Half the misunderstandings between Britain and America are due to the fact that neither will regard the other as what it is—in an important sense of the word—a foreign country. Each thinks of the other as a part of itself which has somehow gone off the lines. . . . What would have been pardonable and even commendable in a foreigner is blameworthy in a cousin.

Sir John Buchan

Let America realize that self-scrutiny is not treason, self-examination is not disloyalty.

Richard James Cushing

This Administration believes that we must not and need not tolerate a boom-and-bust America. We believe that America's prosperity does not and need not depend upon war or the preparation for war.

Dwight David Eisenhower

America is another name for opportunity. Our whole history appears like a last effort of divine Providence in behalf of the human race.

Ralph Waldo Emerson

The source of a nation's strength is its domestic life, and if America has a service to perform in the world it is in large part the service of its own example.

James William Fulbright

If all Europe were to become a prison, America would still present a loop-hole of escape; and, God be praised! that loop-hole is larger than the dungeon itself.

Heinrich Heine

America—a place where the people have the right to complain about the lack of freedom.

Louis Hirsch

The American system of rugged individualism.

Herbert Clark Hoover

A great social and economic experiment, noble in motive and far-reaching in purpose.

Herbert Clark Hoover

Let America be America again,
Let it be the dream it used to be.

(James) Langston Hughes

I am certain that, however great the hardships and the trials which loom ahead, our America will endure and the cause of human freedom will triumph.

Cordell Hull

America has meant to the world a land in which the common man who means well and is willing to do his part has access to all the necessary means of a good life.

Alvin Saunders Johnson

If there is one word that describes our form of society in America, it may be the word-voluntary.

Lyndon Baines Johnson

America is a tune. It must be sung together.

Gerald Stanley Lee

Intellectually I know that America is no better than any other country; emotionally I know she is better than every country.

Sinclair Lewis

AMIABILITY

To be amiable is most certainly a duty, but it is not to be exercised at the expense of any virtue. He who seeks to do the amiable always, can at times be successful only by the sacrifice of his manhood.

William Gilmore Simms

How easy to be amiable in the midst of happiness and success.

Anne Sophie Swetchine

AMUSEMENT

If those who are the enemies of innocent amusements had the direction of the world, they would take away the spring and youth, the former from the year, the latter from human life.

Honoré de Balzac

Amusement to an observing mind is and youth, the former from the year, the study.

Benjamin Disraeli

Dwell not too long upon sports; for as they refresh a man that is weary, so they weary a man that is refreshed.

Thomas Fuller

I am a great friend to public amusements, for they keep people from vice.

Samuel Johnson

Amusement that is excessive and followed only for its own sake, allures and deceives us, and leads us down imperceptibly in thoughtlessness to the grave.

Blaise Pascal

The mind ought sometimes to be diverted, that it may return the better to thinking.

Phaedrus

All amusements to which virtuous women are not admitted, are, rely upon it, deleterious in their nature.

William Makepeace Thackeray

See also: **Pleasure**

ANARCHY

Anarchy is hatred of human authority; atheism of divine authority—two sides of the same whole.

James Macpherson

When the rich assemble to concern themselves with the business of the poor it is called charity. When the poor assemble to concern themselves with the business of the rich it is called anarchy.

Paul Richard

There lives no greater fiend than Anarchy; She ruins states, turns houses out of doors, Breaks up in rout the embattled soldiery.

Sophocles

See also: **Communism, Crime, Freedom, Revolution, Riot, Violence**

ANCESTRY

Honorable descent is, in all nations, greatly esteemed. It is to be expected that the children of men of worth will be like the progenitors; for nobility is the virtue of a family.

Aristotle

Some decent, regulated pre-eminence, some preference given to birth, is neither unnatural nor unjust nor impolitic.

Edmund Burke

We inherit nothing truly, but what our actions make us worthy of.

George Chapman

It is a shame for a man to desire honor only because of his noble progenitors, and not to deserve it by his own virtue.

John Chrysostom

It is of no consequence of what parents a man is born, so he be a man of merit.

Horace

It is the highest of earthly honors to be descended from the great and good. They alone cry out against a noble ancestry who have none of their own.

Ben (Benjamin) Jonson

He that can only boast of a distinguished lineage, boast of that which does not belong to himself; but he that lives worthily of it is always held in the highest honor.

Junius

It is fortunate to come of distinguished ancestry. It is not less so to be such that people do not care to inquire whether you are of high descent or not.

Jean de La Bruyère

Some men by ancestry are only the shadow of a mighty name.

Lucan

It would be more honorable to our distinguished ancestors to praise them in words less, but in deeds to imitate them more.

Horace Mann

Blood will tell but often it tells too much.

Donald Robert Perry (Don) Marquis

Birth is nothing where virtue is not.

Molière (Jean Baptiste Poquelin)

Everyone has ancestors and it is only a question of going back far enough to find a good one.

Howard Kenneth Nixon

The man who has nothing to boast of but his illustrious ancestry, is like the potato—the best part under ground.

Sir Thomas Overbury

Nothing is more disgraceful than for a man who is nothing, to hold himself honored on account of his forefathers; and yet hereditary honors are a noble and splendid treasure to descendants.

Plato

Remember, remember always, that all of us, and you and I especially, are descended from immigrants and revolutionists.

Franklin Delano Roosevelt

What can we see in the longest kingly line in Europe, save that it runs back to a successful soldier?

Sir Walter Scott

The origin of all mankind was the same: it is only a clear and good conscience that makes a man noble, for that is derived from heaven itself.

Seneca

See also: **Birth, Parent**

ANGER

Men often make up in wrath what they want in reason.

William Rounseville Alger

I was angry with my friend;
I told my wrath, my wrath did end.
I was angry with my foe;
I told it not, my wrath did grow.

William Blake

Violence in the voice is often only the death rattle of reason in the throat.

John Frederick Boyes

Life appears to me too short to be spent in nursing animosity or registering wrong.

Charlotte Brontë

An angry man opens his mouth and closes his eyes.

Cato the Elder

The fire you kindle for your enemy often burns yourself more than him.

Chinese Proverb

When anger rises, think of the consequences.

Confucius

Beware of the fury of a patient man.

John Dryden

To rule one's anger is well; to prevent it is still better.

Tryon Edwards

Anger and intolerance are the twin enemies of correct understanding.

Mohandas Karamchand (Mahatma) Gandhi

Anger is a sort of madness and the noblest causes have been damaged by advocates affected with temporary lunacy.

Mohandas Karamchand (Mahatma) Gandhi

When angry, count ten before you speak; if very angry, count a hundred.

Thomas Jefferson

The flame of anger, bright and brief, sharpens the barb of love.

Walter Savage Landor

Anger ventilated often hurries towards forgiveness; anger concealed often hardens into revenge.

Edward G. Bulwer-Lytton (Baron Lytton)

Anger is as a stone cast into a wasp's nest.

Malabar Proverb

Consider how much more you often suffer from your anger and grief, than from those very things for which you are angry and grieved.

Marcus Aurelius

The worst tempered people I've ever met were people who knew they were wrong.

Wilson Mizner

All anger is not sinful, because some degree of it, and on some occasions, is inevitable. But it becomes sinful and contradicts the rule of Scripture when it is conceived upon slight and inadequate provocation, and when it continues long.

William Paley

Temperate anger well becomes the wise.

Philemon

He best keeps from anger who remembers that God is always looking upon him.

Plato

To be angry is to revenge the faults of others on ourselves.

Alexander Pope

An angry man is again angry with himself when be returns to reason.
Pubilius Syrus

Anger begins in folly, and ends in repentance.
Pythagoras

See also: **Aggression, Dissent, Passion, Quarrel, Rage, Resentment**

ANSWER

What is truth? said jesting Pilate; and would not stay for an answer.
Francis Bacon

Examinations are formidable even to the best prepared, for the greatest fool may ask more than the wisest man can answer.
Charles Caleb Colton

Ah, what a dusty answer gets the soul
When hot for certainties in this our life
George Meredith

She who ne'er answers till a husband cools,
Or if she rules him, never shows she rules.
Alexander Pope

An answer is invariably the parent of a great family of new questions.
John Ernst Steinbeck

See also: **Argument, Knowledge, Question**

ANTAGONISM

He that wrestles with us strengthens our nerves, and sharpens our skill. Our antagonist is our helper.
Edmund Burke

In a world which exists by the balance of Antagonism, the respective merit of the Conservator or the Innovator must ever remain debatable.
Thomas Carlyle

In proportion as the antagonism between classes within the nation vanishes, the hostility of one nation to another will come to an end.
Karl Marx

See also: **Aggression, Anger, Difference**

ANTICIPATION

Draw your Salary before Spending it.
George Ade

Nothing is so good as it seems beforehand.
George Eliot (Mary Ann Evans)

Among so many sad realities we can but ill endure to rob anticipation of its pleasant visions.
Henry Giles

To tremble before anticipated evils, is to bemoan what thou hast never lost.
Johann Wolfgang von Goethe

We part more easily with what we possess than with our expectations of what we hope for: expectation always goes beyond enjoyment.
Henry Home (Lord Kames)

Few enterprises of great labor or hazard would be undertaken if we had not the power of magnifying the advantages we expect from them.
Samuel Johnson

It is worse to apprehend than to suffer.
Jean de La Bruyère

Our desires always disappoint us; for though we meet with something that gives us satisfaction, yet it never thoroughly answers our expectation.

Duc François de La Rochefoucauld

Why need a man forestall his date of grief, and run to meet that he would most avoid?

John Milton

He who foresees calamities, suffers them twice over.

Beilby Porteus

Suffering itself does less afflict the senses than the anticipation of suffering.

Quintilian

We often tremble at an empty terror, yet the false fancy brings a real misery.

Johann Christoph Friedrich von Schiller

Nothing is so wretched or foolish as to anticipate misfortunes. What madness is it to be expecting evil before it comes.

Seneca

It is expectation makes blessings dear. Heaven were not heaven if we knew what it were

Sir John Suckling

See also: **Expectation, Forethought, Hope**
Pursuit

ANTIQUITY

Those old ages are like the landscape that shows best in the purple distance, all verdant and smooth, and bathed in mellow light.

Edwin Hubbel Chapin

Antiquity is enjoyed not by the ancients who lived in the infancy of things, but by us who lived live in their maturity.

Charles Caleb Colton

Those we call the ancients were really new in everything.

Blaise Pascal

Time consecrates and what is gray with age becomes religion.

Johann Christoph Friedrich von Schiller

All things now held to be old were once new. What to-day we hold up by example, will rank hereafter as precedent.

Tacitus

See also: **Age, History, Past, Time,**
Tradition

ANXIETY

Never trouble trouble till trouble troubles you.

Anonymous

Where everything's bad it must be good to know the worst.

Francis Herbert Bradley

Better be despised for too anxious apprehensions, than ruined by too confident security.

Edmund Burke

Anxiety is a word of unbelief or unreasoning dread. We have no right to allow it. Full faith in God puts it to rest.

Horace Bushnell

We have a lot of anxieties, and one cancels out another very often.

Sir Winston Leonard Spencer Churchill

Anxiety is the rust of life, destroying its brightness and weakening its power. A childlike and abiding trust in Providence is its best preventive and remedy.

Tryon Edwards

Do not anticipate trouble, or worry about what may never happen. Keep in the sunlight.

Benjamin Franklin

An undivided heart which worships God alone, and trusts him as it should, is raised above anxiety for earthly wants.

John Cunningham Geikie

If pleasures are greatest in anticipation, just remember that this is also true of trouble.

Elbert Green Hubbard

How much have cost us the evils that never happened!

Thomas Jefferson

Borrow trouble for yourself, if that's your nature, but don't lend it to your neighbors.

Rudyard Kipling

Let us be of good cheer, remembering that the misfortunes hardest to bear are those which never come.

James Russell Lowell

Never meet trouble half-way.

John Ray

See also: Fear, Imagination, Worry

APATHY

The tyranny of a prince in not as dangerous to the common good as the apathy of the citizens in a democracy.

.Charles de Secondat (Baron de Montesquieu)

The long mechanic pacings to and fro,
The set gray life, the apathetic end.

Alfred, Lord Tennyson

APOLOGY

Apologies only account for the evil which they cannot alter.

Benjamin Disraeli

No sensible person ever made an apology.

Ralph Waldo Emerson

Apology is only egotism wrong side out. Nine times out of ten the first thing a man's companion knows of his shortcomings, is from his apology.

Oliver Wendell Holmes

I do not trouble my spirit to vindicate itself . . . , I see the elementary laws never apologize.

Walt (Walter) Whitman

See also: Excuse, Humility, Modesty,
Remorse, Repentance

APPEARANCE

Half the work that is done in this world is to make things appear what they are not.

Elias Root Beadle

Foolish men mistake transitory semblances for eternal fact, and go astray more and more.

Thomas Carlyle

The bosom can ache beneath diamond broaches; and many a blithe heart dances under coarse wool.

Edwin Hubbel Chapin

A graceful presence bespeaks acceptance.

John Collier

You are only what you are when no one is looking.

Robert Chambers (Bob) Edwards

Beware, so long as you live, of judging men by their outward appearance.

Jean de La Fontaine

He who observes the speaker more than the sound of his words, will seldom meet with disappointments.

Johann Kaspar Lavater

You may turn into an archangel, or a criminal—no one will see it. but when a button is missing—everyone sees that.

Erich Maria Remarque

There are no greater wretches in the world than many of those whom people in general take to be happy.

Seneca

The shortest and surest way to live with honor in the world, is to be in reality what we would appear to be.

Socrates

How little do they see what is, who frame their hasty judgments upon that which seems.

Robert Southey

You may judge a flower or a butterfly by its looks, but not a human being.

Sir Rabindranath Tagore

The world is governed more by appearances than by realities, so that it is fully as necessary to seem to know something as to know it.

Daniel Webster

See also: Dress, Face, Fashion, Looks

APPETITE

Good cheer is no hindrance to a good life.

Aristippus

Animals feed; man eats. Only the man of intellect and judgment knows how to eat.

Anthelme Brillat-Savarin

Reason should direct and appetite obey.

Cicero

A well-governed appetite is a great part of liberty.

Seneca

See also: Desire, Eating

APPLAUSE

Praise from the common people is generally false, and rather follows the vain than the virtuous.

Francis Bacon

Applause is the spur of noble minds; the end and aim of weak ones.

Charles Caleb Colton

A slowness to applaud betrays a cold temper or an envious spirit.

Hannah More

Neither human applause nor human censure is to be taken as the test of truth; but either should set us upon testing ourselves.

Richard Whately

See also: Appreciation, Compliment, Fame, Flattery, Praise

APPRECIATION

One of the Godlike things of this world is the veneration done to human worth by the hearts of men.

Thomas Carlyle

Contemporaries appreciate the man rather than the merit; but posterity will regard the merit rather than the man.

Charles Caleb Colton

You will find poetry nowhere unless you bring some with you.

Joseph Joubert

It is with certain good qualities as with the senses; those who have them not can neither appreciate nor comprehend them in others.

Duc François de La Rochefoucauld

He is incapable of a truly good action who finds not a pleasure in contemplating the good actions of others.

Johann Kaspar Lavater

Next to excellence is the appreciation of it.

William Makepeace Thackeray

See also: **Applause, Gratitude, Taste**

ARGUMENT

Wise men argue causes; fools decide them.

Anacharsis

Behind every argument is someone's ignorance.

Louis Dembitz Brandeis

The greatest danger in any argument is that real issues are often clouded by superficial ones, that momentary passions may obscure permanent realities.

Mary Ellen Chase

People generally quarrel because they cannot argue.

Gilbert Keith Chesterton

The first duty of a wise advocate is to convince his opponents that he understands their arguments, and sympathizes with their just feelings.

Samuel Taylor Coleridge

Prejudices are rarely overcome by argument; not being founded in reason they cannot be destroyed by logic.

Tryon Edwards

To bung up a man's eyes ain't the way to enlighten him.

Thomas Chandler Haliburton (Sam Slick)

Be calm in arguing; for fierceness makes error a fault, and truth discourtesy.

George Herbert

The best way I know of to win an argument is to start by being in the right.

Quintin McGarel Hogg (Lord Hailsham)

Debate is the death of conversation.

Emil Ludwig

In order to carry on an argument you must descend to the other man's level.

Peter McArthur

He who establishes his argument by noise and command shows that his reason is weak.

• *Michel Eyquem de Montaigne*

Nothing is more certain than that much of the force as well as grace of arguments, as well as of instructions, depends on their conciseness.

Alexander Pope

In argument similes are like songs in love; they describe much, but prove nothing.

Matthew (Matt) Prior

Clear statement is argument.

William Greenough Thayer Shedd

See also: **Agitation, Answer, Difference, Discussion, Quarrel**

ARROGANCE

The arrogance of age must submit to be taught by youth.

Edmund Burke

When men are most sure and arrogant they are commonly most mistaken, giving views to passion without that proper deliberation which alone can secure them from the grossest absurdities.

David Hume

He despises me, I suppose, because I live in an alley: tell him his soul lives in an alley.

Ben (Benjamin) Jonson

See also: **Boldness, Insult, Intolerance, Pride**

ART

Never judge a work of art by its defects.

Washington Allston

Real art is illumination. . . . It adds stature to life.

(Justin) Brooks Atkinson

The arts—those activities whereby man would clamber from the beasts to fly among the gods.

Bernard Iddings Bell

Art and revolt will die only with the last man.

Albert Camus

A product of the untalented, sold by the unprincipled to the utterly bewildered.

Al Capp (Alfred Gerald Caplin)

Art, like morality, consists in drawing the line somewhere.

Gilbert Keith Chesterton

A work that aspires, however humbly, to the condition of art should carry its justification in every line.

Joseph Conrad

Art, as far as it has the ability, follows nature, as a pupil imitates his master, so that art must be, as it were, a descendant of God.

Dante Alighieri

The object of art is to crystallize emotion into thought, and then fix it in form.

François Alexandre Nicolas Chéri Delsarte

As long as art is the beauty parlor of civilization, neither art nor civilization is secure.

John Dewey

Art is the stored honey of the human soul gathered on wings of misery and travail.

Theodore Dreiser

In sculpture did any one ever call the Apollo a fancy piece; or say of the Laocoön how it might be made different? A masterpiece of art has, to the mind, a fixed place in the chain of being, as much as a plant or a crystal.

Ralph Waldo Emerson

Artists are nearest God. Into their souls he breathes his life, and from their hands it comes in fair, articulate forms to bless the world.

Josiah Gilbert Holland

Art has been caught in the vicious circle which chains the artist to publicity and through it to fashion, both of which are again dependent on commercial interests.

Johan Huizinga

The mission of art is to represent nature; not to imitate her.

William Morris Hunt

Sincerity in art is not an affair of will, of a moral choice between honesty and dishonesty. It is mainly an affair of talent.

Aldous Leonard Huxley

See also: **Beauty, Literature, Music**

ARTIST

An artist cannot speak about his art any more than a plant can discuss horticulture.

Jean Cocteau

There are infinite modes of expression in the world of art, and to insist that only by one road can the artist attain his ends is to limit him.

Sir Jacob Epstein

An artist has more than two eyes, that's a fact.

Thomas Chandler Haliburton

An artist creates form from out of what lie needs; the function compels the form.

Alfred Kazin

However skillful an artist may be, and however perfect his technique, if he unhappily has nothing to tell us, his work is valueless.

Jacques Maritain

The only artist who does not deserve respect is the one who works to please the public, for commercial success or for official success.

Jacques Maritain

The artist is the only man who knows what to do with beauty.

Jean Rostand

An artist must try, scrupulously, to render truth, but have the luck of not being able to do so.

Jean Rostand

A marvelous spectacle to behold in art: supreme skill disinterestedly employed.

Jean Rostand

An artist is a dreamer consenting to dream of the actual world.

George *Santayana*

See also: **Art**

ASSASSINATION

An intelligent Russian once remarked to us, "Every country has its own constitution; ours is absolutism moderated by assassination."

Anonymous

Assassination has never changed the history of the world.

Benjamin Disraeli

War is the statesman's game, the
    priest's delight,
The layer's jest, the hired assassin's
    trade.

Percy Bysshe Shelley

See also: **Murder**

ASSERTION

Assertion, unsupported by fact, is nuga-
tory. Surmise and general abuse, in
however elegant language, ought not to
pass for truth.

Junius

It is an impudent kind of sorcery to attempt to blind us with the smoke, without convincing us that the fire has existed.

Junius

Weigh not so much what men assert, as
what they prove. Truth is simple and
naked, and needs not invention to apparel her comeliness.

Sir Philip Sidney

Never assert anything without first being certain of it.

Theresa of Jesus

See also: **Conversation, Word**

ATHEISM

To be an atheist requires an infinitely
greater measure of faith than to receive
all the great truths which atheism would
deny.

Joseph Addison

Atheism is rather in the life than in the
heart of man.

Francis Bacon

There was never miracle wrought by
God to convert an atheist, because the
light of nature might have led him to
confess a God.

Francis Bacon

The three great apostles of practical
atheism that make converts without
persecuting, and retain them without
preaching, are health, wealth, and
power.

Charles Caleb Colton

Virtue in distress, and vice in triumph,
make atheists of mankind.

John Dryden

Atheism is never the error of society, in
any stage or circumstance whatever. In
the belief of a Deity savage and sage
have alike agreed.

Henry Fergus

The atheist is one of the most daring
beings in creation—a contemner of God
who explodes his laws by denying his
existence.

John Foster

Whoever considers the study of anat-
omy can never be an atheist,

Edward Herbert

See also: **Agnosticism, Communism,
        Doubt, God, Unbelief**

ATTENTION

Consideration is the soil in which wisdom may be expected to grow, and
strength be given to every upspringing
plant of duty.

Ralph Waldo Emerson

Few things are impracticable in themselves: and it is for want of application, rather than of means, that men fail of success.

Duc François de La Rochefoucauld

If I have made any improvement in the sciences, it is owing more to patient attention than to anything beside.

Sir Isaac Newton

The power of applying attention, steady and undissipated, to a single object, is the sure mark of a superior genius.

Philip Dormer Stanhope (Lord Chesterfield)

See also: **Diligence, Observation, Thought**

AUDIENCE

The Puritan hated bear-baiting not because it gave pain to the bear but because it gave pleasure to the spectators.

Thomas Babington Macaulay

I never failed to convince an audience that the best thing they could do was to go away.

Thomas Love Peacock

The audience strummed their catarrhs.

Alexander Woollcott

See also: **Applause**

AUTHORITY

Nothing is more gratifying to the mind of man than power or dominion.

Joseph Addison

Every great advance in natural knowledge has involved the absolute rejection of authority.

Thomas Henry Huxley

All authority belongs to the people.

Thomas Jefferson

The highest duty is to respect authority.

Leo XIII (Gioacchino Vincenzo Pecci)

He who is firmly seated in authority soon learns to think security, and not progress, the highest lesson of statecraft.

James Russell Lowell

See also: **Dissent, Government, King, Obedience, Power**

AUTOMATION

The Christian notion of the possibility of redemption is incomprehensible to the computer.

Vance Oakley Packard

We live at a time when automation is ushering in a second industrial revolution.

Adlai Ewing Stevenson

Automation was a new extension of the Industrial Revolution in which machines began to be used to replace the work of men. With automation, machines now began to be used to control other machines.

David Charles Whitney

If it keeps up, man will atrophy all his limbs but the push-button finger.

Frank Lloyd Wright

See also: **Leisure, Science, Work**

AVARICE

Avarice is the vice of declining years.

George Bancroft

Avarice, in old age, is foolish; for what can be more absurd than to increase our provisions for the road the nearer we approach to our journey's end?

Cicero

Poverty wants some things, luxury many, avarice all things.

Abraham Cowley

All the good things of the world are no further good to us than as they are of use; and of all we may heap up we enjoy only as much as we can use, and no more.

Daniel Defoe

The lust of gold, unfeeling and remorseless, the last corruption of degenerate man.

Samuel Johnson

Averrice increases with the increasing pile of gold.

Juvenal

The lust of avarice has so totally seized upon mankind that their wealth seems rather to possess them, than they to possess their wealth.

Pliny the Elder

Avarice is the besetting vice of a propertied society but that avarice is in fact a vice is nowhere questioned.

Max Radin

Avarice, ambition, lust, etc. are species of madness.

Baruch (Benedict) Spinoza

The avaricious man is like the barren sandy ground of the desert which sucks in all the rain and dew with greediness, but yields no fruitful herbs or plants for the benefit of others.

Zeno

See also: **Gain, Miser, Money, Selfishness, Wealth**

AVERAGE

The plain man is the basic clod
From which we grow the demigod;
And in the average man is curled
The hero stuff that rules the world.

Sam Walter Foss

Give me a man that is capable of a devotion to anything, rather than a cold, calculating average of all the virtues!

Francis Bret Harte

I am only an average man but, by George, I work harder at it than the average man.

Theodore Roosevelt

A jury is a group of twelve people of average ignorance.

Herbert Spencer

See also: **Conformity, Majority**

BABBLE

They always talk who never think.

Matthew (Matt) Prior

The arts babblative and scribblative.

Robert Southey

Fire and sword are but slow engines of destruction in comparison with the babbler.

Sir Richard Steele

See also: **Gossip, Rumor**

BABY

A rose with all its sweetest leaves yet folded.

George Gordon Byron (Lord Byron)

There is no finer investment for any community than putting milk into babies.

Sir Winston Leonard Spencer Churchill

A sweet new blossom of humanity, fresh fallen from God's own home, to flower on earth.

Gerald Massey

Man, a dunce uncouth, errs in age and youth: babies know the truth.

Algernon Charles Swinburne

A babe in the house is a well-spring of pleasure, a messenger of peace and love, a resting place for innocence on earth, a link between angels and men.

Martin Farquhar Tupper

See also: **Birth, Birth Control, Family**

BACHELOR

I have no wife or children, good or bad, to provide for; a mere spectator of other men's fortunes and adventures, and how they play their parts; which, methinks, are diversely presented unto me, as from a common theatre or scene.

Richard Eugene Burton

A single man has not nearly the value he would have in a state of union. He is an incomplete animal. He resembles the odd half of a pair of scissors.

Benjamin Franklin

It is impossible to believe that the same God who permitted His own son to die a bachelor regards celibacy as an actual sin.

Henry Louis Mencken

By persistently remaining single a man converts himself into a permanent public temptation.

Oscar Wilde

See also: **Freedom, Independence, Liberty**

BALLAD

Let me write the ballads of a nation, and I care not who may make its laws.

Andrew Fletcher of Saltoun

Ballads are the vocal portraits of the national mind.

Charles Lamb

A well composed song or ballad strikes the mind, and softens the feelings, and produces a greater effect than a moral work, which convinces our reason but does not warm our feelings or effect the slightest alteration of our habits.

Napoleon I (Bonaparte)

See also: **Literature, Music, Poetry, Writing**

BANK

A power bas risen up in the government greater than the people themselves, consisting of many and various and powerful interests, combined into one mass, and held together by the cohesive power of the vast surplus in the banks.

John Caldwell Calhoun

A bank is a place where they lend you an umbrella in fair weather and ask for it back again when it begins to rain.

Robert Lee Frost

Banking establishments are more dangerous than standing armies.

Thomas Jefferson

He couldn't design a cathedral without it looking like the First Supernatural Bank!

Eugene Gladstone O'Neill

See also: Avarice, Gain, Miser, Prosperity, Wealth

BARGAIN

Sometimes one pays most for the things one gets for nothing.

Alfred Einstein

There are very honest people who do not think that they have had a bargain unless they have cheated a merchant.

Anatole France

One of the difficult tasks in this world is to convince a woman that even a bargain costs money.

Edgar Watson (Ed) Howe

Sacrifice is a form of bargaining.

Holbrook Jackson

There are many things in which one gains and the other loses; but if it is essential to any transaction that only one side shall gain, the thing is not of God.

George Macdonald

See also: Advertising, Economy, Frugality, Gain, Thrift

BASEBALL

He was thrown out trying to steal second; his head was full of larceny but his feet were honest.

Arthur (Bugs) Baer

A ball player's got to be kept hungry to become a big-leaguer. That's why no boy from a rich family ever made the big leagues.

Joseph Paul (Joe) DiMaggio

Any ballplayer that don't sign autographs for little kids ain't an American. He's a Communist.

Rogers Hornsby

Speed without control has ruined many a good pitcher.

New York Herald-Tribune

Baseball has the great advantage over cricket of being sooner ended.

George Bernard Shaw

The baseball mind is a jewel in the strict sense—that is to say, a stone of special value, rare beauty, and extreme hardness. Cut, polished and fixed in the Tiffany setting of a club owner's skull, it resists change as a diamond resists erosion.

Walter Wellesley (Red) Smith

See also: Hero

BEAUTY

Beauty is the gift of God.

Aristotle

The best part of beauty is that which no picture can express.

Francis Bacon

It's a sort of bloom on a woman. If you have it you don't need to have anything else; and if you don't have it, it doesn't much matter what else you have.

Sir James Matthew Barrie

To cultivate the sense of the beautiful, is one of the most effectual ways of cultivating an appreciation of the divine goodness.

Christian Nestell Bovee

The need for beauty is as positive a natural impulsion as the need for food.

Luther Burbank

An appearance of delicacy, and even of fragility, is almost essential to beauty.

Edmund Burke

Beauteous, even where beauties most abound.

George Gordon Byron (Lord Byron)

All beauty does not inspire love; some beauties please the sight without captivating the affections.

Miguel de Cervantes Saavedra

Beauty in a modest woman is like fire at a distance, or a sharp sword beyond reach. The one does not burn, or the other wound those that come not too near them.

Miguel de Cervantes Saavedra

Beauty is not caused. It is.

Emily Elizabeth Dickinson

Zest is the secret of all beauty. There is no beauty that is attractive without zest.

Christian Dior

Nothing but beauty and wisdom deserve immortality.

Will (William James) Durant

If you tell a woman she is beautiful, whisper it softly; for if the devil hears it he'll echo it many times.

Francis Alexander Durivage

It would surprise any of us if we realized how much store we unconsciously set by beauty, and how little savor there would be left in life if it were withdrawn.

John Galsworthy

True beauty consists in purity of heart.

Mohandas Karamchand (Mahatma) Gandhi

Beauty is an outward gift which is seldom despised, except by those to whom it has been refused.

Edward Gibbon

Beauty is truth, truth beauty.

John Keats

A thing of beauty is a joy forever.

John Keats

The common foible of women who have been handsome is to forget that they are no longer so.

Duc François de La Rochefoucauld

See also: **Art, Face, Looks**

BEGGING

Borrowing is not much better than begging.

Gotthold Ephraim Lessing

He who begs timidly courts a refusal.

Seneca

Common people do not pray; they only beg.

George Bernard Shaw

A court is an assembly of noble and distinguished beggars.

Charles Maurice de Talleyrand-Périgord

See also: Adversity, Poverty

BEGINNING

Begin; to begin is half the work. Let half still remain; again begin this, and thou wilt have finished.

Ausonius

Let us watch well our beginnings, and results will manage themselves.

Alexander Clark

It is the beginning of the end.

Charles Maurice de Talleyrand-Périgord

The first step, my son, which one makes in the world, is the one on which depends the rest of our days.

Voltaire (François Marie Arouet)

See also: Birth, Discovery, End, Originality, Past

BEHAVIOR

Behavior is a mirror in which every one displays his image

Johann Wolfgang von Goethe

Be nice to people on your way up because you'll meet them on your way down.

Wilson Mizner

Levity of behavior is the bane of all that is good and virtuous.

Seneca

If animals had reason, they would act just as ridiculous as we menfolks do.

Henry Wheeler Shaw (Josh Billings)

I don't say we all ought to misbehave, but we ought to look as if we could.

Orson Welles

He doesn't act on the stage—he behaves.

Oscar Wilde

See Also: Action, Etiquette, Manners, Morality

BENEVOLENCE

In this world it is not what we take up, but what we give up, that makes us rich.

Henry Ward Beecher

It is good for us to think that no grace or blessing is truly ours till we are aware that God has blessed some one else with it through us.

Phillips Brooks

Rare benevolence! the minister of God.

Thomas Carlyle

He who wishes to secure the good of others, has already secured his own.

Confucius

He only does not live in vain, who employs his wealth, his thought, his speech to advance the good of others.

Hindu Maxim

The disposition to give a cup of cold water to a disciple, is a far nobler property than the finest intellect.

William Dean Howells

It is good to think well; it is divine to act well.

Horace Mann

Genuine benevolence is not stationary, but peripatetic; it goes about doing good.

William Nevins

It is no great part of a good man's lot to enjoy himself. To be good and to do good are his ends, and the glory is to be revealed hereafter.

Samuel Irenaeus Prime

Do not wait for extraordinary circumstances to do good actions: try to use ordinary situations.

Jean Paul Richter

The one who will be found in trial capable of great acts of love is ever the one who is always doing considerate small ones.

Frederick William Robertson

I truly enjoy no more of the world's good things than what I willingly distribute to the needy.

Seneca

This is the law of benefits between men; the one ought to forget at once what he has given, and the other ought never to forget what he has received.

Seneca

To feel much for others, and little for ourselves; to restrain our selfish, and exercise our benevolent affections, constitutes the perfection of human nature.

Adam Smith

Benevolent feeling ennobles the most trifling actions.

William Makepeace Thackeray

BEST

The best you get is an even break.

Franklin Pierce Adams

Only a mediocre person is always at his best.

(William) Somerset Maugham

One of the rarest things that a man ever does is to do the best he can.

Henry Wheeler Shaw (Josh Billings)

Everything is for the best in this best of possible worlds.

Voltaire (François Marie Arouet)

I am as bad as the worst but, thank God, I am as good as the best.

Walt (Walter) Whitman

See also: **Excellence, Virtue, Worth**

BILLS

Dreading that climax of all human ills,
The inflammation of his weekly bills.

George Gordon Byron (Lord Byron)

Wilt thou seal up the avenues of ill?
Pay every debt, as if God wrote the bill.

Ralph Waldo Emerson

It is only by not paying one's bills that one can hope to live in the memory of the commercial classes.

Oscar Wilde

See also: **Borrowing, Debt**

BIRTH

Features alone do not run in the blood; vices and virtues, genius and folly, are transmitted through the same sure but unseen channel.

William Hazlitt

About the only thing we have left that actually discriminates in favor of the plain people is the stork.

Frank McKinney (Kin) Hubbard

High birth is a gift of fortune which should never challenge esteem toward those who receive it, since it costs them neither study nor labor.

Jean de La Bruyère

What is birth to a man if it be a stain to his dead ancestors to have left such an offspring?

Sir Philip Sidney

Our birth is nothing but our death begun, As tapers waste the moment they take fire.

Edward Young

See also: **Ancestry, Baby, Birth Control, Death, Family, Father, Mother, Parent**

BIRTH CONTROL

Intercourse with even a legitimate wife is unlawful and wicked if the conception of offspring is prevented.

Augustine of Hippo

Whenever I hear people discussing birth control, I always remember that I was the fifth.

Clarence Seward Darrow

Everyone should remember that the union of the two sexes is meant solely for the purpose of procreation.

Lactantius

Family planning is a necessary complement to the war on poverty effort; it is a program which provides the individual with information necessary for her to make a choice as to whether she wishes to have more children and when she wishes to have them.

Walter F. Mondale

There is an old saying here that a man must do three things during life: plant trees, write books and have sons. I wish they would plant more trees and write more books.

Luis Muñoz Marín

See also: **Abortion, Birth, Sex**

BITTERNESS

The soreness which may not pass the lips is felt the more keenly within.

Sir Rabindranath Tagore

The fairest things have fleetest end,
    Their scent survives their close:
But the rose's scent is bitterness
    To him that loved the rose.

Francis Thompson

But hushed be every thought that springs From out the bitterness of things.

William Wordsworth

See also: **Anger, Dissent, Forgiveness, Hate, Resentment**

BLAME

When the million applaud, you ask yourself what harm you have done; when they censure you, what good.

Charles Caleb Colton

We blame in others only the faults by which we do not profit.
Alexander Dumas (Père)

All of us are prone to put the blame for our inefficiency and failure upon society, environment, early training—any place but on our own precious selves.
Howard Kenneth Nixon

Do not blame your food because you have no appetite.
Sir Rabindranath Tagore

Let not the sword-blade mock its handle for being blunt.
Sir Rabindranath Tagore

See also: **Abuse, Censure, Criticism, Guilt**

BLINDNESS

What a blind person needs is not a teacher but another self.
Helen Adams Keller

O loss of sight, of thee I most complain!
Blind among enemies, O worse than chains,
Dungeon, or beggary, or decrepit age!
John Milton

There's none so blind as they that won't see.
Jonathan Swift

See also: **Eye, Ignorance**

BLOOD

I have nothing to offer but blood, toil, tears and sweat.
Sir Winston Leonard Spencer Churchill

The blood of the martyrs is the seed of the church
Tertullian

The old blood is bold blood, the wide world round.
Byron Webber

See also: **Ancestry, Birth, Parent, Revolution, War**

BLUSH

Blushing is the livery of virtue, though it may sometimes proceed from guilt.
Francis Bacon

The ambiguous livery worn alike by modesty and shame.
Francis Maitland Balfour

Better a blush on the face than a blot on the heart.
Miguel de Cervantes Saavedra

It is better for a young man to blush, than to turn pale.
Cicero

Man is the only animal that blushes. Or needs to.
Samuel Langhorne Clemens (Mark Twain)

A blush is the color of virtue.
Diogenes

The blush is nature's alarm at the approach of sin, and her testimony to the dignity of virtue.
Thomas Fuller

The blush is beautiful, but it is sometimes inconvenient.
Carlo Goldoni

When a girl ceases to blush, she has lost the most powerful charm of her beauty.
Gregory I (Gregory the Great)

Men blush less for their crimes, than for their weaknesses and vanity.
Jean de La Bruyère

Whoever blushes seems to be good.
Menander of Athens

Playful blushes, that seem but luminous escapes of thought.
Thomas Moore

Whoever blushes, is already guilty; true innocence is ashamed of nothing.
Jean Jacques Rousseau

The troubled blood through his pale face was seen to come and go with tidings from his heart, as it a running messenger had been.
Edmund Spenser

See also: Anxiety, Fear

BODY

Our bodies are apt to be our autobiographies.
Frank Gelett Burgess

Our body is a well-set clock, which keeps good time, but if it be too much or indiscreetly tampered with, the alarm runs out before the hour.
Joseph Hall

A human being is an ingenious assembly of portable plumbing.
Christopher Darlington Morley

See also: Health, Soul

BOLDNESS

Boldness is ever blind, for it sees not dangers and inconveniences; whence it is bad in council though good in execution.
Francis Bacon

Fortune befriends the bold.
John Dryden

Carried away by the irresistible influence which is always exercised over men's minds by a bold resolution in critical circumstances.
François Pierre Guillaume Guizot

Fools rush in where angels fear to tread.
Alexander Pope

It is wonderful what strength of purpose and boldness and energy of will are roused by the assurance that we are doing our duty.
Sir Walter Scott

Who bravely dares must sometimes risk a fall.
Tobias George Smollett

See also: Bravery, Confidence, Courage, Cowardice

BOOK

Books are the legacies that genius leaves to mankind, to be delivered down from generation to generation, as presents to those that are yet unborn.
Joseph Addison

All books will become light in proportion as you find light in them.
Mortimer Jerome Adler

That is a good book which is opened with expectation, and closed with delight and profit.
Amos Bronson Alcott

Some books are to be tasted; others swallowed; and some few to be chewed and digested.
Francis Bacon

Books are not men and yet they are alive.
Stephen Vincent Benét

Books are embalmed minds.
Christian Nestell Bovee

In books, it is the chief of all perfections to be plain and brief.
Joseph Butler

If a book come from the heart it win contrive to reach other hearts. All art and authorcraft are of small account to that.
Thomas Carlyle

Every man is a volume if you know how to read him.
William Ellery Channing

The man who does not read good books has no advantage over the man who can't read them.
Samuel Langhorne Clemens (Mark Twain)

The book salesman should be honored because he brings to our attention, as a rule, the very books we need most and neglect most.
Frank Crane

See also: **Literature, Reading**

BORROWING

The borrower runs in his own debt.
Ralph Waldo Emerson

The shoulders of a borrower are always a little straighter than those of a beggar.
Morris Leopold Ernst

Getting into debt, is getting into a tanglesome net.
Benjamin Franklin

If you would know the value of money, go and try to borrow some. He that goes a-borrowing goes a-sorrowing.
Benjamin Franklin

Borrowing is not much better than begging.
Gotthold Ephraim Lessing

Never call a man a fool; borrow from him.
Addison Mizner

It is folly to borrow when there is no prospect of or ability to pay back.
Jawaharlal Nehru

Live within your income, even if you have to borrow money to do so.
Henry Wheeler Shaw (Josh Billings)

See also; **Bank, Debt**

BOY

The fact that boys are allowed to exist at all is evidence of a remarkable Christian forbearance among men.
Ambrose Gwinnett Bierce

It used to be a good hotel, but that proves nothing—I used to be a good boy.
Samuel Langhorne Clemens (Mark Twain)

Boys will be boys, and so will a lot of middle-aged men.
Frank McKinney (Kin) Hubbard

A boy's will is the wind's will.
Henry Wadsworth Longfellow

Just at the age 'twixt boy and youth,
When thought is speech, and speech is truth.
Sir Walter Scott

You save an old man and you save a unit; but save a boy, and you save a multiplication table.
Gipsy Rodney Smith

Who feels injustice; who shrinks before a slight; who has a sense of wrong so acute, and so glowing a gratitude for kindness, as a generous boy?

William Makepeace Thackeray

See also: *Age*

BRAINS

The brain is a wonderful organ; It starts working the moment you get up in the morning, and does not stop until you get into the office.

Robert Lee Frost

Brains well prepared are the monuments where human knowledge is more surely engraved.

Jean Jacques Rousseau

When God endowed human beings with brains, He did not intend to guarantee them.

Charles de Secondat (Baron de Montesquieu)

See also: *Ability, Character, Genius, Intelligence, Mind*

BRAVERY

The brave man is not he who feels no fear, for that were stupid and irrational; but he whose noble soul subdues its fear, and bravely dares the danger nature shrinks from.

Joanna Baillie

At the bottom of not a little of the bravery that appears in the world, there lurks a miserable cowardice. Men will face powder and steel because they have not the courage to face public opinion.

Edwin Hubbel Chapin

No man can be brave who considers pain the greatest evil of life; or temperate, who regards pleasure as the highest good.

Cicero

Nature often enshrines gallant and noble hearts in weak bosoms; oftenest, God bless her, in woman's breast.

Charles John Huffam Dickens

All brave men love; for he only is brave who has affections to fight for, whether in the daily battle of life, or in physical contests.

Nathaniel Hawthorne

Let us act in the spirit of Thucydides that "the bravest are surely those who have the clearest vision of what is before them, glory and danger alike, and yet notwithstanding go out to meet it."

Henry Alfred Kissinger

True bravery is shown by performing without witnesses what one might be capable of doing before all the world.

Duc François de La Rochefoucauld

Physical bravery is an animal instinct; moral bravery is a much higher and truer courage.

Wendell Phillips

Some one praising a man for his foolhardy bravery, Cato, the elder said, "There is a wide difference between true courage and a mere contempt of life."

Plutarch

The best hearts are ever the bravest.

Lawrence Sterne

Bravery ceases to be bravery at a certain point, and becomes mere foolhardiness.

Sir Rabindranath Tagore

See also: *Courage, Hero*

BREVITY

Brevity is the best recommendation of speech, whether in a senator or an orator.

Cicero

Have something to say; say it, and stop when you've done.

Tryon Edwards

Never be so brief as to become obscure.

Tryon Edwards

The one prudence of life is concentration.

Ralph Waldo Emerson

One rare, strange virtue in speeches, and the secret of their mastery, is, that they are short.

Fitz-Greene Halleck

When you introduce a moral lesson let it be brief.

Horace

I saw one excellency within my reach—it was brevity, and I determined to obtain it.

William Jay

The fewer the words, the better the prayer.

Martin Luther

Words are like leaves, and where they most abound, much fruit of sense beneath is rarely found.

Alexander Pope

See also: **Simplicity**

BROTHERHOOD

Grant us brotherhood, not only for this day but for all our years—a brotherhood not of words but of acts and needs.

Stephen Vincent Benét

Our doctrine of equality and liberty and humanity comes from our belief in the brotherhood of man, through the fatherhood of God.

(John) Calvin Coolidge

The universe is but one great city, full of beloved ones, divine and human, by nature endeared to each other.

Epictetus

There is no brotherhood of man without the fatherhood of God.

Henry Martyn Field

Help thy brother's boat across, and lo! thine own has reached the shore.

Hindu Proverb

If God is thy father, man is thy brother.

Alphonse Marie Louis de Prat de Lamartine

The crest and crowning of all good, life's final star, is Brotherhood.

(Charles) Edwin Markham

To live is not to live for one's self alone; let us help one another.

Menander of Athens

Humanity cannot go forward, civilization cannot advance, except as the philosophy of force is replaced by that of human brotherhood.

Francis Bowes Sayre

However degraded or wretched a fellow mortal may be, he is still a member of our common species.

Seneca

It is clear that for Pope John the human race is not a cold abstraction, but a single precious family whose life, interests, responsibilities and well-being are a constant and loving preoccupation.

Adlai Ewing Stevenson

On this shrunken globe, men can no longer live as strangers.

Adlai Ewing Stevenson

We cannot hope to command brotherhood abroad unless we practice it at home.

Harry S Truman

We do not want the men of another color for our brothers-in-law, but we do want them for our brothers.

Booker Taliaferro Washington

See also: **Christianity, Communism, Equality, Friendship, Man, Selfishness, Society, United Nations**

BUSINESS

Business without profit is not business any more than a pickle is candy.

Charles Frederick Abbott

There is nothing more requisite in business than dispatch.

Joseph Addison

In civil business; what first? boldness; what second and third? boldness: and yet boldness is a child of ignorance and baseness.

Francis Bacon

We should keep in mind that the humanities come before the dollars. Our first duty runs to man before business, but we must not forget that sometimes the two are interchangeable.

Bernard Mannes Baruch

That I should make him that steals my coat a present of my cloak—what would become of business?

Katharine Lee Bates

The gambling known as business looks with austere disfavor upon the business known as gambling.

Ambrose Gwinnett Bierce

It is in the interest of the community that a man in a free business, in a competitive business, shall have the incentive to make as much money as he can.

Louis Dembitz Brandeis

The goals of business are inseparable from the goals of the whole community. Every attempt to sever the organic unity of business and the community inflicts equal hardship on both.

Earl Bunting

The best mental effort in the game of business is concentrated on the major problem of securing the consumer's dollar before the other fellow gets it

Stuart Chase

There are two times in a man's life when he should not speculate; when he can't afford it and when he can.

Samuel Langhorne Clemens (Mark Twain)

I do not believe government can run any business as efficiently as private enterprise, and the victim of every such experiment is the public.

Thomas Edmund Dewey

The man who is above his business may one day find his business above him.

Samuel Drew

All business proceeds on beliefs, or judgments of probabilities, and not on certainties.

Charles William Eliot

The "tired business man" is one whose business is usually not a successful one.

Joseph Ridgeway Grundy

Punctuality is the soul of business.
Thomas Chandler Haliburton

Anybody can cut prices, but it takes brains to make a better article.
Alice Hub

The art of winning in business is in working hard—not taking things too seriously.
Elbert Green Hubbard

A man's success in business today turns upon his power of getting people to believe he has something that they want.
Gerald Stanley Lee

See also: *Advertising, Capitalism, Career, Employment, Finance, Money, Vocation, Work*

CALAMITY

Calamity is man's true touchstone.
Francis Beaumont and John Fletcher

Calamity is the perfect glass wherein we truly see and know ourselves.
Sir William Davenant

When any calamity has been suffered, the first thing to be remembered, is, how much has been escaped.
Samuel Johnson

It is only from the belief of the goodness and wisdom of a supreme being, that our calamities can be home in the manner which becomes a man.
Henry Mackenzie

He who foresees calamities, suffers them twice over.
Beilby Porteus

See also: *Adversity, Crisis, War*

CANDOR

Examine what is said, not him who speaks.
Arabian Proverb

Candor is the brightest gem of criticism.
Benjamin Disraeli

There is no wisdom like frankness.
Benjamin Disraeli

Friends, if we be honest with ourselves, we shall be honest with each other.
George Macdonald

Innocence in genius, and candor in power, are both noble qualities.
Madame de Staël

It is great and manly to disdain disguise; it shows our spirit, and proves our strength.
Edward Young

See also: *Truth*

CAPITALISM

In arguing that capitalism as such is not the cause of war, I must not be taken as arguing that capitalists do not often believe in war. Believe that they and their country benefit from it.
Sir Norman Angell

The organization of society on the principle of private profit . . . is leading both to the deformation of humanity by unregulated industrialism, and to the exhaustion of natural resources.
Thomas Stearns Eliot

The dynamo of our economic system is self-interest which may range from mere greed to admirable types of self-expression.
Felix Frankfurter

The fundamental idea of modern capitalism is not the right of the individual to possess and enjoy what he has earned, but the thesis that the exercise of this right redounds to the general good.
Ralph Barton Perry

What we mean when we say we are for or against capitalism is that we like or dislike a certain civilization or scheme of life.
Joseph Alois Schumpeter

See also: **Business, Finance, Money**

CAREER

People don't choose their careers: they are engulfed by them.
John Roderigo Dos Passos

In a free market, in an age of endemic inflation, it is unquestionably more rewarding, in purely pecuniary terms, to be a speculator or a prostitute than a teacher, preacher, or policeman.
John Kenneth Galbraith

Analyzing what you haven't got as well as what you have is a necessary ingredient of a career.
Grace Moore

To find a career to which you are adapted by nature, and then to work hard at it,' is about as near to a formula for success and happiness as the world provides.
Mark Sullivan

See also: **Ambition, Employment, Guidance, Opportunity, Vocation, Work**

CAUSE

We are tired of great causes.
Francis Scott Key

The cause is everything. Those even who dearest to us must be shunted for the sake the cause.
Mohandas Karamchand (Mahatma) Gandhi

Great causes and little men go ill together.
Jawaharlal Nehru

When a person is prepared to die for a cause, and indeed to glory in such a death, it impossible to suppress him or the cause represents.
Jawaharlal Nehru

No cause can command the deepest loyalties and the greatest sacrifices of men till it is presented under a moral aspect.
Arthur Meier Schlesinger

God is the free cause of all things.
Baruch (Benedict) Spinoza

See also: **Beginning, Result**

CAUTION

It is better to be safe than sorry.
American Proverb

I don't like these cold, precise, perfect people, who, in order not to speak wrong, never speak at all, and in order not to do wrong, never do anything.
Henry Ward Beecher

Whenever our neighbor's house is on fire, it cannot be amiss for the engines to play a little on our own. Better to be despised for too anxious apprehensions, than ruined by too confident security.
Edmund Burke

All is to be feared where all is to be lost.
George Gordon Byron (Lord Byron)

None pities him that's in the snare, who warned before, would not beware.
Robert Herrick

It is well to learn caution by the misfortunes of others.
Publilius Syrus

See also: *Cowardice, Discretion, Prudence, Reflection*

CENSORSHIP

Only the suppressed word is dangerous.
Ludwig Börne

So many new ideas are at first strange and horrible though ultimately valuable that a very heavy responsibility rests upon those who would prevent their dissemination.
John Burdon Sanderson Haldane

I am opposed to censorship. Censors are pretty sure to be fools. I have no confidence in the suppression of every-day facts.
James Harvey Robinson

Censorship reflects a society's lack of confidence in itself. It is a hallmark of an authoritarian regime.
Potter Stewart

See also: *Books, Freedom*

CENSURE

There is no defense against reproach but obscurity; it is a kind of concomitant to greatness, as satires and invectives were an essential part of a Roman triumph.
Joseph Addison

It is impossible to indulge in habitual severity of opinion upon our fellow-men without injuring the tenderness and delicacy of our own feelings.
Henry Ward Beecher

The readiest and surest way to get rid of censure, is to correct ourselves.
Demosthenes

Most of our censure of others is only oblique praise of self, uttered to show the wisdom and superiority of the speaker. It has all the invidiousness of self-praise, and all the ill-desert of falsehood.
Tryon Edwards

If anyone speak ill of thee, consider whether he hath truth on his side; and if so, reform thyself, that his censures may not affect thee.
Epictetus

Few persons have sufficient wisdom to prefer censure, which is useful, to praise which deceives them.
Duc François de La Rochefoucauld

He is always the severest censor on the merits of others who has the least worth of his own.
Elias Lyman Magoon

The villain's censure is extorted praise.
Alexander Pope

The censure of those who are opposed to us, is the highest commendation that can be given us.
Seigneur de Saint-Evremond

See also: *Abuse, Criticism*

CERTAINTY

Years make men restless—they needs
    must spy
Some certainty, some sort of end
    assured,
Some sparkle, though from topmost
    beacon-tip,
That warrants life a harbor through the
    haze.

Robert Browning

Certainty generally is illusion, and repose is not the destiny of man.

Oliver Wendell Holmes, Jr.

Certitude is not the test of certainty. We
have been cocksure of many things that
were not so.

Oliver Wendell Holmes, Jr.

He is no wise man that will quit a certainty for an uncertainty.

Samuel Johnson

In these matters the only certainty is
that there is nothing certain.

Pliny the Elder

Ah, what a dusty answer gets the soul
When hot for certainties in this our life!

George Meredith

See also: **Doubt, Facts, Knowledge,**
        Question, Success, Truth

CHALLENGE

If we face our tasks with the resolution
to solve them, who shall say that anything is impossible.

Sir Wilfred Thomason Grenfell

The new frontier of which I speak is not
a set of promises—it is a set of
challenges. It sums up not what I intend
to offer the American people, but what I
intend to ask of them. It appeals to their
pride, not their pocketbook—it holds out
the promise of more sacrifice instead of
more security.

John Fitzgerald Kennedy

My greatest inspiration is a challenge to
attempt the impossible.

Albert Abraham Michelson

It does not cost much courage to challenge.

Sir Rabindranath Tagore

CHANCE

Chance and the moment, what we call
the breaks, so often influence our lives
that they cannot be ignored.

Frank Case

Chance is a nickname of Providence.

Sébastien Roch Nicolas Chamfort

There is no such thing as chance or accident, the words merely signify our ignorance of some real and immediate cause.

Adam Clarke

Great things spring from casualties.

Benjamin Disraeli

Many shining actions owe their success
to chance, though the general or statesmen runs away with the applause.

Henry Home (Lord Kames)

Chance generally favors the prudent.

Joseph Joubert

Though men pride themselves on their
great deeds, they are often not the result
of design, but of chance.

Duc François de La Rochefoucauld

How often events, by chance, and unexpectedly, come to pass, which you had not dared even to hope for

Terence

Chance is a word void of sense; nothing can exist without a cause.

Voltaire (François Marie Arouet)

See also: **Accident, Luck**

CHANGE

He that will not apply new remedies must expect new evils.

Francis Bacon

We are restless because of incessant change, but we would be frightened if change were stopped.

Lyman Lloyd Bryson

Encourage as much change as is possible in your environment.

Frank Gelett Burgess

Today is not yesterday. We ourselves change. How then, can our works and thoughts, if they are always to be the fittest, continue always the same. Change, indeed, is painful, yet ever needful; and if memory have its force and worth, so also has hope.

Thomas Carlyle

The world is a scene of changes; to be constant in nature were inconstancy.

Abraham Cowley

Change is an easy panacea. It takes character to stay in one place and be happy there.

Elizabeth Clarke Dunn

Most of the change we think we see in life is due to truths being in and out of favor.

Robert Lee Frost

All change is not growth, as all movement is not forward.

Ellen Anderson Gholson Glasgow

To blind oneself to change is not therefore to halt it.

Isaac Goldberg

The world hates change, yet it is the only thing that has brought progress.

Charles Franklin Kettering

It isn't so much that hard times are coming; the change observed is mostly soft times going.

Groucho (Julius Henry) Marx

We need courage to throw away old garments which have had their day and no longer fit the requirements of the new generations . . .

Fridtjof Nansen

Everything changes continually. What is history, indeed, but a record of change. And if there had been very few changes in the past, there would have been little of history to write.

Jawaharlal Nehru

The circumstances of the world are so variable, that an irrevocable purpose or opinion is almost synonymous with a foolish one.

William Henry Seward

See also: **Improvement, Instability
    Novelty, Progress, Reform,
    Variety**

CHARACTER

A man's character is the reality of himself. His reputation is the opinion others have formed of him. Character is in him; reputation is from other people—that is the substance, this is the shadow.

Henry Ward Beech

Nothing can work me damage, except myself. The harm that I sustain I carry about me, and never am a real sufferer but by my own fault.

Bernard of Clairvaux

In each human heart are a tiger, a pig, an ass, and a nightingale; diversity of character is due to their unequal activity.

Ambrose Gwinnett Bierce

Let us not say, Every man is the architect his own fortune; but let us say, Every man is the architect of his own character.

George Dana Boardman

No amount of ability is of the slightest avail without honor.

Andrew Carnegie

The miracle, or the power, that elevates the few in their industry, application, and perseverance under the promptings of a brave, determined spirit.

Samuel Langhorne Clemens (Mark Twain)

Truthfulness is a cornerstone in character, and if it be not firmly laid in youth, there will ever after be a weak spot in the foundation.

Jefferson Davis

Characters do not change. Opinions alter, but characters are only developed.

Benjamin Disraeli

Do what you know and perception is converted into character.

Ralph Waldo Emerson

Taste and habits change progressively. In the old days the lady with a past repented and died; to-day she repents and lives happily ever after.

Daniel Frohman

You cannot dream yourself into a character; you must hammer and forge one for yourself.

James Anthony Froude

A man of character will make himself worthy of any position he is given.

Mohandas Karamchand (Mahatma) Gandhi

There are no two opinions about the fact that intellect rather than riches will lead. It might equally be admitted that the heart rather than the intellect will eventually lead. Character, not brain, will count at the crucial moment.

Mohandas Karamchand (Mahatma) Gandhi

The great thing in this world is not so much where we are, but in what direction we are moving.

Oliver Wendell Holmes

If you can talk with crowds and keep your virtue, or walk with kings—nor lose the common touch, if neither foes nor loving friends can hurt you, if all men count with you, but none too much: if you can fill the unforgiving minute with sixty seconds' worth of distance run, yours is the earth and everything that is in it, and—which is more—you'll be a man, my son.

Rudyard Kipling

Weakness of character is the only defect which cannot be amended.

Duc François de La Rochefoucauld

A sound body is a first-class thing; a sound mind is an even better thing; but the thing that counts for most in the individual as in the nation, is character, the sum of those qualities which make a man a good man and a woman a good woman.

Theodore Roosevelt

The most tragic thing in the world is a man of genius who is not also a man of honor.

George Bernard Shaw

The shortest and surest way to live with honor in the world, is to be in reality what we would appear to be; all human virtues increase and strengthen themselves by the practice and experience of them.

Socrates

Character is made by what you stand for; reputation by what you fall for.

Alexander Woolcott

See also: **Individuality, Integrity, Looks, Nature, Temper**

CHARITY

A man should fear when he enjoys only the good he does publicly. Is it not publicity rather than charity, which he loves? Is it not vanity, rather than benevolence, that gives such charities?

Henry Ward Beecher

First daughter to the love of God, is charity to man.

William Drennan

One must be poor to know the luxury of giving.

George Eliot (Mary Ann Evans)

Not he who has much is rich, but he who gives much.

Erich Fromm

The more charity, the more peace.

Hillel

The truly generous is truly wise, and he who loves not others, lives unblest.

Henry Home (Lord Kames)

The charity that hastens to proclaim its good deeds, ceases to be charity, and is only pride and ostentation.

William Hutton

Be charitable and indulgent to every one but thyself.

Joseph Joubert

A bone to the dog is not charity. Charity is the bone shared with the dog, when you are just as hungry as the dog.

Jack London

Charity is infinitely divisible. He who has a little can always give a little.

Peter McArthur

I would have none of that rigid and circumspect charity which is never exercised without scrutiny, and which always mistrusts the reality of the necessities laid open to it.

Jean Baptiste M

Charity is never lost: it may meet with ingratitude, or be of no service to those on whom it was bestowed, yet it ever does a work of beauty and grace upon the heart of the giver.

Conyers Middleton

See also: **Benevolence, Generosity, Help, Kindness, Selfishness**

CHARM

If you have charm, you don't need to have anything else; and if you don't have it, it doesn't matter what else you have.

Sir James Matthew Barrie

Charm is almost as poor a butter for parsnips as good intentions.

(Matthew) Heywood Campbell Brown

Charm is more than beauty.

Yiddish Proverb

See also: ***Beauty***

CHEERFULNESS

To be free-minded and cheerfully disposed at hours of meals, and of sleep, and of exercise, is one of the best precepts of long-lasting.

Francis Bacon

You find yourself refreshed by the presence of cheerful people. Why not make earnest effort to confer that pleasure on others? Half the battle is gained if you never allow yourself to say anything gloomy.

Lydia Maria Francis Child

To make knowledge valuable, you must have the cheerfulness of wisdom. Goodness smiles to the last

Ralph Waldo Emerson

If the soul be happily disposed everything becomes capable of affording entertainment, and distress will almost want a name.

Oliver Goldsmith

The mind that is cheerful at present will have no solicitude for the future, and will meet the bitter occurrences of life with a smile.

Horace

Honest good humor is the oil and wine of a merry meeting, and there is no jovial companionship equal to that where the jokes are rather small and the laughter abundant.

Washington Irving

The habit of looking on the best side of every event is worth more than a thousand pounds a year.

Samuel Johnson

Keep your face to the sunshine and you cannot see the shadow

Helen Adams Keller

If good people would but make their goodness agreeable, and smile instead of frowning in their virtue, how many would they win to the good cause.

James Usher

See also: ***Amiability, Happiness, Smile***

CHILDREN

If a child annoys you, quiet him by brushing his hair. If this doesn't work, use the other side of the brush on the other end of the child.

Anonymous

Children sweeten labors, but they make misfortunes more bitter. They increase the cares of life, but they mitigate the remembrance of death.

Francis Bacon

You cannot teach a child to take care of himself unless you will let him try to take care of himself. He will make mistakes; and out of these mistakes will come his wisdom.

Henry Ward Beecher

Many children, many cares; no children, no felicity.

Christian Nestell Bovee

The child's heart curseth deeper in the silence than the strong man in his wrath.

Elizabeth Barrett Browning

The first duty to children is to make them happy. If you have not made them so, you have wronged them. No other good they may get can make up for that.
Charles Buxton

Bachelors' wives and old maids' children are always perfect.
Sébastien Roch Nicolas Chamfort

I have often thought what a melancholy world this would be without children; and what an inhuman world, without the aged.
Samuel Taylor Coleridge

Children do not know how their parents love them, and they never will till the grave closes those parents, or till they have children of their own.
Philip Pendleton Cooke

When children sound silly, you will always find that it is in imitation of their elders.
Ernest Dimnet

Beware of fatiguing them by ill-judged exactness. If virtue offers itself to the child under a melancholy and constrained aspect, while liberty and license present themselves under an agreeable form, all is lost, and your labor is in vain.
François de Salignac de La Mothe-Fénelon

It is dangerous to confuse children with angels.
David Patrick Maxwell Fyfe

In praising or loving a child, we love and praise not that which is, but that which we hope for.
Johann Wolfgang von Goethe

Feel the dignity of a child. Do not feel superior to him, for you are not.
Robert Henri

Children have neither past nor future; and what scarcely ever happens to us, they enjoy the present.
Jean de La Bruyère

Children generally hate to be idle. All the care then should be, that their busy humor should be constantly employed in something that is of use to them.
John Locke

A torn jacket is soon mended, but hard words bruise the heart of a child.
Henry Wadsworth Longfellow

Many a man spanks his children for things his own father should have spanked out of him.
Donald Robert Perry (Don) Marquis

By the time the youngest children have learned to keep the place tidy, the oldest grandchildren are on hand to tear it to pieces again.
Christopher Darlington Morley

Before you beat a child, be sure you yourself are not the cause of the offense.
Austin O'Malley

See also: **Baby, Family, Infancy, Youth**

CHOICE

Be ignorance thy choice where knowledge leads to woe.
James Beattie

Life often presents us with a choice of evils rather than of good.
Charles Caleb Colton

Between two evils, choose neither; between two goods, choose both.
Tryon Edwards

God offers to every mind its choice between truth and repose.

Ralph Waldo Emerson

The measure of choosing well is, whether a man likes and finds good in what he has chosen.

Charles Lamb

Choose always the way that seems the best, however rough it may be; custom will soon render it easy and agreeable.

Pythagoras

See also: **Freedom, Liberty, Necessity, Resolution, Will, Wish**

CHRISTIANITY

The distinction between Christianity and all other systems of religion consists largely in this, that in these others men are found seeking after God, while Christianity is God seeking after men.

Thomas Arnold

There was never law, or sect, or opinion did so much magnify goodness, as the Christian religion doth.

Francis Bacon

There's not much practical Christianity in the man who lives on better terms with angels and seraphs, than with his children, servants, and neighbors.

Henry Ward Beecher

Christianity has not been tried and found wanting; it has been found difficult and not tried.

Gilbert Keith Chesterton

Let any of those who renounce Christianity. write fairly down in a book all the absurdities they believe instead of it, and they will find it requires more faith to reject Christianity than to embrace it.

Charles Caleb Colton

The steady discipline of intimate friendship with Jesus results in men becoming like him.

Harry Emerson Fosdick

As to Jesus of Nazareth, my opinion of whom you particularly desire, I think the system of morals and his religion, as he left them to us, is the best the world ever saw, or is likely to see.

Benjamin Franklin

Had the doctrines of Jesus been preached always as pure as they came from his lips, the whole civilized world would now have been Christians.

Thomas Jefferson

Too often an institution serves to bless the majority opinion. Today when too many move to the rhythmic beat of the status quo, whoever would be a Christian must be a nonconformist.

Martin Luther King, Jr.

See also: **Brotherhood, Church, Faith, Religion, Worship**

CHURCH

Business checks up on itself frequently to be sure that it still is headed for its original goals. Is there not need for a similar check-up on the part of the church?

Bruce Barton

See also: **Christianity, Religion, Worship**

CHURCH AND STATE

No religion can long continue to maintain its purity when the church becomes the subservient vassal of the state.
Felix Adler

In the relationship between man and religion, the state is firmly committed to a position of neutrality.
Thomas Campbell (Tom) Clark

Religion cannot sink lower than when somehow it is raised to a state religion ... it becomes then an avowed mistress.
Heinrich Heine

I believe in an America where the separation of church and state is absolute— where no Catholic prelate would tell the President, should he be a Catholic, how to act, and no Protestant minister would tell his parishioners for whom to vote— where no church or church school is granted any public funds or political preference—and where no man is denied public office merely because his religion differs fron the president who might appoint him or the people who might elect him.
John Fitzgerald Kennedy

See also: **Christianity, Church**

CITIZENSHIP

The most important office, ... that of private citizen.
Louis Dembitz Brandeis

Voting is the least arduous of a citizen's duties. He has the prior and harder duty of making up his mind.
Ralph Barton Perry

Finally, whether you are citizens of America or citizens of the world, ask of us here the same high standards of strength and sacrifice which we ask of you. With a good conscience our only sure reward, with history the final judge of our deeds, let us go forth to lead the land we love, asking His blessing and His help, but knowing that here on earth God's work must truly be our own.
John Fitzgerald Kennedy

Citizenship consists in the service of the country.
Jawaharlal Nehru

Now the trumpet summons us again— not as a call to bear arms, though arms we need–not as a call to battle, though embattled we are—but a call to bear the burden of a long twilight struggle year in and year out, "rejoicing in hope, patient in tribulation" —a struggle against the common enemies of man: tyranny, poverty, disease and war itself.
John Fitzgerald Kennedy

See also: *America, Beneficence, Duty,*
    Hero, Patriotism, Rights, Soldier

CIVIL RIGHTS: See RIGHTS

CIVILIZATION

In civilization no man can have wholly to or for himself, and whoever would achieve power, influence, or success must cater to the tastes and whims of those who have the granting of these things in their hands.
James Truslow Adams

Civilization is a constant quest for nonviolent means of solving conflicts; it is a common quest for peace.
Max Ascoli

Civilization is the upward struggle of mankind, in which millions are trampled to death that thousands may mount on their bodies.

Francis Maitland Balfour

No civilization other than that which is Christian, is worth seeking or possessing.

Otto Edward Leopold von Bismarck

Human wants are continually shaped and reshaped by civilization, its technical and social standards and its progress.

Karl Brandt

Civilizations are never made up of wholly consistent parts.

Lyman Lloyd Bryson

You think that a wall as solid as the earth separates civilization from barbarism. I tell you the division is a thread, a sheet of glass. A touch here, a push there, and you bring back the reign of Saturn.

Sir John Buchan

The test of a civilization is in the way that it cares for its helpless members.

Pearl Sydenstricker Buck

Can you tell me, in a world that is flagrant with the failures of civilizations, what there is particularly immortal about yours?

Gilbert Keith Chesterton

Civilization will not last, freedom will not survive, peace will not be kept, unless a very large majority of mankind unite together to defend them and show themselves possessed of a constabulary power before which barbaric and atavistic forces will stand in awe.

Sir Winston Leonard Spencer Churchill

The ease, the luxury, and the abundance of the highest state of civilization, are as productive of selfishness as the difficulties, the privations, and the sterilities of the lowest.

Charles Caleb Colton

Increased means and leisure are the two civilizers of man.

Benjamin Disraeli

A sufficient and sure method of civilization is the influence of good women.

Ralph Waldo Emerson

The true test of civilization is, not the census, nor the size of cities, nor the crops, but the kind of man that the country turns out.

Ralph Waldo Emerson

The greatest danger to a civilized nation is the man who has no stake in it, and nothing to lose by rejecting all that civilization stands for.

Henry Ford II

Civilization, in the real sense of the term, consists not in the multiplication, but in the deliberate and voluntary reduction of wants. This alone promotes real happiness and contentment, and increases the capacity for service.

Mohandas Karamchand (Mahatma) Gandhi

The quality of a civilization depends on a balance of body, mind and spirit in its people, measured on a scale less human than divine. . . . To survive, we must keep this balance. To progress, we must improve it. Science is upsetting it with an overemphasis of mind and a neglect of spirit and body.

Charles Augustus Lindbergh

See also: **Culture, Improvement, Progress**

CLASS

There may be said to be two classes of people in the world: those who constantly divide the people of the world into classes, and those who do not.

Robert Charles Bench

As property has its duties as well as its rights, rank has its bores as well as its pleasures.

Benjamin Disraeli

The middle class, that prisoner of the barbarian 20th century.

Sinclair

There was one point by which it [Israel] was distinguished from the other nations of antiquity, namely, its comparative absence of caste, its equality of religious relations.

Arthur Penrhyn Stanley

There is nothing to which men cling more tenaciously than the privileges of class.

Leonard Sidney Woolf

See also: **Rank**

CLEMENCY

Clemency, which we make a virtue of, proceeds sometimes from vanity, sometimes from indolence, often from fear, and almost always from a mixture of all three.

Duc François de La Rochefoucauld

It is not right to show promiscuous and general clemency; and to forgive everyone is as much cruelty as to forgive no one.

Seneca

If you preserve me uninjured, I shall be a lasting example of your clemency.

Tacitus

See also: **Compassion, Cruelty,**
Forgiveness, Leniency, Mercy,
Patience, Pity, Sympathy

CLEVERNESS

Clever men are good, but they are not the best.

Thomas Carlyle

The doctrine of human equality reposes on this: that there is no man really clever who has not found that he is stupid.

Gilbert Keith Chesterton

It takes a clever man to turn cynic, and a wise man to be clever enough not to.

Fannie Hurst

It is great cleverness to know how to conceal our cleverness.

Duc François de La Rochefoucauld

The worst part of an eminent man's conversation is, nine times out of ten, to be found in that part which he means to be clever.

Edward G. Bulwer-Lytton (Baron Lytton)

See also: **Ability, Intelligence**

COMMON SENSE

If common sense has not the brilliancy of the sun, it has the fixity of the stars.

Fernan Caballero

Common sense is, of all kinds, the most uncommon. It implies good judgment, sound discretion, and true and practical wisdom applied to common life.

Tryon Edwards

No man is quite sane. Each has a vein of folly in his composition—a slight determination of blood to the head, to make sure of holding him hard to some one point which he has taken to heart.
Ralph Waldo Emerson

There is nobody so irritating as somebody with less intelligence and more sense than we have.
Don Herold

He was one of those men who possess almost every gift, except the gift of the power to use them.
Charles Kingsley

Common sense is only a modification of talent. Genius is an exaltation of it. The difference is, therefore, in degree, not nature.
Edward G. Bulwer-Lytton (Baron Lytton)

The crown of all faculties is common sense. It is not enough to do the right thing, it must be done at the right time and place. Talent knows what to do; tact knows when and how to do it.
William Matthews

One pound of learning requires ten pounds of common sense to apply it.
Persian Proverb

Fine sense, and exalted sense, are not half as useful as common sense. There are forty men of wit to one man of sense. He that will carry nothing about him but gold, will be every day at a loss for readier change.
Alexander Pope

Common sense is the knack of seeing things as they are, and doing things as they ought to be done.
Calvin Ellis Stowe

See also: **Intelligence, Prudence**

COMMUNICATIONS MEDIA

I think everybody in the television and radio professions has a right to think of himself as a man bearing a great responsibility as a crusader, and help to do this job of education, of ourselves and others about us, and to bring home here an understanding of what goes on in the rest of the world.
Dwight David Eisenhower

It is a medium of entertainment which permits millions of people to listen to the same joke at the same time, and yet remain lonesome.
Thomas Stearns Eliot

A world community can exist only with world communication, which means something more than extensive short-wave facilities scattered about the globe. It means common understanding, a common tradition, common ideas, and common ideals.
Robert Maynard Hutchins

At the high speeds of electric communication, purely visual means of apprehending the world are no longer possible; they are just too slow to be relevant or effective.
(Herbert) Marshall McLuhan

Media, by altering the environment, evoke in us unique ratios of sense perceptions. The extension of any one sense alters the way we think and act—the way we perceive the world.
(Herbert) Marshall McLuhan

We shall never be able to remove suspicion and fear as potential causes of war until communication is permitted to flow, free and open, across intentional boundaries.
Harry S Truman

The modern world is not given to uncritical admiration. It expects its idols to have feet of clay, and can be reasonably sure that press and camera will report their exact dimensions.

Barbara Ward (Lady Jackson)

The fantastic advances in the field of electronic communication constitute a greater danger to the privacy of the individual.

Earl Warren

See also: **Space**

COMMUNISM

An iron curtain has descended across the Continent.

Sir Winston Leonard Spencer Churchill

We cannot successfully combat Soviet Communism in the world and frustrate its methods of fraud, terrorism, and violence unless we have a faith with spiritual appeal that translates itself into practices which, in our modern complex society, get rid of the sordid, degrading conditions of life in which the spirit cannot grow.

John Foster Dulles

What is a communist?—One who has yearnings for equal division of unequal earnings. Idler or bungler, he is willing to fork out his penny and pocket your shilling.

Ebenezer Elliott

The evil of communism is not its doctrinal content, which at worst is utopian, but its fanatical certainty of itself, its messianic zeal and its brutal intolerance of dissent.

James William Fulbright

Communism possesses a language which every people can understand. Its elements are hunger, envy, and death.

Heinrich Heine

There are many people in the world who really don't understand—or say they don't understand—or say they don't—what is the great issue between the free world and the Communist world . . . There are some who say that Communism is the wave of the future . . . And there are some who say in Europe and elsewhere "we can work with the Communists." . . . And there are even a few who say that it's true that Communism is an evil system but it permits us to make economic progress. Let them come to Berlin!

John Fitzgerald Kennedy

See also: **Capitalism, Democracy, Equality, Revolution**

COMPASSION

It is the crown of justice and the glory, where it may kill with right, to save with pity.

Francis Beaumont and John Fletcher

Far from being a handicap to command, compassion is the measure of it. For unless one values the lives of his soldiers and is tormented by their ordeal he is unfit to command.

Omar Nelson Bradley

The dew of compassion is a tear.

George Gordon Byron (Lord Byron)

Man may dismiss compassion from his heart, but God will never.

William Cowper

The mind is no match with the heart in persuasion; constitutionality is no match with compassion.

Everett McKinley Dirksen

Compassion to an offender who has grossly violated the laws, is, in effect, a cruelty to the peaceable subject who has observed them.

Junius

See also: **Clemency, Mercy, Pity**

COMPETITION

To vie is not to rival.

Benjamin Disraeli

Today we are competing for men's hearts and minds, and trust all over the world. such a competition, what we are at home and what we do at home is even more important than what we say abroad.

Dwight David Eisenhower

Competition is the very life of science.

Horace Meyer Kallen

See also: **Rivalry**

COMPLAINT

It is a general popular error to imagine the loudest complainers for the public to be the most anxious for its welfare.

Edmund Burke

I have always despised the whining yelp of complaint, and the cowardly feeble resolve.

Robert Burns

Murmur at nothing: if our ills are irreparable, it is ungrateful; if remediless, it is vain.

Charles Caleb Cotton

We do not wisely when we vent complaint and censure. We cry out for a little pain, when we do but smile for a great deal of contentment.

Owen Felltham

Had we not faults of our own, we should take less pleasure in complaining of others.

François de Salignac de La Mothe-Fénelon

I will not be as those who spend the day in complaining of headache, and the night in drinking the wine that gives it.

Johann Wolfgang von Goethe

The usual fortune of complaint is to excite contempt more than pity.

Samuel Johnson

COMPLIMENT

Soft soap is always a sign that there's dirty water about.

John Dickson Carr

Compliments are pleasant but tend towards complacency and laziness, while complaints stir you to new and necessary effort.

Frank Case

A deserved and discriminating compliment is often one of the strongest encouragements and incentives to the diffident and self-distrustful.

Tryon Edwards

Some people pay a compliment as if they expected a receipt.

Frank McKinney (Kin) Hubbard

See also: **Applause, Flattery, Praise**

COMPROMISE

An appeaser is one who feeds a crocodile hoping it will eat him last.

Sir Winston Leonard Spencer Churchill

CONFESSION

The confession of evil works is the first beginning of good works.

Augustine of Hippo

Confession is good for the soul only in the sense that a tweed coat is good for dandruff—it is a palliative rather than a remedy.

Peter De Vries

There could not be a cleansing without a clean confession.

Mohandas Karamchand (Mahatma) Gandhi

A man should never be ashamed to own he has been in the wrong, which is but saying, in other words, that he is wiser to-day than he was yesterday.

Alexander Pope

Why does no man confess his vices? because he is yet in them. It is for a waking man to tell his dream.

Seneca

No person is ever made better by having someone else tell him how rotten he is; but many are made better by avowing the guilt themselves.

Fulton John Sheen

See also: Conscience, Guilt, Morality, Sin, Truth

CONFIDENCE

Let us have a care not to disclose our hearts to those who shut up theirs against us.

Francis Beaumont

When young, we trust ourselves too much; and we trust others too little when old. Rashness is the error of youth; timid caution of age.

Charles Caleb Colton

They can conquer who believe they can.

John Dryden

Self-trust is the essence of heroism.

Ralph Waldo Emerson

Trust men and they will be true to you; treat them greatly and they will show themselves great.

Ralph Waldo Emerson

That man who has inspired confidence in another has never lost anything in this world.

Mohandas Karamchand (Mahatma) Gandhi

Confidence is a plant of slow growth; especially in an aged bosom.

Samuel Johnson

Confidence always gives pleasure to the man in whom it is placed. It is a tribute which we pay to his merit; it is a treasure which we entrust to his honour; it is a pledge which gives him a right over us, and a kind of dependence to which we subject ourselves voluntarily.

Duc François de La Rochefoucauld

Confidence, in conversation, has a greater share than wit.

Duc François de La Rochefoucauld

Trust him little who praises all; him less who censures all; and him least who is indifferent to all.

Johann Kaspar Lavater

Confidence imparts a wondrous inspiration to its possessor. It bears him on in security, either to meet no danger, or to find matter of glorious trial.

John Milton

See also: Boldness, Doubt, Faith, Self-Confidence, Trust

CONFORMITY

These are the days when men of all disciplines and all political faiths seek the comfortable and the accepted; when the man of controversy is looked upon as a disturbing influence; when originality is taken to be a mark of instability; and when, in minor modification of the scriptural parable, the bland lead the bland.

John Kenneth Galbraith

If we conform too much, we become conventional nobodies, and lose our individuality; on the other hand, if we rebel too much, we are on the "outs" with the rest of our fellow men, and get nowhere.

Joseph Jastrow

You must adjust . . . This is the legend imprinted in every schoolbook, the invisible message on every blackboard. Our schools have become vast factories for the manufacture of robots.

Robert Linder

Fair fame is won as a rule by all who cheerfully take things as they find them and interfere with no established custom.

Philo

See also: Custom, Tradition

CONSCIENCE

Blind is he who sees not his own conscience; lame is he who wanders from the right way.

Anthony of Padua

A good conscience is to the soul what health is to the body; it preserves constant ease and serenity within us, and more than countervails all the calamities and afflictions which can befall us without.

Joseph Addison

A good conscience is the palace of Christ; the temple of the Holy Ghost; the paradise of delight; the standing Sabbath of the saints.

Augustine of Hippo

What we call conscience, is, in many instances, only a wholesome fear of the constable.

Christian Nestell Bovee

Conscience is a great ledger book in which all our offenses are written and registered, and which time reveals to the sense and feeling of the offender.

Richard Eugene Burton

That conscience approves of any given course of action, is, of itself, an obligation.

Joseph Butler

Man's conscience is the oracle of God.

George Gordon Byron (Lord Byron)

There is no future pang can deal that justice on the self-condemned, he deals on his own soul.

George Gordon Byron (Lord Byron)

The torture of a bad conscience is the hell of a living soul.

John Calvin

A good digestion depends upon a good conscience.

Benjamin Disraeli

My dominion ends where that of conscience begins.

Napoleon I (Bonaparte)

Conscience—that vicegerent of God in human heart, whose still, small voice loudest revelry cannot drown.

William Henry Harrison

We cannot live better than in seeking to become better, nor more agreeably than in having a clear conscience.

Socrates

There is no witness so terrible–no accuser so powerful as conscience which dwells within us

Sophocles

The voice of conscience is so delicate that it is easy to stifle it; but it is also so clear that it is impossible to mistake it.

Madame de Staël

Conscience, honor, and credit, are all in our interest; and without the concurrence of the former, the latter are but impositions upon ourselves and others.

Sir Richard Steele

Trust that man in nothing who has not a conscience in everything.

Laurence Sterne

Conscience tells us that we ought to do right, but it does not tell us what right is —that we are taught by God's word.

Henry Clay Trumbull

CONSERVATION

As soils are depleted, human health, vitality and intelligence go with them.

Louis Bromfield

The conservation of natural resources is, and has been for a half a century, the paramount domestic issue before the American people.

Henry Steele Commager

Conservation is ethically sound. It is rooted in our love of the land, our respect for the rights of others, our devotion to the rule of law.

Lyndon Baines Johnson

To sustain an environment suitable for man we must fight on a thousand battlegrounds. Despite all of our wealth and knowledge, we cannot create a redwood forest, or a wild or a gleaming seashore. But we can keep those we have.

Lyndon Baines Johnson

There is no sin punished more implacably by nature than the sin of resistance to change.

Anne Spencer Morrow Lindbergh

See also: **Forethought, Frugality, Water Pollution**

CONTENTMENT

A contented mind is the greatest blessing a man can enjoy in this world; and if, in the present life, his happiness arises from the subduing of his desires, it will arise in the next from the gratification of them,

Joseph Addison

A wise man will always be contented with his condition, and will live rather according to the precepts of virtue, than according to the customs of his country.

Antisthenes

True contentment depends not upon what we have; a tub was large enough for Diogenes, but a world was too little for Alexander.

Charles Caleb Colton

Whether happiness may come or not, one should try and prepare one's self to do without it.

George Eliot (Mary Ann Evans)

I am always content with what happens; for I know that what God chooses is better than what I choose.

Epictetus

You traverse the world in search of happiness, which is within the reach of every man; a contented mind confers it all.

Horace

If we fasten our attention on what we have, rather than on what we lack, a very little wealth is sufficient.

Francis Johnson

A man who finds no satisfaction in himself, seeks for it in vain elsewhere.

Duc François de La Rochefoucauld .

If two angels were sent down from heaven, one to conduct an empire, and the other to sweep a street, they would feel no inclination to change employments.

John Newton

One should be either sad or joyful. Contentment is a warm sty for eaters and sleepers.

Eugene Gladstone O'Neill

Contentment is natural wealth, luxury artificial poverty.

Socrates

The noblest mind the best contentment has.

Edmund Spenser

When loss and gain are alike to one that is real gain.

Sir Rabindranath Tagore

See also: *Amusement, Happiness, Peace, Pleasure*

CONTRAST

Where there is much light, the shadow is deep.

Johann Wolfgang von Goethe

The lustre of diamonds is invigorated by the interposition of darker bodies; the lights of a picture are created by the shades; the highest pleasure which nature has indulged to sensitive perception is that of rest after fatigue.

Samuel Johnson

Joy and grief are never far apart. In the same street the shutters of one house are closed, while the curtains of the next are brushed by the shadows of the dance. A wedding party returns from the Church; and a funeral winds to its door. The smiles and sadness of life are the tragi-comedy of Shakespeare. Gladness and sighs brighten and dim the mirror he beholds.

Robert Eldridge Aris Willmott

CONVERSATION

In private conversation between intimate friends the wisest men very often talk like the weakest; for, indeed, the talking with a friend is nothing else but thinking aloud.

Joseph Addison

For good or ill, your conversation is your advertisement. Every time you open your mouth you let men look into your mind. Do they see it well clothed, neat, businesslike?

Bruce Barton

Generally speaking, poverty of speech is the outward evidence of poverty of mind.

Bruce Barton

Drawing on my fine command of language, I said nothing.

Robert Charles Benchley

A single conversation across the table with a wise man is worth a month's study of books.

Chinese Proverb

Conversation is an art in which a man has all mankind for competitors.

Ralph Waldo Emerson

Conversation warms the mind, enlivens the imagination, and is continually starting fresh game that is immediately pursued and taken, which would never have occurred in the duller intercourse of epistolary correspondence.

Benjamin Franklin

COURAGE

Courage that grows from constitution, often forsakes a man when he has occasion for it; courage which arises from a sense of duty, acts in a uniform manner.

Joseph Addison

Courage is rightly esteemed the first of human qualities because it is the quality which guarantees all others.

Sir Winston Leonard Spencer Churchill

Conscience is the root of all true courage; if a man would be brave let him obey his conscience.

James Freeman Clarke

To see what is right and not to do it, is want of courage.

Confucius

Courage from hearts and not from numbers grows.

John Dryden

Those nervous persons who may be terrified by imaginary dangers are often courageous in the face of real danger.

Henry Havelock Ellis

The courage of life is often a less dramatic spectacle than the courage of a final moment; but it is no less than a magnificent mixture of triumph and tragedy. A man does what he must—in spite of personal consequences, in spite of obstacles and dangers and pressures and that is the basis of all human morality.

John Fitzgerald Kennedy

We can never be certain of our courage till we have faced danger.

Duc François de La Rochefoucauld

A coward flees backward, away from new things. A man of courage flees forward, in the midst of new things.

Jacques Maritain

If we survive danger it steels our courage more than anything else.

Barthold Georg Niebuhr

Courage in danger is half the battle.

Plautus

Courage consists not in hazarding without fear, but being resolutely minded in a just cause.

Plutarch

Courage consists, not in blindly overlooking danger, but in seeing and conquering it.

Jean Paul Richter

Far better it is to dare mighty things, to win glorious triumphs, even though checkered by failure, than to take rank with those poor spirits who neither enjoy much nor suffer much, because they live in the gray twilight that knows neither victory nor defeat.

Theodore Roosevelt

A great deal of talent is lost in this world for the want of a little courage.

Sydney Smith

True courage is not the brutal force of vulgar heroes, but the firm resolve of virtue and reason.

Alfred North Whitehead

See also: **Boldness, Bravery, Confidence, Cowardice, Firmness, Hero**

COURT

The place of justice is a hallowed place.

Francis Bacon

The penalty for laughing in a courtroom is six months in jail; if it were not for this penalty, the jury would never hear the evidence.

Henry Louis Mencken

See also: **Crime, Justice, Rights**

COURTESY

The small courtesies sweeten life; the greater, ennoble it.

Christian Nestell Bovee

We should be as courteous to a man as we are to a picture, which we are willing to give the advantage of the best light.

Ralph Waldo Emerson

When saluted with a salutation, salute the person with a better salutation, or at least return the same, for God taketh account of all things.

Koran

Approved valor is made precious by natural courtesy.

Sir Philip Sidney

How beautiful is humble courtesy!

Sir Rabindranath Tagore

See also: **Manners**

COWARDICE

Bullies are always to be found where there are cowards.

Mohandas Karamchand (Mahatma) Gandhi

Fear has its use but cowardice has none.

Mohandas Karamchand (Mahatma) Gandhi

Cowardice is not synonymous with prudence. —It often happens that the better part of discretion is valor.

William Hazlitt

Cowardice . . . is almost always simply a lack of ability to suspend the functioning of the imagination.

Ernest Hemingway

It is the coward who fawns upon those above him. It is the coward who is insolent whenever he dares be so.

Junius

See also: **Bravery, Fear**

CREATIVITY

Creative people are especially obser-
vant, and they value accurate observation (telling themselves the truth) more
than other people do . . . . They are by
constitution more vigorous, and have
available to them an exceptional fund of
psychic and physical energy.

Frank X. Barron

Creation is a drug I can't do without.

Cecil Blount De Mille

Man is made to create, from the poet to
the potter.

Benjamin Disraeli

Few of the great creators have bland
personalities. They are cantankerous
egotists, the kind of men who are un-
welcome in the modern corporation.

David Mackenzie Ogilvy

See also: *Art, Artist, Literature*

CREDITOR

It takes a man to make a devil; and the
fittest man for such a purpose is a
snarling, waspish red-hot, fiery, creditor.

Henry Ward Beecher

Creditors have better memories than
debtors; they are a superstitious sect,
great observers of set days and times.

Benjamin Franklin

The creditor whose appearance glad-
dens the heart of a debtor may hold his
head in sunbeams, and his foot on
storms.

Johann Kaspar Lavater

See also: *Debt*

CREDULITY

There's a sucker born every minute.

Phineas Taylor Barnum

The more gross the fraud, the more
glibly will it go down and the more
greedily will it be swallowed, since folly
will always find faith wherever impos-
tors will find impudence.

Christian Nestell Bovee

Your noblest natures are most credulous.

George Chapman

Beyond all credulity is the credulous-
ness of atheists, who believe that chance
could make the world, when it cannot
build a house.

McDonald Clarke

When people are bewildered they tend
to become credulous.

(John) Calvin Coolidge

Generous souls are still most subject to
credulity.

Sir William Davenant

Credulity is the common failing of inex-
perienced virtue; and he who is sponta-
neously suspicious may justly be
charged with radical corruption.

Samuel Johnson

To take for granted as truth all against
the fame of others, is a species of credulity that men would blush at on any
other subject.

Jane Porter

The only disadvantage of an honest
heart is credulity.

Sir Philip Sidney

You believe easily that which you hope
for earnestly.

Terence

See also: *Doubt, Faith, Ignorance, Innocence, Lying, Simplicity*

CRIME

Crimes lead into one another. They who are capable of being forgers, are capable of being incendiaries.

Edmund Burke

The real significance of crime is its being a breach of faith with the community of mankind.

Joseph Conrad

Physical deformity calls forth our charity. But the infinite misfortunate of moral deformity calls forth nothing but hatred and vengeance.

Clarence Seward Darrow

One crime is everything; two nothing.

Madame Dorothée Deluzy

There is no den in the wide world to hide a rogue. Commit a crime and the earth is made of glass. Commit a crime, and it seems as if a coat of snow fell on the ground, such as reveals in the woods the track of every partridge, and fox, and squirrel.

Ralph Waldo Emerson

Set a thief to catch a thief.

English Proverb

Crime will last as long as old and gloomy humanity. But the number of criminals has lessened with the number of the wretched. The slums of the great cities are the feeding grounds of crime.

Anatole France

Whoever profits by the crime is guilty of it.

French Proverb

Crime is not punished as an offense against God, but as prejudicial to society.

James Anthony Froude

All crime is a kind of disease and should be treated as such.

Mohandas Karamchand (Mahatma) Gandhi

Crimes sometimes shock us too much; vices almost always too little.

Augustus and Julius Hare

We are a fact-gathering organization only. We don't clear anybody. We don't condemn anybody. Just the minute the F.B.I. begins making recommendations on what should be done with its information, it becomes a Gestapo.

John Edgar Hoover

Organized crime constitutes nothing less than a guerrilla war against society.

Lyndon Baines Johnson

Revolvers and nightsticks are clearly inadequate for the many different crises faced by the police. New weapons and chemicals—effective but causing no permanent injury—have been and are being developed.

Lyndon Baines Johnson

We easily forget crimes that are known only to ourselves.

Duc François de La Rochefoucauld

Whenever man commits a crime heaven finds a witness.

Edward G. Bulwer-Lytton (Baron Lytton)

The idea of having a lawyer present before you can ask a man a question about whether he has committed a crime is taking absurdity to the extreme.

John L. McClellan

The contagion of crime is like that of the plague. Criminals collected together corrupt each other! They are worse than ever when, at the termination of their punishment, they return to society.

Napoleon I (Bonaparte)

If people starve what are they to do? Judges and magistrates wax eloquent about the increase of crime; but are blind to the obvious economic causes of it.

Jawaharlal Nehru

Ignorant people imagine that if the punishment is not severe enough crimes will increase. As a matter of fact, the exact reverse is the truth.

Jawaharlal Nehru

Small crimes always precede great ones. Never have we seen timid innocence pass suddenly to extreme licentiousness.

Jean Baptiste Racine

A man may be disconcerted because of unconscious wants. For instance, Americans need rest, but do not know it. I believe this to be a large part of the explanation of the crime wave in the United States.

Bertrand Arthur William Russell

And who are the greater criminals—those who sell instruments of death, or those who buy them and use them?

Robert Emmet Sherwood

Fear follows crime, and is its punishment.

Voltaire (François Marie Arouet)

See also: **Dishonesty, Fraud, Guilt, Murder, Riot, Sin, Vice, Wickedness, Wrong**

CRISIS

Crises and deadlocks when they occur have at least this advantage, that they force us to think.

Jawaharlal Nehru

Every little thing counts in a crisis .

Jawaharlal Nehru

These are the times that try men's souls.

Thomas Paine

The turning points of lives are not the great moments. The real crises are often concealed in occurrences so trivial in appearance that they pass unobserved.

William E. Woodward

CRITICISM

It is ridiculous for any man to criticize the works of another if he has not distinguished himself by his own performances.

Joseph Addison

I am bound by my own definition of criticism: a disinterested endeavour to learn and propagate the best that is known and thought in the world.

Matthew Arnold

It is a maxim with me, that no man was ever written out of a reputation but by himself.

Richard Bentley

The legitimate aim of criticism is to direct attention to the excellent. The bad will dig its own grave, and the imperfect may safely be left to that final neglect from which no amount of present undeserved popularity can rescue it.

Christian Nestell Bovee

Is it in destroying and pulling down that skill is displayed? The shallowest understanding, the rudest hand, is more than equal to that task.

Edmund Burke

The rule in carving holds good as to criticism; never cut with a knife what you can cut with a spoon.

Charles Buxton

Criticism is dangerous, because it wounds a man's precious pride, hurts his sense of importance, and arouses his resentment.

Dale Carnegie

I have adhered to my rule of never criticizing any measure of war or policy after the event unless I had before expressed publicly or formally my opinion or warning about it. Indeed in the afterlight I have softened many of the severities of contemporary controversy.

Sir Winston Leonard Spencer Churchill

It is much easier to be critical than to be correct.

Benjamin Disraeli

The most noble criticism is that in which the critic is not the antagonist so much as the rival of the author.

Benjamin Disraeli

CRUELTY

Cruelty and fear shake hands together.

Honoré de Balzac

Man's inhumanity to man, makes countless thousands mourn.

Robert Burns

One of the ill effects of cruelty is that it makes the by-standers cruel.

Sir Thomas Fowell Buxton

Detested sport, that owes its pleasures to another's pain.

William Cowper

I would not enter on my list of friends the man who needlessly sets foot upon a worm.

William Cowper

Cruelty is the child of ignorance.

Clarence Seward Darrow

Cruelty, like every other vice, requires no motive outside of itself; it only requires opportunity.

George Eliot (Mary Ann Evans)

Cruelty to dumb animals is one of the distinguishing vices of the lowest and basest of the people. Wherever it is found, it is a certain mark of ignorance and meanness.

William Jones of Nayland

Brutality degrades everybody. It degrades the sufferer; it degrades also the person who makes others suffer.

Jawaharld Nehru

All cruelty springs from hard-heartedness and weakness.

Seneca

See also: *Abuse, Punishment, Violence, War.*

CULTURE

The great aim of culture [is] the aim of setting ourselves to ascertain what perfection is and how to make it prevail.

Matthew Arnold

Culture of the mind must be subservient to the heart.

Mohandas Karamchand (Mahatma) Gandhi

Culture exists the moment man discovers that the hand armed with the flint is capable of things which without it would have been beyond his reach.

Johan Huizinga

Culture cannot be copied suddenly; it has to take root. A backward nation merely aping advanced nations changes the gold and silver of real culture into tinsel.

Jawaharlal Nehru

Culture is the widening of the mind and of the spirit.

Jawaharlal Nehru

See also: **Art, Literature, Manners**

CURIOSITY

The first and simplest emotion which we discover in the human mind, is curiosity.

Edmund Burke

Curiosity is one of the permanent and certain characteristics of a vigorous intellect. Every advance into knowledge opens new prospects and produces new incitements to further progress.

Samuel Johnson

There are different kinds of curiosity: one the offspring of interested motives, leading us to the desire of learning what may be useful to us; and the other arising from feelings of pride, which makes us desire to know what others are ignorant of.

Duc François de La Rochefoucauld

CUSTOM

Men commonly think according to their inclinations, speak according to their learning and imbibed opinions, but generally act according to custom.

Francis Bacon

There is no tyrant like custom, and no freedom where its edicts are not resisted.

Christian Nestell Bovee

There are not infrequently substantial reasons underneath for customs that appear to us absurd.

Charlotte Brontë

Customs may not be as wise as laws, but they are always more popular.

Benjamin Disraeli

The custom and fashion of to-day will be the awkwardness and outrage of to-morrow—so arbitrary are these transient laws.

Alexandre Dumas (père)

In this great society wide lying around us, a critical analysis would find very few spontaneous actions. It is almost all custom and gross sense.

Ralph Waldo Emerson

See also: **Conformity, Fashion, Habit, Tradition.**

CYNIC

The cynic is one who never sees a good quality in a man, and never fails to see a bad one. He is the human owl, vigilant in darkness and blind to light, mousing for vermin, and never seeing noble game.

Henry Ward Beecher

Don't be a cynic, and bewail and bemoan. Omit the negative propositions. Don't waste yourself in rejection, nor bark against the bad, but chant the beauty of the good.—Set down nothing that will help somebody.

Ralph Waldo Emerson

It takes a clever man to turn cynic, and a wise man to be clever enough not to.

Fannie Hurst

A cynic is a man who knows the price of everything, and the value of nothing.

Oscar Wilde

See also: **Doubt, Prejudice, Skepticism**

DEATH

Every minute dies a man, and one and one-sixteenth is born.

Anonymous

It is as natural to man to die, as to be born; and to a little infant, perhaps the one is as painful as the other.

Francis Bacon

As long as we are living, God will give us living grace, and he won't give us dying grace till it's time to die. What's the use of trying to feel like dying when you ain't dying, nor anywhere near it?

Henry Ward Beecher

Certainly there is no happiness within this circle of flesh, nor is it in the optics of these eyes to behold felicity; the first day of our Jubilee is death.

Sir Thomas Browne

Each person is born to one possession which outvalues all the others—his last breath.

Samuel Langhorne Clemens (Mark Twain)

Whoever has lived long enough to find out what life is, knows how deep a debt of gratitude we owe to Adam, the first great benefactor of our race. He brought death into the world.

Samuel Langhorne Clemens (Mark Twain)

Time is a system of folds which only death can unfold.

Jean Cocteau

Death is the liberator of him whom freedom cannot release; the physician of him whom medicine cannot cure; the comforter of him whom time cannot console.

Charles Caleb Colton

Death has nothing terrible which life has not made so. A faithful Christian life in this world is the best preparation for the next.

Tryon Edwards

I never think he is quite ready for another world who is altogether weary of this.

Hugh Hamilton

What is certain in death is somewhat softened by what is uncertain: it is an indefiniteness in the time, which holds a certain relation to the infinite, and to what is called eternity.

Jean de La Bruyère

Death is not a foe, but an inevitable adventure.

Sir Oliver Joseph Lodge

There is no death! What seems so is transition; this life of mortal breath is but a suburb of the life elysian, whose portal we call death.

Henry Wadsworth Longfellow

Death is the golden key of eternity.

John Milton

On death and judgment, heaven and hell, who oft doth think, must needs die well.

Sir Walter Raleigh

Is death the last sleep? No, it is the last and final awakening.

Sir Walter Scott

Be of good cheer about death, and know this of a truth, that no evil can happen to a good man, either in life or after death.

Socrates

One may live as a conqueror, a king, or a magistrate; but he must die a man. The bed of death brings every human being to his pure individuality, to the intense contemplation of that deepest and most solemn of all relations—the relation between the creature and his Creator.

Daniel Webster

Men may live fools, but fools they cannot die.

Edward Young

See also: **Epitaph, Grave, Immortality, Life**

DEBT

Do not accustom yourself to consider debt only as an inconvenience; you will find it a calamity.

Samuel Johnson

Youth is in danger until it learns to look upon debts as furies.

Edward G. Bulwer-Lytton (Baron Lytton)

Debt is the secret foe of thrift, as vice and idleness are its open foes. The debt-habit is the twin brother of poverty.

Theodore Thornton Munger

A small debt produces a debtor; a large one, an enemy.

Publilius Syrus

I have discovered the philosopher's stone, that turns everything into gold: it is, "Pay as you go."

John Randolph

See also: **Borrowing**

DECEIT

He that has no real esteem for any of the virtues, can best assume the appearance of them all.

Charles Caleb Colton

Idiots only may be cozened twice

John Dryden

Of all the evil spirits abroad in the world, insincerity is the most dangerous.

James Anthony Froude

Have I not told you times without number that ultimately a deceiver only deceives himself?

Mohandas Karamchand (Mahatma) Gandhi

No man, for any considerable period, can wear one face to himself and another to the multitude, without finally getting bewildered as to which may be true.

Nathaniel Hawthorne

It is double pleasure to deceive the deceiver.

Jean de La Fontaine

It is as easy to deceive one's self without perceiving it, as it is difficult to deceive others without their finding it out.

Duc François de La Rochefoucauld

We must make a difference between speaking to deceive and being silent to be impenetrable.

> *Voltaire (François Marie Arouet)*

There are three persons you should never deceive: your physician, your confessor, and your lawyer.

> *Horace Walpole*

See also: ***Dishonesty, Fraud, Hypocrisy, Lying***

DECENCY

Virtue and decency are so nearly related that it is difficult to separate them from each other but in our imagination.

> *Cicero*

Decency is the least of all laws, but yet it is the law which is most strictly observed.

> *Duc François de La Rochefoucauld*

See also: ***Censorship, Modesty***

DECEPTION: See DECEIT

DEED

Good actions ennoble us, and we are the sons of our own deeds.

> *Miguel de Cervantes Saavedra*

See also: ***Action***

DEFEAT

Defeat is a school in which truth always grows strong.

> *Henry Ward Beecher*

Defeat never comes to any man until he admits it.

> *Josephus Daniels*

Heroes are made in the hour of defeat. Success is, therefore, well described as a series of glorious defeats.

> *Mohandas Karamchand (Mahatma) Gandhi*

No man is defeated without some resentment, which will be continued with obstinacy while he believes himself in the right, and asserted with bitterness, if even to his own conscience he is detected in the wrong.

> *Samuel Johnson*

Those who are prepared to die for any cause are seldom defeated.

> *Jawaharlal Nehru*

What is defeat? Nothing but education; nothing but the first step to something better.

> *Wendell Phillips*

Give me the heart to fight and lose.

> *Louis Untermeyer*

See also: ***Failure, Victory***

DELIGHT

I am convinced that we have a degree of delight, and that no small one, in the real misfortunes and pains of others.

> *Edmund Burke*

Sensual delights soon end in loathing, quickly bring a glutting surfeit, and degenerate into torments when they are continued and unintermitted.

> *John Howe*

What more felicity can fall to man than to enjoy delight with liberty?

> *Edmund Spenser*

As high as we have mounted in delight, in our dejection do we sink as low.

> *William Wordsworth*

See also: ***Happiness, Joy***

DELUSION

No man is happy without a delusion of some kind. Delusions are as necessary to our happiness as realities.
Christian Nestell Bovee

The worst deluded are the self-deluded.
Christian Nestell Bovee

The disappointment of manhood succeeds the delusion of youth.
Benjamin Disraeli

You think a man to be your dupe. If he pretends to be so, who is the greatest dupe—he or you?
Jean de La Bruyère

Were we perfectly acquainted with the object, we should never passionately desire it.
Duc François de La Rochefoucauld

When our vices quit us, we flatter ourselves with the belief that it is we who quit them.
Duc François de La Rochefoucauld

See also: **Error**

DEMOCRACY

There can be no democracy unless it is a dynamic democracy. When our people cease to participate—to have a place in the sun—then all of us will wither in the darkness of decadence. All of us will become mute, demoralized, lost souls.
Saul David Alinsky

The real democratic American idea is, not that every man shall be on a level with every other, but that every one shall have liberty, without hindrance, to be what God made him.
Henry Ward Beecher

Democracy is a culture—that is, the deliberate cultivation of an intellectual passion in people with intellects and feelings. Like most passions it is at times vague, heedless, even unpractical but always as real as the affinity of dog and bone.
Jacques Martin Barzun

The democratic faith is this: that the most terribly important things must be left to ordinary men themselves—the mating of the sexes, the rearing of the young, the laws of the state.
Gilbert Keith Chesterton

The first of all democratic doctrines is that all men are interesting.
Gilbert Keith Chesterton

If our democracy is to flourish, it must have criticism; if our government is to function it must have dissent.
Henry Steele Commager

It would be folly to argue that the people cannot make political mistakes. They can and do make grave mistakes. They know it, they pay the penalty, but compared with the mistakes which have been made by every kind of autocracy they are unimportant.
(John) Calvin Coolidge

In a democracy, the individual enjoys not only the ultimate power but carries the ultimate responsibility.
Norman Cousins

Democracy is based upon the conviction that there are extraordinary possibilities in ordinary people.
Harry Emerson Fosdick

Democracy is always a beckoning goal, not a safe harbor. For freedom is an unremitting endeavor, never a final achievement.

Felix Frankfurter

Nature herself vindicates democracy. For nature plants gifts and graces where least expected, and under circumstances that defy all the little artifices of man.

Felix Frankfurter

The measure of a democracy is the measure of the freedom of its humblest citizens.

John Galsworthy

While democracy must have its organization and controls, its vital breath is individual liberty.

Charles Evans Hughes

A democracy is the most difficult kind of government to operate. It represents the last flowering, really, of the human experience.

John Fitzgerald Kennedy

We hold the view that the people come first, not the government.

John Fitzgerald Kennedy

Democracy is the most demanding of all forms of government in terms of the energy, imagination and public spirit required of the individual.

George Catlett Marshall

You don't have a democracy. It's a photocracy.

Sir Robert Gordon Menzies

Democracy has many virtues, but one of its concomitants is wastage of time and energy.

Jawaharlal Nehru

Envy is the basis of democracy.

Bertrand Arthur William Russell

Democracy is both the best and the most difficult form of political organization—the most difficult because it is the best.

Ralph Barton Perry

Democracy, the practice of self-government, is a covenant among free men to respect the rights and liberties of their fellows.

Franklin Delano Roosevelt

We must be the great arsenal of democracy.

Franklin Delano Roosevelt

If there were a people consisting of gods, they would be governed democratically. So perfect a government is not suitable to men.

Jean Jacques Rousseau

In a democracy both deep reverence and a sense of the comic are requisite.

Carl Sandburg

In this critical time in the affairs of the world, it is vital that the democratic nations show their concern for the wellbeing of men everywhere and their desire for a better life for mankind.

Harry S Truman

In art, democracy means that some thought of your own, some feeling you have about the thing yourself, should enter into everything you have to do, so that everything you have may be your own and everything you do be sincerely yourself.

Frank Lloyd Wright

The essential problem is how to govern a large-scale world with small-scale minds.

Sir Alfred Zimmern

See also: *America, Equality, Liberty*

DESIRE

We trifle when we assign limits to our desires, since nature hath set none.
Christian Nestell Bovee

Nothing is far and nothing is dear, if one desires. The world is little, human life is little. There is only one big thing—desire. And before it, when it is big, all is little.
Willa Sibert Cather

The thirst of desire is never filled, nor fully satisfied.
Cicero

There is nothing capricious in nature; and the implanting of a desire indicates that its gratification is in the constitution of the creature that feels it.
Ralph Waldo Emerson

However rich or elevated we may be, a nameless something is always wanting to our imperfect fortune.
Horace

Every desire bears its death in its very gratification. Curiosity languishes under repeated stimulants, and novelties cease to excite surprise, until at length we do not wonder even at a miracle.
Washington Irving

Some desire is necessary to keep life in motion; he whose real wants are supplied, must admit those of fancy.
Samuel Johnson

Before we passionately desire anything which another enjoys, we should examine as to the happiness of its possessor.
Duc François de La Rochefoucauld

There are two tragedies in life. One is not to get your heart's desire. The other is to get it.
George Bernard Shaw

The stoical schemes of supplying our wants by lopping off our desires, is like cutting off our feet when we want shoes.
Jonathan Swift

See also: **Ambition, Appetite, Love, Wish.**

DESPAIR

Now Giant Despair had a wife, and her name was Diffidence.
John Bunyan

Beware of desperate steps. The darkest day, live till to-morrow, will have passed away.
William Cowper

Despair is the conclusion of fools.
Benjamin Disraeli

Despair is the damp of hell, as joy is the serenity of heaven.
John Donne

It is possible, even probable, that hopelessness among a people can be a far more potent cause of war than greed. War—in such case—is a symptom, not the disease.
Dwight David Eisenhower

What we call despair is often only the painful eagerness of unfed hope.
George Eliot (Mary Ann Evans)

See also: **Disappointment, Hope, Poverty, Sorrow**

DESTINY

Destiny is the scapegoat which we make responsible for all our crimes and follies; a necessity we set down for invincible when we have no wish to strive against it.
Arthur James Balfour

Destiny is not a matter of chance, it is a matter of choice; it is not a thing to be waited for, it is a thing to be achieved.
William Jennings Bryan

Death and life have their determined appointments; riches and honors depend upon heaven.
Confucius

We make our fortunes, and we call them fate.
Benjamin Disraeli

Thoughts lead on to purposes; purposes go in action; actions form habits; habits decide character; and character fixes our destiny.
Tryon Edwards

No man of woman born, coward or brave, can shun his destiny.
Homer

There is a destiny that makes us brothers—none goes his way alone.
(Charles) Edwin Markham

The acts of this life are the destiny of the next.
Oriental Proverb

See also: **Chance, Fate, Fortune, God**

DIFFERENCE

If men would consider not so much wherein they differ, as wherein they agree, there would be far less of uncharitableness and angry feeling in the world.
Joseph Addison

Diversity in the Creed, Unanimity in the Deed.
Felix Adler

The difference is no less real because it is of degree.
Benjamin Nathan Cardozo

Even differences prove helpful, where there are tolerance, charity and truth.
Mohandas Karamchand (Mahatma) Gandhi

That among all the differences which exist, the only ones which interest us strongly are those we do not take for granted.
William James

It is only those who have no culture and no belief in culture who resent differences among men and the exploration of the human imagination.
Alfred Kazin

See also: **Argument, Quarrel.**

DIFFICULTY

The best way out of a difficulty is through it.
Anonymous

Difficulties are God's errands; and when we are sent upon them we should esteem it a proof of God's confidence—as a compliment from him.
Henry Ward Beecher

Difficulties show men what they are. In case of any difficulty God has pitted you against a rough antagonist that you may be a conqueror, and this cannot be without toil.
Epictetus

The greatest difficulties lie where we are not looking for them.
Johann Wolfgang von Goethe

The greater the obstacle, the more glory we have in overcoming it; the difficulties with which we are met are the maids of honor which set off virtue.
Moliére (Jean Baptiste Poquelin)

Life would be dull and colourless but for the obstacles that we have to overcome and the fights that we have to win.

Jawaharlal Nehru

Difficulties strengthen the mind, as labor does the body.

Seneca

No man who is occupied in doing a very difficult thing, and doing it very well, ever loses his self-respect.

George Bernard Shaw

See also: **Adversity, Simplicity, Trouble**

DIGNITY

When nothing is permitted to retain dignity, nothing retains for long the allegiance of man.

Herbert Sebastian Agar

Dignity consists not in possessing honors, but in the consciousness that we deserve them.

Aristotle

Dignity is like a top hat. Neither is very much use when you are standing on it.

Christopher Hollis

True dignity is never gained by place, and never lost when honors are withdrawn.

Philip Massinger

Dignity and love do not blend well, nor do they continue long together.

Ovid

See also: **Honor, Pride, Rights, Work**

DILIGENCE

What we hope ever to do with ease, we must learn first to do with diligence.

Samuel Johnson

The expectations of life depend upon diligence; the mechanic that would perfect his work must first sharpen his tools.

Confucius

Diligence is the mother of good luck, and God gives all things to industry. Work while it is called to-day, for you know not how much you may be hindered to-morrow. One to-day is worth two to-morrows; never leave that till to-morrow which you can do to-day.

Benjamin Franklin

Who makes quick use of the moment, is a genius of prudence.

Johann Kaspar Lavater

He who labors diligently need never despair; for all things are accomplished by diligence and labor.

Menander of Athens

See also: **Effort, Labor, Perseverance, Work.**

DIPLOMACY

When a diplomat says yes he means perhaps; when he says perhaps he means no; when he says no he is no diplomat.

Anonymous

I never refuse. I never contradict. I sometimes forget.

Benjamin Disraeli

When the world thermometer registers, "not war, not peace," it is hard to decide whether to follow military judgments or political judgments.

John Foster Dulles

Modern diplomats approach every problem with an open mouth.

Arthur J. Goldberg

Governments are quite familiar with the process of sending inaccurate messages to each other.

David Dean Rusk

High in the art of living comes the wisdom of never letting anyone do anything for you until he so longs to do it that you know he is doing it with real joy.

David Seabury

See also: **Discretion, Government, Judgment, Politics, Tact**

DISAPPOINTMENT

We mount to heaven mostly on the ruins of our cherished schemes, finding our failures were successes.

Amos Bronson Alcott

It is sometimes of God's mercy that men in the eager pursuit of worldy aggrandizement are baffled; for they are very like a train going down an inclined plane—putting on the brake is not pleasant, but it keeps the car on the track and from ruin.

Henry Ward Beecher

The disappointment of manhood succeeds to the delusion of youth.

Benjamin Disraeli

He who expects much will be often disappointed; yet disappointment seldom cures us of expectation, or has any other effect than that of producing a moral sentence or peevish exclamation.

Samuel Johnson

Mean spirits under disappointment, small beer in a thunder-storm, always turn sour.

John Randolph

Man must be disappointed with the lesser things of life before he can comprehend the full value of the greater.

Edward G. Bulwer-Lytton (Baron Lytton)

There is many a thing which the world calls disappointment, but there is no such a word in the dictionary of faith. What to others are disappointments are to believers intimations of the way of God.

John Newton

See, also: **Defeat, Failure.**

DISCIPLINE

In the order named, these are the hardest to control: Wine, Women and Song.

Franklin Pierce Adams

A disciplined army of a few hundred picked men has, time without number, routed countless undisciplined hordes.

Mohandas Karamchand (Mahatma) Gandhi

I am myself a believer in discipline. And yet I suppose there can be too much of discipline.

Jawaharlal Nehru

No pain, no palm; no thorns, no throne; no gall, no glory; no cross, no crown.

William Penn

A stern discipline pervades all nature, which is a little cruel that it may be very kind.

Edmund Spenser

See also: **Authority, Education, Order, Parent, Punishment, Self-Improvement, Study**

DISCOVERY

Through every rift of discovery some seeming anomaly drops out of the darkness, and falls, as a golden link, into the great chain of order.

Edwin Hubbel Chapin

A new principle is an inexhaustible source of new views.

Luc de Clapiers (Marquis de Vauvenargues)

It is a mortifying truth, and ought to teach the wisest of us humility, that many of the most valuable discoveries have been the result of chance rather than of contemplation, and of accident rather than of design.

Charles Caleb Colton

If I have ever made any valuable discoveries, it has been owing more to patient attention, than to any other talent.

Sir Isaac Newton

All great discoveries are made by men whose feelings run ahead of their thinking.

Charles Henry Parkhurst

See also: **Novelty, Originality**

DISCRETION

Discretion in speech, is more than eloquence.

Francis Bacon

Discretion is the salt, and fancy the sugar of life; the one preserves, the other sweetens it.

Christian Nestell Bovee

A sound discretion is not so much indicated by never making a mistake, as by never repeating it.

Christian Nestell Bovee

I have never been hurt by anything I didn't say.

(John) Calvin Coolidge

If thou art a master, be sometimes blind, if a servant, sometimes deaf.

Thomas Fuller

The greatest parts, without discretion, may be fatal to their owner. Polyphemus, deprived of his eye, was only the more exposed on account of his enormous strength and stature.

David Hume

Discretion is the perfection of reason, and a guide to us in all the duties of life. It is only found in men of sound sense and good understanding.

Jean de La Bruyère

Be discreet in all things, and so render it unnecessary to be mysterious about any.

Arthur Wellesley (First Duke Wellington)

Open your mouth and purse cautiously, and your stock of wealth and reputation shall, at least in repute, be great.

Johann Georg von Zimmerman

See also: **Common Sense, Intelligence, Prudence, Reflection**

DISCUSSION

It is not the facts which guide the conduct of men, but their opinions about facts; which may be entirely wrong. We can only make them right by discussion.

Sir Norman Angell

A good discussion increases the dimensions of everyone who takes part.

Randolph Silliman Bourne

Free and fair discussion will ever be found the firmest friend to truth.

George Campbell

Public discussions are useful because they disturb complacency and lead to the restless uncertainty about one's self that has long been known as the beginning of wisdom.

Lyman Lloyd Bryson

In debate, rather pull to pieces the argument of thine antagonist, than offer him any of thine own; for thus thou will fight him in his own country.

Henry Fielding

Whosoever is afraid of submitting any question, civil or religious, to the test of free discussion, is more in love with his own opinion than with truth.

Thomas Watson

He that is not open to conviction, is not qualified for discussion.

Richard Whately

See also: **Argument, Controversy, Conversation, Silence.**

DISEASE

It is with disease of the mind, as with those of the body; we are half dead before we understand our disorder, and half cured when we do.

Charles Caleb Colton

If I had my way I'd make health catching instead of disease.

Robert Green Ingersoll

We live longer than our forefathers but we suffer more, from a thousand artificial anxieties and cares. They fatigued only the muscles; we exhaust the finer strength of the nerves.

Edward G. Bulwer-Lytton (Baron Lytton)

When the Czar has a cold all Russia coughs.

Russian Proverb

See also: **Death, Doctor, Health, Medicine, Pain**

DISHONESTY

So grasping is dishonesty, that it is no respecter of persons; it will cheat friends as well as foes; and were it possible, would cheat even God himself.

George Bancroft

He who purposely cheats his friend, would cheat his God.

Johann Kaspar Lavater

I could never draw the line between meanness and dishonesty. What is mean, so far as I can see, slides by indistinguishable gradations into what is dishonest.

George Macdonald

See also: **Crime, Deceit, Fraud, Hypocrisy, Injustice, Lying**

DISSENT

If all mankind minus one were of one opinion, and only one person were of the contrary opinion, mankind would be no more justified in silencing that one person, than he, if he had the power, would be justified in silencing mankind.

John Stuart Mill

The United States can . . . be proud that it has institutions and a structure that permit its citizens to express honest dissent, even though those who do so may be maligned by the highest official in the land.

New York Times

Dissent does not include the freedom to destroy the system of law which guarantees freedom to speak, assemble and march in protest. Dissent is not anarchy.

Seymour F. Simon

Who is there to say what is good dissent and what is bad dissent. Who can frame fair and meaningful standards to measure what is creative, constructive or responsible in disagreement and what is destructive. Are these decisions which can safely be left to a local police chief or a municipal administrator or the majority or to public opinion or perhaps to those good people who simply want to remain comfortable and uninvolved?

Seymour F. Simon

Mere unorthodoxy or dissent from the prevailing mores is not to be condemned. The absence of such voices would be a symptom of grave illness in our society.

Earl Warren

See also: **Argument, Difference**

DISTRUST

The disease of mutual distrust among nations is widely spread and is the bane of modern civilization.

Franz Boas

What loneliness is more lonely than distrust?

George Eliot (Mary Ann Evans)

To think and feel we are able, is often to be so.

Joel Hawes

However much we may distrust men's sincerity, we always believe that they speak to us more sincerely than to others.

Duc François de La Rochefoucauld

Our want of trust justifies the deceit of others.

Duc François de La Rochefoucauld

As health lies in labor, and there is no royal road to it but through toil, so there is no republican road to safety but in constant distrust.

Wendell Phillips

The feeling of distrust is always the last which a great mind acquires.

Jean Baptiste Racine

Nothing is more certain of destroying any good feelings that may be cherished toward us than to show distrust. On the contrary, confidence leads us naturally to act kindly; we are affected by the good opinion others entertain of us, and are not easily induced to lose it.

Marquise de Sévigné

See also: **Doubt, Suspicion, Trust.**

DOUBT

In contemplation, if a man begins with certainties he shall end in doubts; but if he be content to begin with doubts, he shall end in certainties.

Francis Bacon

Who never doubted, never half believed. Where doubt is, there truth is—it is her shadow.

Gamaliel Bailey

A bitter and perplexed, "What shall I do?" is worse to man than worse necessity.

Samuel Taylor Coleridge

The doubter's dissatisfaction with his doubt is as great and widespread as the doubt itself.

Jan De Witt

Doubt is a pain too lonely to know that faith is his twin brother.

Kahlil Gibran

We know accurately only when we know little; with knowledge doubt increases.

Johann Wolfgang von Goethe

Human knowledge is the parent of doubt.

Fulke Greville (First Baron Brooke)

The worst of worms: the dagger thoughts of doubt.

Heinrich Heine

To have doubted one's own first principles, is the mark of a civilized man.

Oliver Wendell Holmes

Doubt comes in at the window when inquiry is denied at the door.

Benjamin Jowett

I respect faith, but doubt is what gets you an education.

Wilson Mizner

Doubt is brother devil to despair.

John Boyle O'Reilly

The end of doubt is the beginning of repose.

Petrarch

Never do anything concerning the rectitude of which you have a doubt.

Pliny the Elder

Beware of doubt—faith is the subtle chain that binds us to the infinite.

Elizabeth Oakes Smith

Misgive, that you may not mistake.

Richard Whately

When you doubt, abstain.

Zoroaster

See also: **Agnosticism, Distrust, Incredulity, Skepticism**

DREAM

Dreams full oft are found of real events the forms and shadows.

Joanna Baillie

As dreams are the fancies of those that sleep, so fancies are but the dreams of those awake.

Sir Thomas Pope Blount

Children of the night, of indigestion bred.

Charles Churchill

Nothing so much convinces me of the boundlessness of the human mind as its operations in dreaming.

William Benton Clulow

A lost but happy dream may shed its light upon our waking hours, and the whole day may be infected with the gloom of a dreary or sorrowful one; yet of neither may we be able to recover a trace.

Walter John de la Mare

Dreaming permits each and every one of us to be quietly and safely insane every night of our lives.

William Charles Dement

Existence would be intolerable if we were never to dream.

Anatole France

I am a dreamer. I am, indeed, a practical dreamer. My dreams are not airy nothings. I want to convert my dreams into realities, as far as possible.

Mohandas Karamchand (Mahatma) Gandhi

Sir, do not mock our dreamers. . . . Their words become the seeds of freedom.
Heinrich Heine

A world of the dead in the hues of life.
Felicia Dorothea Browne Hemans

Men never cling to their dreams with such tenacity as at the moment when they are losing faith in them, and know it, but do not dare to confess it to themselves.
William Graham Sumner

If you have built castles in the air, your work need not be lost, there is where they should be. Now put foundations under them.
Henry David Thoreau

See also: **Imagination**

DRESS

A fine coat is but a livery when the person who wears it discovers no higher sense than that of a footman.
Joseph Addison

Had Cicero himself pronounced one of his orations with a blanket about his shoulders, more people would have laughed at his dress than admired his eloquence.
Joseph Addison

The body is the shell of the soul, and dress the husk of that shell; but the husk often tells what the kernel is.
Anonymous

If honor be your clothing, the suit will last a lifetime; but if clothing be your honor, it will soon be worn threadbare.
William Arnot

The perfection of dress is in the union of three requisites—in its being comfortable, cheap, and tasteful.
Christian Nestell Bovee

Eat to please thyself, but dress to please others.
Benjamin Franklin

An emperor in his night-cap would not meet with half the respect of an emperor with a crown.
Oliver Goldsmith

The vanity of loving fine clothes and new fashions, and valuing ourselves by them, is one of the most childish pieces of folly.
Sir Matthew Hale

In clothes clean and fresh there is a kind of youth with which age should surround itself.
Joseph Joubert

In the indications of female poverty there can be no disguise. No woman dresses below herself from caprice.
Charles Lamb

I hate to see men overdressed; a man ought to look like he's put together by accident, not added up on purpose.
Christopher Darlington Morley

No man is esteemed for gay garments, but by fools and women.
Sir Walter Raleigh

The only medicine which does women more good than harm, is dress.
Jean Paul Richter

A loose and easy dress contributes much to give to both sexes those fine proportions of body that are observable in the Grecian statues, and which serve as models to our present artists.
Jean Jacques Rousseau

The plainer the dress with greater luster does beauty appear. Virtue is the greatest ornament, and good sense the best equipage.

George Savile (Marquis of Halifax)

Persons are often misled in regard to their choice of dress by attending to the beauty of colors, rather than selecting such colors as may increase their own beauty.

William Shenstone

Next to clothes being fine, they should be well made, and worn easily: for a man is only the less genteel for a fine coat, if, in wearing it, he shows a regard for it, and is not as easy in it as if it were a plain one.

Philip Dormer Stanhope (Lord Chesterfield)

Clothes don't make the man, but good clothes have got many a man a good job.

Herbert Harold Vreeland

As to matters of dress, I would recommend one never to be first in the fashion nor the last out of it.

John Wesley

There is new strength, repose of mind, and inspiration in fresh apparel.

Ella Wheeler Wilcox

See also: **Fashion, Looks, Taste**

DRUNKENNESS

Drunkenness is a flattering devil, a sweet poison, a pleasant sin, which whosoever hath, hath not himself, which whosoever doth commit, doth not commit sin, but he himself is wholly sin.

Augustine of Hippo

All the armies on earth do not destroy so many of the human race, nor alienate so much property, as drunkenness.

Francis Bacon

There is scarcely a crime before me that is not, directly or indirectly, caused by strong drink.

Sir John Duke Coleridge

Some of the domestic evils of drunkenness are houses without windows, gardens without fences, fields without tillage, barns without roofs, children without clothing, principles, morals, or manners.

Benjamin Franklin

Habitual intoxication is the epitome of every crime.

Douglas William Jerrold

Let there be an entire abstinence from intoxicating drinks throughout this country during the period of a single generation, and a mob would be as impossible as combustion without oxygen.

Horace Mann

A drunkard is like a whisky bottle, all neck and belly and no head.

Austin O'Malley

The sight of a drunkard is a better sermon against that vice than the best that was ever preached on the subject.

John Faucit Saville

Drunkenness is nothing else but a voluntary madness.

Seneca

Drunkenness places man as much below the level of the brutes, as reason elevates him above them.

Sir John Sinclair

DUTY

When the soul resolves to perform every duty, immediately it is conscious of the presence of God.

Francis

Duty by habit is to pleasure turned.
Sir Samuel Egerton Bydges

To what gulfs a single deviation from the path of human duties leads!
George Gordon Byron (Lord Byron)

Men do less than they ought, unless they do all that they can.
Thomas Carlyle

Our grand business is not to see what lies' dimly in the distance, but to do what lies clearly at hand.
Thomas Carlyle

Think ever that you are born to perform great duties.
Benjamin Disraeli

So nigh is grandeur to our dust, so near is God to man, when duty whispers low, "Thou must," the youth replies, "I can."
Ralph Waldo Emerson

See also: Obligation, Responsibility, Rights, Trust

EARTH

The earth's a stage which God and nature do with actors fill.
Thomas Heywood

How far must suffering and misery go before we see that even in the day of vast cities and powerful machines, the good earth is our mother and that if we destroy her, we destroy ourselves?
Paul Bigelow Sears

The Earth, it seems to me, may well be the Siberia, the Perth Amboy, of the inhabited planets of the Universe.
James Grover Thurber

Earth, thou great footstool of our God, who reigns on high; thou fruitful source of all our raiment, life, and food; our house, our parent, and our nurse.
Isaac Watts

See also: Nature, World.

EATING

Part of the secret of success in life is to eat what you like and let the food fight it out inside.
Samuel Langhorne Clemens (Mark Twain)

One should eat to live, not live to eat.
Benjamin Franklin

The difference between a rich man and a poor man, is this—the former eats when be pleases, and the latter when he can get it.
Sir Walter Raleigh

The turnpike road to most people's hearts, I find, lies through their mouths, or I mistake mankind.
John Wolcot (Peter Pindar)

See also: Gluttony

ECONOMICS

There is always present the two twin dangers of deflation and inflation. And the function of government so far as it affects this matter at all is to be watchful, to be vigilant and alert, and to take measures from time to time that tend to move in one direction if the signs are we are moving in another.
Dwight David Eisenhower

We cannot forever be an Atlas . . . supporting the rest of the world.
Dwight David Eisenhower

A stable American economy cannot be sustained if the world's economy is in chaos. International cooperation is absolutely essential and vital.
Gerald Rudolph Ford

The most impressive increases in output in the history of both the United States and other western countries have occurred since men began to concern themselves with reducing the risks of the competitive system.
John Kenneth Galbraith

One of the greatest pieces of economic wisdom is to know what you do not know.
John Kenneth Galbraith

The face which we present to the world . . . is the face of the individual or the family as a high consumption unit with minimal social links or responsibilities—father happily drinking his beer, mother dreamily fondling soft garments newly rinsed in a wonderful new detergent, the children gaily calling from the new barbecue pit for a famous sauce for their steak.
Adlai Ewing Stevenson

The life and spirit of the American economy is progress and expansion.
Harry S Truman

See also: **Business, Capitalism, Communism, Economy, Government**

ECONOMY

If you know how to spend less than you get you have the philosopher's stone.
Benjamin Franklin

The man who will live above his present circumstances, is in great danger of soon living much beneath them; or as the Italian proverb says, "The man that lives by hope, will die by despair."
Joseph Addison

A man's ordinary expenses ought to be but to the half of his receipts, and if he thinks to wax rich, but to the third part.
Francis Bacon

There are but two ways of paying a debt; increase of industry in raising income, or increase of thrift in laying out.
Thomas Carlyle

Without economy none can be rich, and with it few will be poor.
Samuel Johnson

He who is taught to live upon little owes more to his father's wisdom than he that has a great deal left him does to his father's care.
William Penn

The art of living easily as to money is to pitch your scale of living one degree below your means.
Sir Henry Taylor

See also: **Business, Economics, Money**

EDUCATION

Nothing in education is so astonishing as the amount of ignorance it accumulates in the form of inert facts.
Henry Brooks Adams

There are obviously two educations. One should teach us how to make a living and the other how to live.
James Truslow Adams

There can be but a single goal of education, and that—education to courage.
Alfred Adler

Observation more than books, experience rather than persons, are the prime educators.
Amos Bronson Alcott

What is fatal to the humanities is that they have been professionalized as if their end and purpose were the same as that of the sciences.
William Arrowsmith

The aim of education should be to teach us rather how to think, than what to think—rather to improve our minds, so as to enable us to think for ourselves, than to load the memory with the thoughts of other men.
James Beattie

Education is the knowledge of how to use the whole of oneself. Many men use but one or two faculties out of the score with which they are endowed. A man is educated who knows how to make a tool of every faculty—how to open it, how to keep it sharp, and how to apply it to all practical purposes.
Henry Ward Beecher

The academic community has in it the biggest concentration of alarmists, cranks and extremists this side of the giggle house.
William Frank Buckley, Jr.

Education is the cheap defense of nations.
Edmund Burke

I have never let my schooling interfere with my education.
Samuel Langhorne Clemens (Mark Twain)

Soap and education are not as sudden as a massacre, but they are more deadly in the long run.
Samuel Langhorne Clemens (Mark Twain)

It is essential that the student acquire an understanding of and a lively feeling for values. He must acquire a vivid sense of the beautiful and of the morally good. Otherwise he—with his specialized knowledge—more closely resembles a well-trained dog than a harmoniously developed person.
Albert Einstein

We know that education, centrally controlled, finally would lead to a kind of control in other fields which we don't want and will never have. So we are dedicated to the proposition that the responsibility for educating our young is primarily local.
Dwight David Eisenhower

In some small field each child should . . . attain, within the limited range of its experience and observation, the power to draw a justly limited inference from observed facts.
Charles William Eliot

The secret of education lies in respecting the pupil.
Ralph Waldo Emerson

I wish every immigrant could know that Lincoln spent only one year in school under the tutelage of five different teachers, and that the man still could be the author of the Gettysburg address.
John Huston Finley

Education in its widest sense includes everything that exerts a formative influence, and causes a young person to be, at a given point, what he is.
Mark Hopkins

The first thing education teaches you is to walk alone.

Alfred Aloysius (Trader) Horn

I care not what subject is taught if only it be taught well.

Thomas Henry Huxley

A child miseducated is a child lost.

John Fitzgerald Kennedy

The human mind is our fundamental resource.

John Fitzgerald Kennedy

I want to emphasize in the great concentration which we now place upon scientists and engineers how much we still need the men and women educated in the liberal tradition, willing to take the long look, undisturbed by prejudices and slogans of the moment, who attempt to make an honest judgment on difficult events.

John Fitzgerald Kennedy

See also: *Discipline, Instruction, Learning, Reading, Study, Teaching, Truth, University.*

EFFICIENCY

Loyal and efficient work in a great cause, even though it may not be immediately recognized, ultimately bears fruit.

Jawaharld Nehru

Obviously, the highest type of efficiency is that which can utilize existing material to the best advantage.

Jawaharld Nehru

It is more than probable that the average man could, with no injury to his health, increase his efficiency fifty percent.

Walter Dill Scott

See also: *Ability, Diligence, Genius, Order*

EFFORT

Remember that the faith that removes mountains always carries a pick.

Anonymous

The fact is, nothing comes; at least, nothing good. All has to be fetched.

Charles Buxton

If you would relish food, labor for it before you take it; if enjoy clothing, pay for it before you wear it; if you would sleep soundly, take a clear conscience to bed with you.

Benjamin Franklin

Things don't turn up in this world until some body turns them up.

James Abram Garfield

It is common sense to take a method and try it. If this fails, admit it frankly and try another. But above all, try something.

Franklin Delano Roosevelt

It is hard to fail, but it is worse never to have tried to succeed. In this life we get nothing save by effort.

Theodore Roosevelt

See also: *Action, Energy, Labor, Perseverance, Work*

EMOTION

By starving emotions we become humorless, rigid and stereotyped; by repressing them we become literal, reformatory and holier-than-thou; encouraged, they perfume life; discouraged, they poison it.

Joseph Collins

The stress of passion often discloses an aspect of the personality completely ignored till then by its closest intimates.

Joseph Conrad

Emotion is not something shameful, subordinate, second-rate; it is a supremely valid phase of humanity at its noblest and most mature.

Joshua Loth Liebman

All loving emotions, like plants, shoot up most rapidly in the tempestuous atmosphere of life.

Jean Paul Richter

Emotion turning back on itself, and not leading on to thought or action, is the element of madness.

John Sterling

Intellect is to emotion as our clothes are to our bodies: we could not very well have civilized life without clothes, but we would be in a poor way if we had only clothes without bodies.

Alfred North Whitehead

See also: **Heart, Passion**

EMPLOYMENT

Every man's task is his life-preserver.

George Barrell Emerson

Employment is nature's physician, and is essential to human happiness.

Galen

The employer generally gets the employees he deserves.

Sir Walter Gilbey

Be always employed about some rational thing, that the devil find thee not idle.

Jerome (Eusebius Hieronymus)

Employment gives health, sobriety and morals. Constant employment and well-paid labor produce, in a country like ours, general prosperity, content, and cheerfulness.

Daniel Webster

See also: **Business, Diligence, Effort Labor, Poverty, Work**

END

If well thou hast begun, go on; it is the end that crowns us, not the fight.

Robert Herrick

In everything we ought to look to the end.

Jean de La Fontaine

The end must justify the means.

Matthew Prior

It is the beginning of the end.

Charles Maurice de Talleyrand-Périgord

See also: **Aim, Beginning, Death, Purpose**

ENDURANCE

Not in the achievement, but in the endurance of the human soul, does it show its divine grandeur, and its alliance with the infinite God.

Edwin Hubbel Chapin

The greater the difficulty, the more glory in surmounting it. Skilful pilots gain their reputation from storms and tempests.

Epicurus

He conquers who endures.

Persius

By bravely enduring, an evil which cannot be avoided is overcome.

Proverb

To endure is the first thing that a child ought to learn, and that which he will have most need to know.

Jean Jacques Rousseau

Happy the man who can endure the highest and lowest fortune. He who has endured such vicissitudes with equanimity has deprived misfortune of its power.

Seneca

There is nothing in the world so much admired as a man who knows how to bear unhappiness with courage.

Seneca

See also: **Strength, Will, Zeal**

ENEMY

Though all things do to harm him what they can, no greater enemy to himself than man.

William Alexander (Earl of Stirling)

The fine and noble way to destroy a foe, is not to kill him; with kindness you may so change him that he shall cease to be so; then he's slain.

Charles Aleyn

Observe your enemies, for they first find out your faults.

Antisthenes

Some men are more beholden to their bitterest enemies than to friends who appear to be sweetness itself. The former frequently tell the truth, but the latter never.

Cato the Elder

If you want enemies, excel others; if friends, let others excel you.

Charles Caleb Colton

Make no enemies.—He is insignificant indeed who can do thee no harm.

Charles Caleb Colton

There is no little enemy.

Benjamin Franklin

Instead of loving your enemies, treat your friends a little better.

Edgar Watson

Have you fifty friends?—it is not enough. Have you one enemy?—it is too much.

Italian Proverb

Our enemies come nearer the truth in the opinions they form of us than we do in our opinion of ourselves.

Duc François de La Rochefoucauld

If we could read the secret history of our enemies, we should find in each man's life sorrow and suffering enough to disarm all hostility.

Henry Wadsworth Longfellow

A merely fallen enemy may rise again, but the reconciled one is truly vanquished.

Johann Christoph Frederick von Schiller

A man cannot be too careful in the choice of his enemies.

Oscar Wilde

See also: **Friendship, Quarrel, Violence, War**

ENERGY

The reward of a thing well done, is to have done it.

Ralph Waldo Emerson

This world belongs to the energetic.

Ralph Waldo Emerson

Energy will do anything that can be done in the world; and no talents, no circumstances, no opportunities will make a two legged animal a man without it.

Johann Wolfgang von Goethe

He alone has energy who cannot be deprived of it.

Johann Kaspar Lavater

There is no genius in life like the genius of energy and activity.

Donald Grant Mitchell (Ik Marvel)

The truest wisdom, in general is a resolute determination.

Napoleon I (Bonaparte)

See also: *Effort, Nuclear Energy, Power, Work*

ENTHUSIASM

Every production of genius must be the production of enthusiasm.

Benjamin Disraeli

Truth is never to be expected from authors whose understandings are warped with enthusiasm; for they judge all actions and their causes by their own perverse principles, and a crooked line can never be the measure of a straight one.

John Dryden

Every great and commanding movement in the annals of the world is the triumph of enthusiasm. Nothing great was ever achieved without it.

Ralph Waldo Emerson

Enthusiasts soon understand each other.

Washington Irving

We act as though comfort and luxury were the chief requirements of life, when all that we need to make us really happy is something to be enthusiastic about.

Charles Kingsley

See also: *Zeal*

EQUALITY

The doctrine of human equality reposes on this: that there is no man really clever who has not found that he is stupid.

Gilbert Keith Chesterton

There are many humorous things in the world: among them the white man's notion that he is less savage than the other savages.

Samuel Langhorne Clemens (Mark Twain)

Kings and their subjects, masters and slaves, find a common level in two places—at the foot of the cross and in the grave.

Charles Caleb Colton

Those who might themselves be subject to equalization have rarely been enthusiastic about equality as a subject of social comment.

John Kenneth Galbraith

I have no respect for the passion for equality, which seems to me merely idealizing envy.

Oliver Wendell Holmes

So far is it from being true that men are naturally equal, that no two people can be half an hour together but one shall acquire an evident superiority over the other.

Samuel Johnson

Even though we face the difficulties of today and tomorrow, I still have a dream. I have a dream that one day this nation will rise up and live out the true meaning of its creed: "We hold these truths to be self-evident, that all men are created equal."

Martin Luther King, Jr.

We must recover the element of quality in our traditional pursuit of equality. We must not, in opening our schools to everyone, confuse the idea that all should have equal chance with the notion that all have equal endowments.

Adlai Ewing Stevenson

In the gates of eternity the black hand and the white hold each other with an equal clasp.

Harriet Elizabeth Beecher Stowe

We conclude that in the field of public education the doctrine of "separate but equal" has no place. Separate educational facilities are inherently unequal [Brown vs. Board Education of Topeka, May 17, 1954].

United States Supreme Court

Men are equal; it is not birth but virtue that makes the difference.

Voltaire (François Marie Arouet)

They who say all men are equal speak an undoubted truth, if they mean that all have an equal right to liberty, to their property and to their protection of the laws. But they are mistaken if they think men are equal in their station and employments, since they are not so by their talents.

Voltaire (François Marie Arouet)

The Constitution does not provide for first and second class citizens.

Wendell Lewis Wilkie

It is not tolerance that one is entitled to in America. It is the right of every citizen in America to be treated by other citizens as an equal.

Wendell Lewis Wilkie

See also: **Democracy, Justice, Rights**

ERROR

An error doesn't become a mistake until you refuse to correct it.

Orlando A. Battista

There are errors which no wise man will treat with rudeness, while there is a probability that they may be the refraction of some great truth still below the horizon.

Samuel Taylor Coleridge

No tempting form of error is without some latent charm derived from truth.

Alexander Keith

Find earth where grows no weed, and you may find a heart wherein no error grows.

Thomas Knowles

We live in terror of doing the wrong thing instead of in hope of finding the right.

Harold Joseph Laski

Errors that last the shortest time are always the best.

Molière (Jean Baptiste Poquelin)

My principal method for defeating error and heresy, is, by establishing the truth. One purposes to fill a bushel with tares; but if I can fill it first with wheat, I may defy his attempts.

John Newton

Half the truth will very often amount to absolute falsehood.

Richard Whately

See also: *Crime, Delusion, Forgiveness, Sin, Understanding, Vice, Wickedness, Wrong*

ESTEEM

The chief ingredients in the composition of those qualities that gain esteem and praise, are good nature, truth, good sense, and good breeding.

Joseph Addison

The esteem of wise and good men is the greatest of all temporal encouragements to virtue; and it is a mark of an abandoned spirit to have no regard to it.

Edmund Burks

Esteem has more engaging charms than friendship and even love. It captivates hearts better, and never makes ingrates.

Duc François de La Rochefoucauld

All true love is founded on esteem.

George Villaers (2d Duke of Buckingham)

See also: *Love, Respect.*

ETERNITY

Eternity is in love with the productions of time.

William Blake

Eternity is not an everlasting flux of time, but time is a short parenthesis in a long period.

John Donne

I saw Eternity the other night
Like a great ring of pure and endless light,
All calm, as it was bright.

Henry Vaughan

Eternity has no gray hairs! The flowers fade, the heart withers, man grows old and dies, the world lies down in the sepulchre of ages, but time writes no wrinkles on the brow of eternity.

Reginald Heber

This is eternal life; a life of everlasting love, showing itself in everlasting good works; and whosoever lives that life, he lives the life of God, and hath eternal life.

Charles Kingsley

See also: *Future, God, Heaven, Hell, Immortality, Time*

ETIQUETTE

The propriety of some persons seems to consist in having improper thoughts about their neighbors.

Francis Herbert Bradley

Good taste rejects excessive nicety; it treats little things as little things, and is not hurt by them.

Frangois Salignac de La Mothe-Fénelon

We must conform, to a certain extent, to the conventionalities of society, for they are the ripened results of a varied and long experience.

Archibald Alexander Hodge

Who needs a book of etiquette? Everyone does . . . for we must all learn the socially acceptable ways of living . . . . Even in primitive societies there are rules, some . . . as complex and inexplicable as many of our own. Their original *raison d'être* or purpose is lost, but their acceptance is still unquestioned.

Amy Vanderbilt

See also: *Custom, Manners*

EVIL

He who is good is free, even if he is a
   slave;
he who is evil is a slave, even if he is a
   king.

Augustine of Hippo

The caterpillar on the leaf
Repeats to thee thy mother's grief.
Kill not the moth nor butterfly,
For the Last Judgement draweth nigh.

William Blake

He who shall hurt the little wren
Shall never be belov'd by men.
He who the ox to wrath has mov'd
Shall never be by woman lov'd.

William Blake

The only thing necessary for the triumph of evil is for good men to do
nothing.

Edmund Burke

Often even an entire city has reaped the
evil of a bad man.

Hesiod

Here lies one whose name was writ in
water.

John Keats

All good to me is lost;
Evil, be thou my good.

John Milton

The oldest and best known evil was ever
more supportable than the one that was
new and untried.

Michel Eyquem de Montaigne

What is evil?—Whatever springs from
weakness.

Friedrich Wilhelm Nietzsche

The war against physical evil, like every
other war, must not be conducted with
such fury as to render men incapable of
the arts of peace.

Bertrand Arthur William Russell

There are a thousand hacking at the
branches of evil to one who is striking at
the root.

Henry David Thoreau

See also: **Adversity, Crime, Injustice,
   Punishment, Sin, Wrong**

EVOLUTION

The expression often used by Mr. Herbert Spencer of the Survival of the Fittest
is more accurate, and is sometimes
equally convenient.

Charles Robert Darwin

I have called this principle, by which
each slight variation, if useful, is preserved, by the term of Natural Selection.

Charles Robert Darwin

Every form of consciousness is a reaction to a way of life that existed before,
and an adaptation to new realities.

Charles Alan Reich

Civilization is a progress from an in-
definite, incoherent homogeneity toward a definite, coherent heterogeneity.

Herbert Spencer

This survival of the fittest, which I have
here sought to express in mechanical
terms is that which Mr. Darwin has
called "natural selection or the preservation of favoured races in the struggle for
life."

Herbert Spencer

See also: **Change, Improvement, Science**

EXAGGERATION

The speaking in a perpetual hyperbole is comely in nothing but in love.

Francis Bacon

Some so speak in exaggerations and superlatives, that we need to make a large discount from their statements before we can come at their real meaning.

Tryon Edwards

We always weaken whatever we exaggerate.

Jean François de Laharpe

We are not helped in fighting evil by exaggerating its extent. In rejecting or refuting the exaggeration, men often make the truth a victim.

Norman Mattoon Thomas

See also: **Deceit, Dishonesty, Lying**

EXAMPLE

Example is the school of mankind; they will learn at no other.

Edmund Burke

Few things are harder to put up with than the annoyance of a good example.

Samuel Langhorne Clemens (Mark Twain)

I am absolutely convinced that no wealth in the world can help humanity forward, even in the hands of the most devoted worker in this cause. The example of great and pure individuals is the only thing that can lead us to noble thoughts and deeds. Money only appeals to selfishness and irresistibly invites abuse. Can anyone imagine Moses, Jesus, or Gandhi armed with the moneybags of Carnegie?

Albert Einstein

I am only coming to Princeton to do research, not to teach. There is too much education altogether, especially in American schools. The only rational way of educating is to be an example—if one can't help it, a warning example.

Albert Einstein

Example is not the main thing in life—it is the only thing.

Albert Schweitzer

Men trust rather to their eyes than to their ears. The effect of precepts is, therefore, slow and tedious, while that of examples is summary and effectual.

Seneca

Noble examples stir us up to noble actions, and the very history of large and public souls inspires a man with generous thoughts.

Seneca

See also: **Influence**

EXCELLENCE

Nothing is such an obstacle to the production of excellence as the power of producing what is good with ease and rapidity.

John Aikin

There are three marks of a superior man: being virtuous, he is free from anxiety; being wise, he is free from perplexity; being brave, he is free from fear.

Confucius

Those who attain to any excellence commonly spend life in some one single pursuit, for excellence is not often gained upon easier terms.

Samuel Johnson

The pursuit of excellence is less profitable than the pursuit of bigness, but it can be more satisfying.

David Mackenzie Ogilvy

All things excellent are as difficult as they are rare.

Baruch (Benedict) Spinoza

See also: Merit, Perfection, Worth

EXCEPTION

No rule is so general, which admits not some exception.

Robert Burton

How glorious it is—and also how painful—to be an exception.

(Louis Charles) Alfred de Musset

Every system should allow loopholes and exceptions, for if it does not it will in the end crush all that is best in man.

Bertrand Arthur William Russell

See also: Dissent

EXCUSE

He that is good for making excuses, is seldom good for anything else.

Benjamin Franklin

Don't make excuses—make good.

Frank McKinney (Kin) Hubbard

Uncalled for excuses are practical confessions.

Charles Simmons

See also: Apology

EXPECTATION

What we anticipate seldom occurs; what we least expect generally happens.

Benjamin Disraeli

Nothing is so good as it seems beforehand.

George Eliot (Mary Ann Evans)

We love to expect, and when expectation is either disappointed or gratified, we want to be again expecting.

Samuel Johnson

It is folly to expect men to do all that they may reasonably be expected to do.

Richard Whately

Blessed are those that nought expect, For they shall not be disappointed.

John Wolcot (Peter Pindar)

See also: Anticipation, Hope, Pursuit

EXPEDIENCY

Expediency may tip the scales when arguments are nicely balanced.

Benjamin Nathan Cardozo

When private virtue is hazarded on the perilous cast of expediency, the pillars of the republic, however apparent their stability, are infected with decay at the very centre.

Edwin Hubbel Chapin

No man is justified in doing evil on the ground of expediency.

Theodore Roosevelt

See also: Compromise, Interest, Opportunity

EXPENSE

Riches are for spending, and spending for honor and good actions; therefore extraordinary expense must be limited by the worth of the occasion.

Francis Bacon

Gain may be temporary and uncertain; but ever while you live, expense is constant and certain: and it is easier to build two chimneys than to keep one in fuel.

Benjamin Franklin

Never buy a thing you don't want merely because it is dear.

Oscar Wilde

See also: **Bargain, Extravagance, Money**

EXPERIENCE

All experience is an arch to build upon.
Henry Brooks Adams

Experience is one thing you can't get for nothing.

Anonymous

When I was a boy of fourteen, my father was so ignorant I could hardly stand to have the old man around. But when I got to be twenty-one, I was astonished at how much the old man had learned in seven years.

Samuel Langhorne Clemens (Mark Twain)

A sadder and a wiser man,
He rose the morrow morn.

Samuel Taylor Coleridge

Experience cannot deliver to us necessary truths; truths completely demonstrated by reason. Its conclusions are particular, not universal.

John Dewey

Experience keeps a dear school; but fools will learn in no other, and scarce in that; for it is true, we may give advice, but we cannot give conduct.

Benjamin Franklin

Men are wise in proportion, not to their experience, but to their capacity for experience.

George Bernard Shaw

See also: **Suffering, Wisdom**

EXTRAVAGANCE

The passion of acquiring riches in order to support a vain expense, corrupts the purest souls.

François de Salignac de La Mothe-Fénelon

The covetous man never has money; the prodigal will have none shortly.

Ben (Benjamin) Jonson

Waste of time is the most extravagant and costly of all expenses.

Theophrastus

That is suitable to a man, in point of ornamental expense, not which he can afford to have, but which he can afford to lose.

Richard Whately

See also: **Expense**

EXTREMES

Neither great poverty, nor great riches will hear reason.

Henry Fielding

I never dared be radical when young
For fear it would make me conservative
    when old.

Robert Lee Frost

There is a mean in everything. Even virtue itself hath its stated limits, which, not being strictly observed, it ceases to be virtue.

Horace

The greatest flood has soonest ebb: the sorest tempest, the most sudden calm; the hottest love, the coldest end; and from the deepest desire often ensues the deadliest hate.

Socrates

EYE

The eye is the pulse of the soul; as physicians judge the heart by the pulse, so we by the eye.

Thomas Adams

Men are born with two eyes, but only one tongue, in order that they should see twice as much as they say.

Charles Caleb Colton

An eye can threaten like a loaded and levelled pistol, or can insult, like hissing or kicking; or in its altered mood, can, by beams of kindness, make the heart dance with joy. Some eyes have no more expression than blueberries, while others are as deep as a well which you fall into.

Ralph Waldo Emerson

One of the most wonderful things in nature is a glance of the eye; it transcends speech; it is the bodily symbol of identity.

Ralph Waldo Emerson

The eye of the master will do more work than both his hands.

Benjamin Franklin

It is the eyes of other people that ruin us. if all but myself were blind I should neither want a fine house nor fine furniture.

Benjamin Franklin

Eyes will not see when the heart wishes them to be blind. Desire conceals truth, as darkness does the earth.

Seneca

Her eyes are homes of silent prayer.

Alfred, Lord Tennyson

See also: **Face, Looks, Vision**

FABLE

Fables take off from the severity of instruction, and enforce at the same time that they conceal it.

Joseph Addison

The virtue which we gather from a fable or an allegory, is like the health we get by hunting, as we are engaged in an agreeable pursuit that draws us on with pleasure, and makes us insensible of the fatigues that accompany it.

Joseph Addison

Fables, like parables, are more ancient than formal arguments and are often the most effective means of presenting and impressing both truth and duty.

Tryon Edwards

See also: **Literature, Religion**

FACE

When I see a man with a sour, shriveled face, I cannot forbear pitying his wife; and when I meet with an open ingenuous countenance, I think on the happiness of his friends, his family, and his relations.

Joseph Addison

A beautiful face is a silent commendation.

Francis Bacon

I more and more see this, that we judge men's abilities less from what they say or do, than from what they look. 'Tis the man's face that gives him weight. His doings help, but not more than his brow.

Charles Buxton

It matters more what's in a woman's face than what's on it.

Claudette Colbert

There is in every human countenence, either a history or a prophecy, which must sadden, or at least soften, every reflecting observer.

Samuel Taylor Coleridge

A cheerful face is nearly as good for an invalid as healthy weather.

Benjamin Franklin

The faces which have charmed us the most escape us the soonest.

Sir Walter Scott

We are all sculptors and painters, and our material is our own flesh and blood and bones. Any nobleness begins, at once, to refine a man's features; any meanness or sensuality to imbrute them.

Henry David Thoreau

He had the sort of face that, once seen, is never remembered.

Oscar Wilde

See also: *Appearance, Eye, Looks*

FACTS

Facts are God's arguments; we should be careful never to misunderstand or pervert them.

Tryon Edwards

Any fact is better established by two or three good testimonies than by a thousand arguments.

Nathaniel Emmons

Facts, as such, never settled anything. They are working tools only. It is the implications that can be drawn from facts that count, and to evaluate these requires wisdom and judgment that are unrelated to the computer approach to life.

Clarence Belden Randall

See also: **Credulity, Science, Truth**

FAILURE

We are all of us failures—at least, the best of us are.

Sir James Matthew Barrie

They never fail who die in a great cause.

George Gordon Byron (Lord Byron)

The only people who never fail are those who never try.

Ilka Chase

Failure, when sublime, is not without its purpose.

Benjamin Disraeli

Sometimes a noble failure serves the world as faithfully as a distinguished success.

Edward Dowden

I never blame failure—there are too many complicated situations in life—but I am absolutely merciless towards lack of effort.

Francis Scott Key Fitzgerald

One who fears failure limits his activities. Failure is only the opportunity to more intelligently begin again.

Henry Ford

Failure is, in a sense, the highway to success, inasmuch as every discovery of what is false leads us to seek earnestly after what is true, and every fresh experience points out some form of error which we shall afterward carefully avoid.

John Keats

We have forty million reasons for failure, but not a single excuse.

Rudyard Kipling

See also: Defeat, Despair, Success

FAITH

There never was found in any age of the world, either philosopher or sect, or law, or discipline which did so highly exalt the public good as the Christian faith.

Francis Bacon

Faith without works is like a bird without wings; though she may hop about on earth, she will never fly to heaven. But when both are joined together, then doth the soul mount up to her eternal rest.

Francis Beaumont

Man is not naturally a cynic; he wants pitifully to believe, in himself, in his future, in his community and in the nation in which he is a part.

Louis Bromfield

No coward soul is mine,
No trembler in the world's storm-
troubled sphere:
I see Heaven's glories shine,
And faith shines equal, arming me from
fear.

Emily Brontë

Faith and works are as necessary to our spiritual life as Christians, as soul and body are to our life as men; for faith is the soul of religion, and works, the body.

Charles Caleb Colton

All I have seen teaches me to trust the Creator for all I have not seen.

Ralph Waldo Emerson

Strike from mankind the principle of faith, and men would have no more history than a flock of sheep.

Edward G. Bulwer-Lytton (Baron Lytton)

The errors of faith are better than the best thoughts of unbelief.

Thomas Russell

See also: Religion

FAME

Our admiration of a famous man lessens upon our nearer acquaintance with him; and we seldom hear of a celebrated person without a catalogue of some of his weaknesses and infirmities.

Joseph Addison

Fame is no sure test of merit, but only a probability of such, it is an accident, not a property of man.

Thomas Carlyle

Fame is a fickle food
Upon a shifting plate.

Emily Elizabeth Dickinson

Few people make much noise after their deaths who did not do so while living.

William Hazlitt

Fame is the perfume of heroic deeds.

Socrates

He that pursues fame with just claims, trusts his happiness to the winds; but he that endeavors after it by false merit, has to fear, not only the violence of the storm, but the leaks of his vessel

Samuel Johnson

Time has a doomsday book, on whose pages he is continually recording illustrious names. But as often as a new name is written there, an old one disappears. Only a few stand in illuminated characters never to be effaced.

Henry Wadsworth Longfellow

Even the best things are not equal to their fame.

Henry David Thoreau

See also: **Esteem, Glory, Honor**

FAMILIARITY

When a man becomes familiar with his goddess, she quickly sinks into a woman.

Joseph Addison

A good neighbor is a fellow who smiles at you over the back fence but doesn't climb over it.

Arthur (Bugs) Baer

Familiarity breeds contempt —and children.

Samuel Langhorne Clemens (Mark Twain)

All objects lose by too familiar a view.

John Dryden

See also: **Acquaintance, Friendship** .

FAMILY

A happy family is but an earlier heaven.

Sir John Bowring

The family is the miniature common upon whose integrity the safety of the commonwealth depends.

Felix *Adler*

The greatest thing in family life is to take a hint when a hint is intended— and not to take a hint when a hint isn't intended.

Robert Lee Frost

In my judgment, one of the basic reasons we have had crime, lawlessness, and disorder in the United States has been the breakdown of the family unit.

Robert Francis Kennedy

Where can a man better be than with his family?

Jean François Marmontel

See also: **Birth, Father, Mother, Parent**

FANATICISM

Of all things wisdom is the most terrified with epidemical fanaticism, because, of all enemies, it is that against which she is the least able to furnish any kind of resource.

Edmund Burke

A fanatic is one who can't change his mind and won't change the subject.

Sir Winston Leonard Spencer Churchill

We often excuse our own want of philanthropy by giving the name of fanaticism to the more ardent zeal of others.

Henry Wadsworth Longfellow

Fanatic faith, once wedded fast to some dear falsehood, hugs it to the last.

Thomas Moore

Fanaticism harkens only to its own counsel, which it believes to be inspired.

Francis Wilson

See also: **Intolerance**

FASHION

The customs and fashions of men change like leaves on the bough, some of which go, and others come.

· *Dante Alighieri*

Thus grows up fashion, an equivocal semblance; the most puissant, the most fantastic and frivolous, the most feared and followed, and which morals and violence assault in vain.

Ralph Waldo Emerson

Fashion is only the attempt to realize art in living forms and social intercourse.

Oliver Wendell Holmes

Be not too early in the fashion, nor too long out of it; nor at any time in the extremes of it.

Johann Kaspar Lavater

Fashion is, for the most part, nothing but the ostentation of riches.

John Locke

Fashion must be forever new, or she becomes insipid.

James Russell Lowell

Every generation laughs at the old fashions, but follows religiously the new.

Henry David Thoreau

Fashion seldom interferes with nature without diminishing her grace and efficiency.

Henry Theodore Tuckerman

Fashion is a form of ugliness so intolerable that we have to alter it every six months.

Oscar Wilde

Fashion is what one wears oneself. What is unfashionable is what other people wear.

Oscar Wilde

See also: **Appearance, Dress**

FATE

Fate is the friend of the good, the guide of the wise, the tyrant of the foolish, the enemy of the bad.

William Rounseville Alger

All things are ordered by God, but his providence takes in our free agency, as well as his own sovereignty.

Tryon Edwards

All is created and goes according to order, yet o'er our lifetime rules an uncertain fate.

Johann Wolfgang von Goethe

Fate is not the ruler, but the servant of Providence.

Edward G. Bulwer-Lytton (Baron Lytton)

Fate! there is no fate. Between the thought and the success God is the only agent.

Edward G. Bulwer-Lytton (Baron Lytton)

In two senses we are precisely what we worship. Ourselves are Fate.

Herman Melville

The Moving Finger writes; and having writ,
Moves on; nor all your Piety nor Wit
Shall lure it back to cancel half a Line,
Nor all your Tears wash out a Word of it.

Omar Khayyám

What must be shall be; and that which is a necessity to him that struggles, is little more than choice to him that is willing.

Seneca

See also: **Destiny, Fortune**

FATHER

My son is 7 years old. I am 54. It has taken me a great many years to reach that age. I am more respected in the community, I am stronger, I am more intelligent, and I think am better than he is. I don't want to be a pal, I want to be a father.

Clifton Fadiman

By profession I am a soldier and take pride in that fact. But I am prouder—infinitely prouder—to be a father. A soldier destroys in order to build; the father only builds, never destroys. The one has the potentiality of death; the other embodies creation and life. And while the hordes of death are mighty, the battalions of life are mightier still. It is my hope that my son, when I am gone, will remember me not from the battle but in the home repeating with him our simple daily prayer.

Douglas MacArthur

There was a time when father amounted to something in the United States. He was held with some esteem in the community; he had some authority in his own household; his views were sometimes taken seriously by his children; and even his wife paid heed to him from time to time.

Adlai Ewing Stevenson

The fundamental defect of fathers is that they want their children to be a credit to them.

Bertrand Arthur William Russell

See also: **Mother, Parent.**

FAULT

There is so much good in the worst of us,
And so much bad in the best of us,
That it ill behooves any of us
To find fault with the rest of us.

Anonymous

To reprove small faults with undue vehemence, is as absurd as if a man should take a great hammer to kill a fly on his friend's forehead.

Anonymous

Observe your enemies for they first find out your faults.

Antisthenes

When I feel like finding fault I always begin with myself and then I never get any further.

Ray Stannard Baker (David Grayson)

We should correct our own faults by seeing how uncomely they appear in others.

Francis Beaumont

The greatest of faults is to be conscious of none.

Thomas Carlyle

Think of your own faults the first part of the night when you are awake, and of the faults of others the latter part of the night when you are asleep.

Chinese Proverb

Faults of the head are punished in this world, those of the heart in another; but as most of our vices are compound, so also is their punishment.

Charles Caleb Colton

To acknowledge our faults when we are blamed, is modesty; to discover them to one's friends, in ingenuousness, is confidence; but to proclaim them to the world, if one does not take care, is pride.

Confucius

Every one is eagle-eyed to see another's faults and deformity.

John Dryden

FEAR

No one loves the man whom he fears.

Aristotle

Often the fear of one evil leads us into a worse.

Nicolas Boileau-Despréaux

The most dangerous person is the fearful; he is the most to be feared.

Ludwig Börne

Early and provident fear is the mother of safety.

Edmund Burke

No passion so effectually robs the mind of all its powers of acting and reasoning as fear.

Edmund Burke

The most drastic and usually the most effective remedy for fear is direct action.

William Burnham

Nothing in life is to be feared. It is only to be understood.

Marie Curie

If a man harbors any sort of fear, it percolates through all his thinking, damages his personality, makes him landlord to a ghost.

Lloyd Cassel Douglas

One of the strange phenomena of the last century is the spectacle of religion dropping the appeal to fear while other human interests have picked it up.

Harry Emerson Fosdick

He who fears being conquered is sure of defeat.

Napoleon I (Bonaparte)

The only thing we have to fear is fear itself.

Franklin Delano Roosevelt

The experience of overcoming fear is extraordinarily delightful.

Bertrand Arthur William Russell

FIDELITY

Nothing is more noble, nothing more venerable than fidelity. Faithfulness and truth are the most sacred excellences and endowments of the human mind.

Cicero

Trust reposed in noble natures obliges them the more.

John Dryden

Fidelity is the sister of justice.

Horace

Faithful found among the faithless, his loyalty he kept, his love, his zeal, nor number, nor example with him wrought to swerve from truth, or change his constant mind.

John Milton

Fidelity is seven-tenths of business success.

James Parton

It goes far toward making a man faithful to let him understand that you think him so; and he that does but suspect I will deceive him gives me a sort of right to do it.

Seneca

Another of our highly prized virtues is fidelity. We are immensely pleased with ourselves when we are faithful.

Ida Alexa Ross Wylie

See also: **Faith**

FINANCE

There is no such thing as an innocent purchaser of stocks.

Louis Dembitz Brandeis

A financier is a pawn-broker with imagination.

Sir Arthur Wing Pinero

A holding company is a thing where you hand an accomplice the goods while the policeman searches you.

Will (William Penn Adair) Rogers

See also: **Bank, Business, Economics, Gain, Money**

FIRMNESS

Firmness, both in suffering and exertion, is a character which I would wish to possess. I have always despised the whining yelp of complaint, and the cowardly feeble resolve.

Robert Burns

The greatest firmness is the greatest mercy.

Henry Wadsworth Longfellow

It is only persons of firmness that can have real gentleness. Those who appear gentle are, in general, only a weak character, which easily changes into asperity.

Duc François de La Rochefoucauld

The firm, without pliancy, and the pliant, without firmness, resemble vessels without water, and water without vessels.

Johann Kaspar Lavater

When firmness is sufficient, rashness is unnecessary.

Napoleon I (Bonaparte)

Firmness of purpose is one of the most necessary sinews of character, and one of the best instruments of success. Without it genius wastes its efforts in a maze of inconsistencies.

Philip Dormer Stanhope (Lord Chesterfield)

Your salvation is in your own hands; in the stubborness of your minds, the tenacity of your hearts, and such blessings as God, sorely tried by His children, shall give us. Nature is indifferent to the survival of the human species, including Americans.

Adlai Ewing Stevenson

FISHING

There is no use in your walking five miles to fish when you can depend on being just as unsuccessful near home.

Samuel Langhorne Clemens (Mark Twain)

I would rather fish than eat, particularly eat fish.

Corey Ford

You must lose a fly to catch a trout.

George Herbert

A fishing-rod is a stick with a hook at one end and a fool at the other.
Samuel Johnson

Angling may be said to be so like the mathematics that it can never be fully learnt.
Izaak Walton

As no man is born an artist, so no man is born an angler.
Izaak Walton

FLATTERY

The most skillful flattery is to let a person talk on, and be a listener.
Joseph Addison

It has well been said that the archflatterer, with whom all petty flatterers have intelligence, is a man's self.
Francis Bacon

Flattery corrupts both the receiver and the giver; and adulation is not of more service to the people than to kings.
Edmund Burke

Flattery is from the teeth out. Sincere appreciation is from the heart out.
Dale Carnegie

Some there are who profess to despise all flattery, but even these are, nevertheless, to be flattered, by being told that they do despise it.
Charles Caleb Colton

Imitation is the sincerest flattery.
Nathaniel Cotton

The lie that flatters I abhor the most.
William Cowper

Flattery is the destruction of all good fellowship: it is like qualmish liqueur in the midst of a bottle of wine.
Benjamin Disraeli

We love flattery, even when we see through it, and are not deceived by it, for it shows that we are of importance enough to be courted.
Ralph Waldo Emerson

A death-bed flattery is the worst of treacheries. Ceremonies of mode and compliment are mightily out of season when life and salvation come to be at stake.
Sir Roger L'Estrange

There is no tongue that flatters like a lover's; and yet in the exaggeration of his feelings, flattery seems to him commonplace.
Edward G. Bulwer-Lytton (Baron Lytton)

The art of flatterers is to take advantage of the foibles of the great, to foster their errors, and never to give advice which may annoy.
Molière (Jean Baptiste Poquelin)

Men find it more easy to flatter than to praise.
Jean Paul Richter

None are more taken in by flattery than the proud, who wish to be the first and are not.
Baruch (Benedict) Spinoza

Flattery is okay if you handle it right. It's like smoking cigarettes. Quite all right, as long as you don't inhale.
Adlai Ewing Stevenson

The only benefit of flattery is that by hearing what we are not, we may be instructed what we ought to be.
Jonathan Swift

See also: **Applause, Compliment, Praise**

FOLLY

A good folly is worth whatever you pay for it.

George Ade

He who lives without folly is not so wise as he imagines.

Duc François de La Rochefoucauld

Folly consists in drawing false conclusions from just principles, by which it is distinguished from madness, which draws just conclusions from false principles.

John Locke

See also: **Fool**

FOOL

A fool may be known by six things: anger, without cause; speech, without profit; change, without progress; inquiry, without object; putting trust in a stranger, and mistaking foes for friends.

Arabian Proverb

Every single forward step in history has been taken over the bodies of empty-headed fools who giggled and snickered.

Bruce Barton

Let us be thankful for the fools; but for them the rest of us could not succeed.

Samuel Langhorne Clemens (Mark Twain)

Nobody can describe a fool to the life, without much patient self-inspection.

Frank Moore Colby

I am always afraid of a fool; one cannot be sure he is not a knave.

William Hazlitt

No fools are so troublesome as those who have some wit.

Duc François de La Rochefoucauld

There are many more fools in the world than there are knaves, otherwise the knaves could not exist.

Edward G. Bulwer-Lytton (Baron Lytton)

To be a man's own fool is bad enough; but the vain man is everybody's.

William Penn

O Heaven! he who thinks himself wise is a great fool.

Voltaire (François Marie Arouet)

See also: **Folly, Ignorance**

FORETHOUGHT

In life, as in chess, forethought wins.

Sir Thomas Fowell Buxton

To have too much forethought is the part of a wretch; to have too little is the part of a fool.

Richard Cecil

As a man without forethought scarcely deserves the name of man, so forethought without reflection is but a phrase for the instinct of the beast.

Samuel Taylor Coleridge

Human foresight often leaves its proudest possessor only a choice of evils.

Charles Caleb Colton

If a man take no thought about what is distant, he will find sorrow near at hand.

Confucius

The pace of events is moving so fast that unless we can find some way to keep our sights on tomorrow, we cannot expect to be in touch with today.

(David) Dean Rusk

It is only the surprise and newness of the thing which makes terrible that misfortune, which by premeditation might be made easy to us; for what some people make light by sufferance, others do by foresight.

Seneca

Whatever is foretold by God will be done by man; but nothing will be done by man because it is foretold by God.

William Wordsworth

See also: **Caution, Providence, Prudence**

FORGIVENESS

"I can forgive, but I cannot forget," is only another way of saying, "I will not forgive." Forgiveness ought to be like a cancelled note—torn in two, and burned up, so that it never can be shown against one.

Henry Ward Beecher

He who is ready to forgive only invites offences.

Pierre Corneille

It is easier to forgive an enemy than a friend.

Madame Dorothée Deluzy

May I tell you why it seems to me a good thing for us to remember wrong that has been done us? That we may forgive it.

Charles John Huffam Dickens

His heart was as great as the world, but there was no room in it to hold the memory of a wrong.

Ralph Waldo Emerson

To err is human; to forgive, divine.

Alexander Pope

A brave man thinks no one his superior who does him an injury; for he has it then in his power to make himself superior to the other by forgiving it.

Alexander Pope

See also: **Clemency, Mercy, Pardon, Pity**

FORTUNE

It cannot be denied that outward accidents conduce much to fortune; favor, opportunity, death of others, occasion fitting virtue: but chiefly, the mold of a man's fortune is in his own hands.

Francis Bacon

Fortune knocks at every man's door once in a life, but in a good many cases the man is in neighboring saloon and does not hear her.

Samuel Langhorne Clemens (Mark Twain)

The wheel of fortune turns round incessantly, and who can say to himself, "I shall to-day be uppermost."

Confucius

It is a madness to make fortune the mistress of events, because in herself she is nothing, but is ruled by prudence.

John Dryden

To be thrown upon one's own resources, is to be cast into the very lap of fortune; for our faculties then undergo a development and display an energy of which they were previously unsusceptible.

Benjamin Franklin

The fortunate circumstances of our lives are generally found, at last, to be of our own producing.

Oliver Goldsmith

Human life is more governed by fortune than by reason.

David Hume

Ill fortune never crushed that man whom good fortune deceived not.
>> *Ben (Benjamin) Jonson*

It requires greater virtues to support good than bad fortune.
>> *Duc François de La Rochefoucauld*

Fortune gives too much to many, but to none enough.
>> *Martial*

The power of fortune is confessed only by the miserable, for the happy impute all their success to prudence or merit.
>> *Jonathan Swift*

From fortune to misfortune is just a span, but from misfortune to fortune is quite a distance.
>> *Yiddish Proverb*

See also: **Accident, Chance, Destiny, Fate, Luck, Wealth**

FRAUD

The first and worst of all frauds is to cheat oneself.
>> *Gamaliel Bailey*

The more gross the fraud the more glibly will it go down, and the more greedily be swallowed, since folly will always find faith where imposters will find impudence.
>> *Charles Caleb Colton*

Though fraud in all other actions be odious, yet in matters of war it is laudable and glorious, and he who overcomes his enemies by stratagem is as much to be praised as he who overcomes them by force.
>> *Niccolò Machiavilli*

For the most part fraud in the end secures for its companions repentance and shame.
>> *Charles Simmons*

All frauds, like the wall daubed with untempered mortar, with which men think to buttress up an edifice, always tend to the decay of what they are devised to support.
>> *Richard Whately*

See also: **Deceit, Dishonesty**

FREEDOM

What is life? It is not to stalk about, and draw fresh air, or gaze upon the sun; it is to be free.
>> *Joseph Addison*

As long as there are in the world countries where the citizens exert an influence on their political future by choosing between different programs, the dictators cannot feel secure.
>> *Max Ascoli*

Freedom is power, a concentrated, skilful capacity to act.
>> *Max Ascoli*

It is by the goodness of God that we have in our country three unspeakably precious things: freedom of speech, freedom of conscience, and the prudence never to practise either.
>> *Samuel Langhorne Clemens (Mark Twain)*

All our freedoms are a single bundle, all must be secure if any is to be preserved.
>> *Dwight David Eisenhower*

It is impossible to enslave, mentally or socially, a Bible-reading people. The principles of the Bible are the groundwork of human freedom.
>> *Horace Greeley*

Martin Luther King stands with out other American martyrs in the cause of freedom and justice. His death is a terrible tragedy and a sorrow to his family, to our nation, to our conscience. The criminal act that took his life brings shame to our country.

The apostle of nonviolence has been the victim of violence. The cause for which he marched and worked I am sure will find a new strength.

The plight of discrimination, poverty and neglect must be erased from America, and an America of full freedom, full and equal opportunity, is the living memorial he deserves, and it shall be his living memorial.

Hubert Horatio Humphrey

Freedom of religion, freedom of the press, and freedom of person under the protection of the habeas corpus, these are principles that have guided our steps through an age of revolution and reformation.

Thomas Jefferson

Until every American, whatever his color or wherever his home, enjoys and uses his franchise, the work which Lincoln began will remain unfinished.

Lyndon Baines Johnson

Education is the first resort as well as the last, for a world-wide solution of the problem of freedom.

Horace Meyer Kallen

All free men, wherever they may live, are citizens of Berlin. And therefore, as a free man, I take pride in the words *"Ich bin ein Berliner"* [I am a Berliner].

John Fitzgerald Kennedy

Freedom is not merely a word or an abstract theory, but the most effective instrument for advancing the welfare of man.

John Fitzgerald Kennedy

If men and women are in chains, anywhere in the world, then freedom is endangered everywhere.

John Fitzgerald Kennedy

We will accept only a world consecrated to freedom of speech and expression-freedom of every person to worship God in his own way—freedom from want—and freedom from terrorism.

Franklin Delano Roosevelt

Freedom rings wherever opinions clash.

Adlai Ewing Stevenson

A hungry man is not a free man.

Adlai Ewing Stevenson

I would rather sit on a pumpkin, and have it all to myself, than to be crowded on a velvet cushion.

Henry David Thoreau

Men and women cannot be really free until they have plenty to eat, and time and ability to read and think and talk things over.

Henry Agard Wallace

The highest and best form of efficiency is the spontaneous cooperation of a free people.

(Thomas) Woodrow Wilson

Only free peoples can hold their purpose and their honor steady to a common end, and prefer the interests of mankind to any narrow interest of their own.

(Thomas) Woodrow Wilson

See also: **Dissent, Equality, Freedom Of The Press, Liberty**

FREEDOM OF THE PRESS

The press is not only free, it is powerful. That power is ours. It is the proudest that man can enjoy. It was not granted by monarchs; it was not gained for us by aristocracies; but it sprang from the people, and, with an immortal instinct, it has always worked for the people.

Benjamin Disraeli

If by the liberty of the press, we understand merely the liberty of discussing the propriety of public measures and political opinions, let us have as much of it as you please; but, if it means the liberty of affronting, calumniating, and defaming one anther, I own myself willing to part with my share of it whenever our legislators shall please to alter the law; and shall cheerfully consent to exchange my liberty of abusing others for the privilege of being abused myself.

Benjamin Franklin

The liberty of the press is a blessing when we are inclined to write against others, and a calamity when we find ourselves overborne by the multitude of our assailants.

Samuel Johnson

The free press is the mother of all our liberties and of our progress under liberty.

Adlai Ewing Stevenson

Freedom of the press is the staff of life for any vital democracy.

Wendell Lewis Willkie

See also: **Freedom, Journalism, Newspaper, Responsibility**

FRIENDSHIP

Friendship improves happiness, and abates misery, by doubling our joy, and dividing our grief.

Joseph Addison

The friendships of the world are oft confederacies in vice, or leagues of pleasure.

Joseph Addison

In poverty and other misfortunes of life, true friends are a sure refuge. The young they keep out of mischief; to the old they are a comfort and aid in their weakness, and those in the prime of life they incite to noble deeds.

Aristotle

Those friends are weak and worthless, that will not use the privilege of friendship in admonishing their friends with freedom and confidence, as well of their errors as of their danger.

Francis Bacon

It is one of the severest tests of friendship to tell your friend his faults. So to love a man that you cannot bear to see a stain upon him, and to speak painful truth through loving words, that is friendship.

Henry Ward Beecher

Do you want to make friends? Be friendly. Forget yourself.

Dale Carnegie

You can make more friends in two months by becoming interested in other people than you can in two years by trying to get other people interested in you.

Dale Carnegie

Never contract a friendship with a man that is not better than thyself.

Confucius

There are three friendships which are advantageous: friendship with the upright, with the sincere, and with the man of much observation. Friendship with the man of specious airs with the insinuatingly soft, and with the glib-tongued, these are injurious.

Confucius

The only way to have a friend is to be one.

Ralph Waldo Emerson

We take care of our health, we lay up money, we make our roof tight and our clothing sufficient, but who provides wisely that he shall not be wanting in the best property of all—friends?

Ralph Waldo Emerson

Be slow to fall into friendship; but when thou art in, continue firm and constant.

Socrates

Friendship is a plant of slow growth, and must undergo and withstand the shocks of adversity before it is entitled to the appellation.

George Washington

Friendship is the only cement that will ever hold the world together.

(Thomas) Woodrow Wilson

See also: **Acquaintance, Brotherhood, Enemy, Love**

FRUGALITY

Eat it up, make it do, wear it out.

(John) Calvin Coolidge

He seldom lives frugally who lives by chance. Hope is always liberal, and they that trust her promises make little scruple of revelling to-day on the profits of to-morrow.

Samuel Johnson

The way to wealth is as plain as the way to market. It depends chiefly on two words, industry and frugality; that is, waste neither time nor money, but make the best use of both. Without industry and frugality nothing will do; with them, everything.

Benjamin Franklin

Frugality is good if liberality be joined with it. The first is leaving off superfluous expenses; the last is bestowing them for the benefit of those who need. The first, without the last, begets covetousness; the last without the first begets prodigality.

William Penn

With parsimony a little is sufficient; without it nothing is sufficient; but frugality makes a poor man rich.

Seneca

See also: **Economy, Miser**

FUN

The mirth and fun grew fast and furious.

Robert Burns

Fun is like life insurance: the older you get, the more it costs.

Frank McKinney (Kin) Hubbard

I live in the crowds of jollity, not so much to enjoy company as to shun myself.

Samuel Johnson

See also: **Amusement**

FUTURE

We should live for the future, and yet should find our life in the fidelities of the present; the last is the only method of the first.

Henry Ward Beecher

When all else is lost, the future still remains.

Christian Nestell Bovee

I never think of the future. It comes soon enough.

Albert Einstein

My interest is in the future because I am going to spend the rest of my life there.

Charles Franklin Kettering

The veil which covers the face of futurity is woven by the hand of mercy.

Edward G. Bulwer-Lytton (Baron Lytton)

Too many people are afraid of Tomorrow—their happiness is poisoned by a phantom.

William Lyon Phelps

My faith! that man is a fool who shall trust the future. He who laughs on Friday will weep on Sunday.

Jean Baptist Racine

See also: **Age, Present**

GAIN

The true way to gain much, is never to desire to gain too much. He is not rich that possesses much, but he that covets no more; and he is not poor that enjoys little, but he that wants too much.

Francis Beaumont

Every joy is gain And gain is gain, however small.

Robert Browning

Sometimes the best gain is to lose.

George Herbert

See also: **Avarice, Property**

GENEROSITY

A man there was, tho' some did count him mad,
The more he cast away, the more he had.

John Bunyan

Men of the noblest dispositions think themselves happiest when others share their happiness with them.

William Duncan

Humanitarianism is a link that binds together all Americans . . . . Whenever tragedy or disaster has struck in any corner of the world, the American people has promptly and generously extended its hand of mercy and help. Generosity has never impoverished the giver; it has enriched the lives of those who have practiced it . . . . And the bread we have cast upon the waters has been returned in blessings a hundredfold.

Dwight David Eisenhower

True generosity is a duty as indispensably necessary as those imposed on us by law. It is a rule imposed by reason, which should be the sovereign law of a rational being.

Oliver Goldsmith

Generosity during life is a very different thing from generosity in the hour of death; one proceeds from genuine liberality and benevolence, the other from pride or fear.

Horace Mann

See also: **Benevolence, Help, Kindness**

GENIUS

Talent, lying in the understanding, is often inherited; genius, being the action of reason and imagination, rarely or never.

Samuel Taylor Coleridge

Fortune has rarely condescended to be the companion of genius.

Isaac D'Israeli

Genius must be born; it never can be taught.

John Dryden

Genius is one per cent inspiration and ninety-nine per cent perspiration.

Thomas Alva Edison

Great geniuses have the shortest biographies.

Ralph Waldo Emerson

Genius is the ability to put into effect what is in your mind, there's no other definition of it.

Francis Scott Key Fitzgerald

Genius is commonly developed in men by some deficiency that stabs them wide awake and becomes a major incentive. Obstacles can be immensely arousing and kindling.

Harry Emerson Fosdick

One of the strongest characteristics of genius is the power of lighting its own fire.

John Watson Foster

Genius is only a superior power of seeing.

John Ruskin

Genius is no snob. It does not run after titles or seek by preference the high circles of society.

(Thomas) Woodrow Wilson

See also: **Ability, Art, Creativity**

GENTLEMAN

A gentleman is any man who wouldn't hit a woman with his hat on.

Fred Allen

I like him. He is every other inch a gentleman.

Noel Fierce Coward

We sometimes meet an original gentleman, who, if manners had not existed, would have invented them.

Ralph Waldo Emerson

See also: **Courtesy, Manners**

GLORY

As to be perfectly just is an attribute of the divine nature, to be so to the utmost of our abilities is the glory of man.

Joseph Addison

Let us not disdain glory too much; nothing is finer, except virtue. The height of happiness would be to unite both in this life.

Vicomte François René de Chateaubriand

True glory takes root, and even spreads; all false pretences, like flowers, fall to the ground; nor can any counterfeit last long.

Cicero

Glory, built on selfish principles, is shame and guilt.

William Cowper

Our greatest glory consists not in never falling, but in rising every time we fall.

Oliver Goldsmith

The glory of a people, and of an age, is always the work of a small number of great men, and disappears with them.

Baron Friedrich Melchior von Grimm

The shortest way to glory is to be guided by conscience.

Henry Home (Lord Kames)

See also: **Fame, Honor, Praise**

GLUTTONY

Their kitchen is their shrine, the cook their priest, the table their altar, and their belly their god.

Charles Buck

As houses well stored with provisions are likely to be full of mice, so the bodies of those who eat much are full of diseases.

Diogenes

I saw few die of hunger—of eating, a hundred thousand.

Benjamin Franklin

Swinish gluttony ne'er looks to heaven amid his gorgeous feast, but with besotted, base ingratitude, crams and blasphemes his feeder.

John Milton

The pleasures of the palate deal with us like the Egyptian thieves, who strangle those whom they embrace.

Seneca

See also: **Abstinence, Eating**

GOD

The nature of God is a circle of which the centre is everywhere and the circumference is nowhere.

Anonymous

Reason in man is rather like God in the world.

Thomas Aquinas

We cannot too often think, that there is a never sleeping eye that reads the heart, and registers our thoughts.

Francis Bacon

There is something in the nature of things which the mind of man, which reason, which human power cannot effect, and certainly that which produces this must be better than man. What can this be but God?

Cicero

You can believe in God without believing in immortality, but it is hard to see how anybody can believe in immortality and not believe in God.

Ernest Dimnet

Nature is too thin a screen; the glory of the omnipresent God bursts through everywhere.

Ralph Waldo Emerson

A man who writes of himself without speaking of God is like one who identifies himself without giving his address.

Ben Hecht

Performing miracles in a crisis—so much easier than loving God selflessly every moment of the day! Which is why most crises arise—because people find it so hard to behave properly at ordinary times.

Aldous Leonard Huxley

See also: **Integrity, Morality.**

GOSSIP

Truth is not exciting enough to those who depend on the characters and lives of their neighbors for all their amusement.

George Bancroft

In private life I never knew any one interfere with other people's disputes but that he heartily repented of it.

Thomas Carlyle

Gossip is the henchman of rumor and scandal.

Octave Feuillet

I hold it to be a fact, that if all persons knew what each said of the other, there would not be four friends in the world.

Blaise Pascal

Tale bearers are just as bad as tale makers.

Richard Brinsley Sheridan

Gossip is the art of saying nothing in a way that leaves practically nothing unsaid.

Walter Winchell

News-hunters have great leisure, with little thought; much petty ambition to be thought intelligent, without any other pretension than being able to communicate what they have just learned.

Johann Georg von Zimmermann

GOVERNMENT

Few consider how much we are indebted to government, because few can represent how retched mankind would be without it.

Joseph Addison

It is better for a city to be governed by a good man than even by good laws.

Aristotle

When any of the four pillars of government, religion, justice, counsel, and treasure, are mainly shaken or weakened, men had need to pray for fair weather.

Francis Bacon

Government is a contrivance of human wisdom to provide for human *wants*. Men have a right that these wants should be provided for by this wisdom.

Edmund Burke

No government ought to exist for the purpose of checking the prosperity of its people or to allow such a principle in its policy.

Edmund Burke

Government alone cannot meet and master the great social problems of our day. It will take public-interest partnerships of a scope we cannot yet perceive.

Joseph Anthony Califano, Jr.

Though the people support the government, the government should not support the people.

(Stephen) Grover Cleveland

Governments are necessarily continuing concerns. They have to keep going in good times and in bad. They therefore need a wide margin of safety. If taxes and debt are made all the people can bear when times are good, there will be certain disaster when times are bad.

(John) Calvin Coolidge

A government of statesmen or of clerks? Of Humbug or of Humdrum?

Benjamin Disraeli

The greatest of all evils is a weak government.

Benjamin Disraeli

The less government we have the better——the fewer laws and the less confided power. The antidote to this abuse of formal government is the influence of private character, the growth of the individual.

Ralph Waldo Emerson

The partnership between the Federal Government and the states and localities is a partnership which requires that all partners are adequately equipped to fully participate in their responsibilities.

Hubert Horatio Humphery

Government is an art and a precious obligation; and when it has a job to do, I believe it should do it. And this requires not only great ends but that we propose concrete means of achieving them.

John Fitzgerald Kennedy

This nation, under God, shall have a new birth of freedom, that government of the people, by the people, for the people, shall not perish from the earth.

Abraham Lincoln

See also: **Authority, Democracy, Law**

GRACE

Grace comes into the soul, as the morning sun into the world; first a dawning; then a light; and at last the sun in his full and excellent brightness.

Thomas Adams

There is no such way to attain to greater measure of grace as for a man to live up to the little grace he has.

Phillips Brooks

"What is grace?" was asked of an old colored man, who, for over forty years, had been a slave. "Grace," he replied, "is what I should call giving something for nothing."

Anonymous

As heat is opposed to cold, and light to darkness, so grace is opposed to sin. Fire and water may as well agree in the same vessel, as grace and sin in the same heart.

Thomas Brooks

Grace is but glory begun, and glory is but grace perfected.

Jonathan Edwards

The being of grace must go before the increase of it; for there is no growth without life, and no building without a foundation.

George Lavington

See also: **God**

GRAMMAR

Everything bows to success, even grammar.

Victor Marie Hugo

The rights of nations and of kings sink into questions of grammar if grammarians discuss them.

Samuel Johnson

George Moore wrote brilliant English until he discovered grammar.

Oscar Wilde

See also: **Book, Writing**

GRATITUDE

If gratitude is due from children to their earthly parent, how much more is the gratitude of the great family of men due to our father in heaven.

Hosea Ballou

He who remembers the benefits of his parents is too much occupied with his recollections to remember their faults.

Pierre Jean de Béranger

A grateful thought toward heaven is of itself a prayer.

Rudolph Block (Bruno Lessing)

He who receives a benefit should never forget it; he who bestows should never remember it.

Pierre Charron

No metaphysician ever felt the deficiency of language so much as the grateful.

Charles Caleb Colton

Gratitude is one of the least articulate of the emotions, especially when it is deep.

Felix Frankfurter

To the generous mind the heaviest debt is that of gratitude, when it is not in our power to repay it.

Benjamin Franklin

When I find a great deal of gratitude in a poor man, I take it for granted there be as much generosity if he were rich.

Alexander Pope

Two kinds of gratitude: the sudden kind
We feel for what we take, the larger kind
We feel for what we give.

Edwin Arlington Robinson

Gratitude to God makes even a temporal blessing a taste of heaven.

William Romaine

He enjoys much who is thankful for little; a grateful mind is both a great and a happy mind.

Thomas Secker

It is another's fault if he be ungrateful, but it is mine if I do not give. To find one thankful man, I will oblige a great many that are not so.

Seneca

See also: **Appreciation**

GRAVE

When I look upon the tombs of the great, every motion of envy dies within me; when I read the epitaphs of the beautiful, every inordinate desire goes out.

Joseph Addison

We weep over the graves of infants and the little ones taken from us by death; but an early grave may be the shortest way to heaven.

Tryon Edwards

A grave, wherever found, preaches a short and pithy sermon to the soul.

Nathaniel Hawthorne

The grave buries every error, covers every defect, extinguishes every resentment. From its peaceful bosom spring none but fond regrets and tender recollections. Who can look down upon the grave of an enemy, and not feel a compunctious throb that he should have warred with the poor handful of dust that lies moldering before him.

Washington Irving

See also: **Death, End**

GRAVITY

Gravity is only the bark of wisdom; but it preserves it.

Confucius

Those wanting wit affect gravity, and go by the name of solid men.

John Dryden

Gravity is a mysterious carriage of the body, invented to cover the defects of the mind.

Duc François de La Rochefoucauld

Too much gravity argues a shallow mind.

Johann Kaspar Lavater

Gravity—the body's wisdom to conceal the mind.

Edward Young

GREED: *See* AVARICE

GRIEF

No grief is so acute but that time ameliorates it.

Cicero

There is no greater grief than to remember days of joy when misery is at hand.

Dante Alighieri

Grief is the agony of an instant; the indulgence of grief the blunder of a life.

Benjamin Disraeli

Great grief makes sacred those upon whom its hand is laid. Joy may elevate, ambition glorify, but only sorrow can consecrate.

Horace Greeley

While grief is fresh, every attempt to divert only irritates. You must wait till it be digested, and then amusement will dissipate the remains of it.

Samuel Johnson

Well has it been said that there is no grief like the grief which does not speak.

Henry Wadsworth Longfellow

See also: **Sorrow**

GUEST

To what happy accident is it that we owe so unexpected a visit?

Oliver Goldsmith

The first day, a guest; the second, a burden; the third, a pest.

Edouard René Laboulaye

True friendship's laws are by this rule expressed:
Welcome the coming, speed the parting guest.

Alexander Pope

GUIDANCE

The divine guidance often comes when the horizon is the blackest.

Mohandas Karamchand (Mahatma) Gandhi

He that takes truth for his guide, and duty for his end, may safely trust to God's providence to lead him aright.

Blaise Pascal

That man may safely venture on his way,
Who is so guided that he cannot stray.

Sir Walter Scott

See also: **Advice, Education**

GUILT

The guilty is he who meditates a crime;
the punishment is his who lays the plot.
Conte Vittorio Alfieri

Adversity, how blunt are all the arrows
of thy quiver in comparison with those
of guilt.
Hugh Blair

God hath yoked to guilt, her pale tor-
mentor, misery.
William Cullen Bryant

Guilt is the very nerve of sorrow.
Horace Bushnell

The greatest incitement to guilt is the
hope of sinning with impunity.
Cicero

The consequences of our crimes long
survive their commission, and, like the
ghosts of the murdered, forever haunt
the steps of the malefactor.
Sir Walter Scott

Let wickedness escape, as it may at the
bar, it never fails of doing justice upon
itself; for every guilty person is his own
hangman.
Seneca

From the body of one guilty deed a
thousand ghostly fears and haunting
thoughts proceed.
William Wordsworth

Let no man trust the first false step of
guilt: it hangs upon a precipice, whose
steep descent in lost perdition ends.
Edward Young

See also: **Conscience, Crime, Remorse,
Repentance, Sin**

HABIT

Habit, if not resisted, soon becomes necessity.
Augustine of Hippo

Habit, if wisely and skillfully formed,
becomes truly a second nature; but un-
skillfully and unmethodically directed, it
will be as it were the ape of nature,
which imitates nothing to the life, but
only clumsily and awkwardly.
Francis Bacon

Habit is the deepest law of human nature.
Thomas Carlyle

Habit is habit and not to be flung out of
the window by any man, but coaxed
downstairs a step at a time.
Samuel Langhorne Clemens (Mark Twain)

Habit converts luxurious enjoyments
into dull and daily necessities.
Aldous Leonard Huxley

The chains of habit are generally too
small to be felt until they are too strong
to be broken.
Samuel Johnson

Habit is a cable. We weave of it every
day, and at last we cannot break it.
Horace Mann

When a man boasts of his bad habits,
you may rest assured they are the best
he has.
(Thomas) Woodrow Wilson

See also: **Custom, Fashion, Tradition**

HAIR

By common consent gray hairs are a
crown of glory; the only object of respect
that can never excite envy.
George Bancroft

Beware of her fair locks, for when she winds them round a young man's neck, she will not set him free again.

Johann Wolfgang von Goethe

The hair is the richest ornament of women. Of old, virgins used to wear it loose, except when they were in mourning.

Martin Luther

Fair tresses mans imperial race ensnare, And beauty draws us with a single hair.

Alexander Pope

HAPPINESS

Happiness consists in the attainment of our desires, and in our having only right desires.

Augustine of Hippo

Happiness sneaks in through a door you didn't know you left open.

John Barrymore

Happiness is not the end of life; character is.

Henry Ward Beecher

All who would win joy, must share it; happiness was born a twin.

George Gordon Byron (Lord Byron)

Happiness is like a sunbeam, which the least shadow intercepts, while adversity is often as the rain of spring.

Chinese Proverb

Happiness lies, first of all, in health.

George William Curtis

To find out what one is fitted to do and to secure an opportunity to do it is the key to happiness.

John Dewey

Happiness makes up in height for what it lacks in length.

Robert Lee Frost

No man is happy who does not think himself so.

Marcus Aurelius

The secret of happiness is this: let your interests be as wide as possible, and let your reactions to the things and persons that interest you be as far as possible friendly rather than hostile.

Bertrand Arthur William Russell

The greatest happiness you can have is knowing that you do not necessarily require happiness.

William Saroyan

The habit of being happy enables one to be freed, or largely freed, from the domination of outward conditions.

Robert Louis Balfour Stevenson

Happiness is possible even in pain and suffering. But pleasure alone can never create happiness.

Paul Tillich

See also: **Contentment, Joy**

HASTE

The more haste ever the worse speed.

Charles Churchill

No two things differ more than hurry and despatch. Hurry is the mark of a weak mind; despatch of a strong one.

Charles Caleb Colton

No man who is in a hurry is quite civilized.

Will (William James) Durant

Manners require time, and nothing is more vulgar than haste.

Ralph Waldo Emerson

Fraud and deceit are ever in a hurry. Take time for all things. Great haste makes great waste.

Benjamin Franklin

Unreasonable haste is the direct road to error.

Molière (Jean Baptiste Poquelin)

Whoever is in a hurry shows that the thing he is about is too big for him. Haste and hurry are very different things.

Philip Dormer Stanhope (Lord Chesterfield)

Though I am always in haste, I am never in a hurry.

John Wesley

HATE

Hatred does not cease by hatred, but only by love; this is the eternal rule.

Buddha

There are glances of hatred that stab, and raise no cry of murder.

George Eliot (Mary Ann Evans)

Hating people is like burning down your own house to get rid of a rat.

Harry Emerson Fosdick

Dislike what deserves it, but never hate, for that is of the nature of malice, which is applied to persons, not to things.

William Penn

It is human nature to hate him whom you have injured.

Tacitus

I shall never permit myself to stoop so low as to hate any man.

Booker Taliaferro Washington

See also: **Enemy, Jealousy, Resentment**

HEALTH

He who has health, has hope; and he who has hope, has everything.

Arabian Proverb

If you want to know if your brain is flabby feel of your legs.

Bruce Barton

Half the spiritual difficulties that men and women suffer arise from a morbid state of health.

Henry Ward Beecher

To become a thoroughly good man is the best prescription for keeping a sound mind in a sound body.

Francis Bowen

What a searching preacher of self-command is the varying phenomenon of health.

Ralph Waldo Emerson

Be sober and temperate, and you will be healthy.

Benjamin Franklin

See also: **Disease**

HEART

All our actions take their hue from the complexion of the heart, as landscapes their variety from light.

Francis Bacon

The heart has reasons that reason does not understand.

Jacques Bénigne Bossuet

There is no instinct like that of the heart.

George Gordon Byron (Lord Byron)

The heart seldom feels what the mouth expresses.

Jean Galbert de Campistron

The heart of a wise man should resemble a mirror, which reflects every object without being sullied by any.

Confucius

A loving heart is the truest wisdom.

Charles John Huffam Dickens

A kind heart is a fountain of gladness, making everything in its vicinity to freshen into smiles.

Washington Irving

It is better to break one's heart than to do nothing with it.

Margaret Kennedy

All who know their own minds, do not know their own hearts.

Duc François de La Rochefoucauld

The human heart is like the millstone in a mill; when you put wheat under it, it turns and grinds the wheat into flour. If you put no wheat in, it still grinds on, but then it is itself it grinds and slowly wears away.

Martin Luther

When the heart speaks, glory itself is an illusion.

Napoleon I (Bonaparte)

The heart of a good man is the sanctuary of God in this world.

Albertine Adrienne Necker de Saussure

The ways of the heart, like the ways of providence, are mysterious.

Henry Ware

See also: **Emotion, Love, Soul**

HEAVEN

It is heaven upon earth to have a man's mind move in charity, rest in providence, and turn upon the poles of truth.

Francis Bacon

To appreciate heaven well 'tis good for a man to have some fifteen minutes of hell.

William Carleton

What a man misses mostly in heaven is company.

Samuel Langhorne Clemens (Mark Twain)

Great Spirit, give to me a heaven not so large as yours but large enough for me.

Emily Elizabeth Dickinson

I would not give one moment of heaven for all the joy and riches of the world, even if it lasted for thousands and thousands of years.

Martin Luther

If I ever reach heaven I expect to find three wonders there: first, to meet some I had not thought to see there; second, to miss some I had expected to see there; and third, the greatest wonder of all, to find myself there.

John Newton

Heav'n is but the vision of fullfill'd desire.
And hell the shadow from a soul on fire.

Omar Khayyám

See also: **Hell**

HELL

Hell is truth seen too late —duty neglected in its season.

Tryon Edwards

Hell is full of good meanings and wishings.

George Herbert

One path leads to paradise, but a thousand to hell.

Yiddish Proverb

Men might go to heaven with half the labor they put to go to hell, if they would but venture their industry in the right way.

Ben (Benjamin) Jonson

See also: Heaven, Punishment, Sin

HELP

Help thyself and God will help thee.
George Herbert

Light is the task where many share the toil.

Homer

When a person is down in the world, an ounce of help is better than a pound of preaching.

Edward G. Bulwer-Lytton (Baron Lytton)

Nothing makes one feel so strong as a call for help.

George MacDonald

God helps them that help themselves.
Proverb

See also: Generosity

HERO

Unbounded courage and compassion joined proclaim him good and great, and make the hero and the man complete.

Joseph Addison

The world's battlefields have been in the heart chiefly; more heroism has been displayed in the household and the closet, than on the most memorable battlefields of history.

Henry Ward Beecher

Let us so bear ourselves that if the British Commonwealth lasts for a thousand years, men will still say, "This was their finest hour."

Sir Winston Leonard Spencer Churchill

Heroes in history seem to us poetic because they are there. But if we should tell the simple truth of some of our neighbors, it would sound like poetry.

George William Curtis

To believe in the heroic makes heroes.
Benjamin Disraeli

Mankind is not disposed to look narrowly into the conduct of great victors when their victory is on the right side.

George Eliot (Mary Ann Evans)

Self-trust is the essence of heroism.
Ralph Waldo Emerson

There is only one gift sufficient to honor [heroes] . . ., namely the assurance to every man in uniform "that their cause is a good cause."

Lyndon Baines Johnson

See also: Bravery, Courage

HISTORY

Neither history nor economics can be intelligently studied without a constant reference to the geographical surroundings which have affected different nations.

Henry Brooks Adams

There is nothing that solidifies and strengthens a nation like reading the nations history, whether that history is recorded in books, or embodied in customs, institutions, and monuments.

Joseph Anderson

Out of monuments, names, words, proverbs, traditions, private records and evidences, fragments of stories, passages of books, and the like, we do save and recover somewhat from the deluge of time.

Francis Bacon

History gives us a kind of chart, and we dare not surrender even a small rushlight in the darkness. The hasty reformer who does not remember the past will find himself condemned to repeat it.

Sir John Buchan

History is the essence of innumerable biographies.

Thomas Carlyle

Truth is very liable to be left-handed in history.

Alexandre Dumas (père)

History is little more than the register of the crimes, follies, and misfortunes of mankind.

Edward Gibbon

The best thing which we derive from history is the enthusiasm that it raises in us.

Johann Wolfgang von Gothe

History is fine, but a country should not live in its past or off its past glories.

Edward Heath

History is but a kind of Newgate calendar, a register of the crimes and miseries that man has inflicted on his fellowman.

Washington Irving

What is history but a fable agreed upon?
Napoleon I (Bonaparte)

We read history through our prejudices.
Wendell Phillips

See also: **Antiquity, Past**

HOME

America's future will be determined by the home and the school. The child becomes largely what it is taught, hence we must watch what we teach it, and how we live before it.

Jane Addams

Eighty per cent of our criminals come from unsympathetic homes.

Hans Christian Andersen

Home is the place where, when you have to go there, they have to take you in.

Robert Lee Frost

It was the policy of the good old gentleman to make his children feel that home was the happiest place in the world; and I value this delicious home feeling as one of the choicest gifts a parent can bestow.

Washington Irving

There is a magic in that little word, home; it is a mystic circle that surrounds comforts and virtues never known beyond its hallowed limits.

Robert Southey

Every house where love abides and friendship is a guest, is surely home, and home, sweet home; for there the heart can rest.

Henry van Dyke

See also: **Family, Father, Mother**

HONESTY

Be so true to thyself as thou be not false to others.

Francis Bacon

I had rather starve and rot and keep the privilege of speaking the truth as I see it, than of holding all the offices that capital has to give from the presidency downward.

Henry Brooks Adams

He who says there is no such thing as an honest man, is himself a knave.

George Berkeley

Make yourself an honest man, and then you may be sure there is one rascal less in the world.

Thomas Carlyle

Don't place too much confidence in a man who boasts of being as honest as the day is long. Wait until you meet him at night.

Robert Chambers (Bob) Edwards

Honesty is the best policy.

Benjamin Franklin

An honest man's the noblest work of God.

Alexander Pope

It would be an unspeakable advantage, both to the public and private, if men would consider that great truth, that no man is wise or safe, but he that is honest.

Sir Walter Raleigh

The best standard by which to judge the honesty of nations as well as men is whether they keep their word.

Lewis Baxter Schwellenbach

I hope I shall always possess firmness and virtue enough to maintain what I consider the most enviable of all titles, the character of an honest man.

George Washington

The shortest and surest way to live with honor in the world, is to be in reality what we would appear to be; and if we observe, we shall find, that all human virtues increase and strengthen themselves by the practice and experience of them.

Socrates

See also: **Candor, Integrity, Justice, Truth**

HONOR

Better to die ten thousand deaths than wound my honor.

Joseph Addison

Our own heart, and not other men's opinion, forms our true honor.

Samuel Taylor Coleridge

The difference between a moral man and a man of honor is that the latter regrets a discreditable act even when it has worked.

Henry Louis Mencken

No man is ever too old to enjoy fancy regalia, a secret password and a salute.

Louis Nizer

Hereditary honors are a noble and splendid treasure to descendants.

Plato

Let honor be to us as strong an obligation as necessity is to others.

Pliny the Elder

The giving of riches and honors to a wicked man is like giving strong wine to him that hath a fever.

Plutarch

Honor and shame from no condition rise;
Act well your part, there all the honor lies.

Alexander Pope

That nation is worthless that will not, with pleasure, venture all for its honor.

Johann Christoph Friedrich von Schiller

See also: **Esteem, Fame, Glory, Honesty, Integrity**

HOPE

Hope is the most beneficial of all the affections and doth much to the prolongation of life, it be not too often frustrated; but entertaineth the fancy with an expectation of good

Francis Bacon

Before you give up hope, turn back and read the attacks that were made upon Lincoln

Bruce Barton

I live on hope, and that I think do all who come into this world.

Robert Seymour Bridges

Man is, properly speaking, based upon hope; he has no other possession but hope; this world of his is emphatically the place of hope.

Thomas Carlyle

He that lives on hope will die fasting.

Benjamin Franklin

My country owes me nothing. It gave me, as it gives every boy and girl, a chance. It gave me schooling, independence of action, opportunity for service and honor. In no other land could a boy from a country village, without inheritance or influential friends, look forward with unbounded hope.

Herbert Clark Hoover

Hope is a delusion; no hand can grasp a wave or a shadow.

Victor Marie Hugo

Unfortunately many Americans live on the outskirts of hope—some because of their poverty, some because of their color, and all too many because of both. Our task is to help replace their despair with opportunity.

Lyndon Baines Johnson

Each time a man stands for an ideal, or acts to improve the lot of others, or strikes out against injustice, he sends forth a tiny ripple of hope.

Robert Francis Kennedy

The worldly hope men set their hearts upon; turns ashes—or it prospers; and anon, like snow upon the desert's dusty face, lighting a little hour or two—is gone.

Omar Khayyám

Hope springs eternal in the human breast, Man never is, but always to be blest.

Alexander Pope

Hope is brightest when it dawns from fears.

Sir Walter Scott

The mighty hopes that make us men.

Alfred, Lord Tennyson

See also: **Anticipation, Confidence, Expectation, Faith, Trust**

HUMILITY

Humility is the solid foundation of all the virtues.

Confucius

The street is full of humiliations to the proud.

Ralph Waldo Emerson

After crosses and losses men grow humbler and wiser.

Benjamin Franklin

To be humble to superiors, is duty; to equals, is courtesy; to inferiors, is nobleness; and to all, safety; it being a virtue that, for all its lowliness, commandeth those it stoops to.

Thomas Moore

Sense shines with a double luster when set in humility.

William Penn

True dignity abides with him only, who, in the silent hour of inward thought, can still suspect, and still revere himself, in lowliness of heart.

William Wordsworth

See also: **Modesty**

HUMOR

True humor springs not more from the head than from the heart. It is not contempt; its essence is love. It issues not in laughter, but in still smiles, which lie far deeper.

Thomas Carlyle

With the fearful strain that is on me night and day, if I did not laugh I should die.

Abraham Lincoln

Good-humor is goodness and wisdom combined.

Edward R. Bulwer Lytton (Owen Meredith)

The longer I live the more I think of humor as in truth the saving sense.

Jacob August Riis

Good humor isn't a trait of character, it is an art which requires practice.

David Seabury

See also: **Jesting, Levity, Ridicule, Wit**

HUNGER

Our own conception of democracy, no matter how earnestly venerated by ourselves, is of little importance to men whose immediate concern is the preservation of physical life. With famine and starvation the lot of half the world, food is of far more current importance to them than are political ideas. The degree of our sacrifice in feeding the hungry is the degree of our understanding of the world today.

Dwight David Eisenhower

More than half the people of the world are living in conditions approaching misery.... For the first time in history humanity possesses the knowledge and the skill to relieve the suffering of these people.

Harry S Truman

Hunger does not breed reform; it breeds madness, and all the ugly distempers that make an ordered life impossible.

(Thomas) Woodrow Wilson

See also: **Poverty**

HUSBAND

All husbands are alike, but they have different faces so you can tell them apart.

Anonymous

An archaeologist is the best husband any woman can have: the older she gets, the more interested he is in her.

Agatha Mary Clarissa Christie

A husband's patience atones for all crimes.

Heinrich Heine

With thee goes Thy husband, him to
   follow thou art bound;
Where he abides, think there thy native
   soil.

John Milton

See also: **Family, Marriage, Wife**

HYPOCRISY

A bad man is worse when he pretends
to be a saint.

Francis Bacon

The worst sort of hypocrite and liar is
the man who lies to himself in order to
feel at ease.

Hilaire Belloc

A man who hides behind the hypocrite
is smaller than the hypocrite.

William Edward Biederwolf

Behavior which appears superficially
correct but is intrinsically corrupt always irritates those who see below the
surface.

James Bryant Conant

No man can, for any considerable time
wear one face to himself, and another to
the multitude, without finally getting
bewildered to which is the true one.

Nathaniel Hawthorne

In modern society everyone faces in
some degree the problem of making his
public face the same as his private face.

Adlai Ewing Stevenson

I hope you have not been leading a
double life, pretending to be wicked and
being really good all the time. That
would be hypocrisy.

Oscar Wilde

See also: **Deceit, Lying**

IDEA

Ideas in the mind are the transcript of
the world; words are the transcript of
ideas; and writing and printing are the
transcript of words.

Joseph Addison

Our land is not more the recipient of the
men of all countries than of their ideas.

George Bancroft

If you want to get across an idea, wrap it
up in a person.

Ralph Bunche

I would swap a whole cartload of prece-
dents any time for one brand new idea.

Luther Burbank

The ideas I stand for are not mine. I borrowed them from Socrates. I swiped
them from Chesterfield. I stole them
from Jesus. And I put them in a book. If
you don't like their rules, whose would
you use?

Dale Carnegie

An idea, like a ghost, according to the
common notion of ghosts, must be spoken to a little before it will explain itself.

Charles John Huffam Dickens

New ideas can be good or bad, just the
same as old ones.

Franklin Delano Roosevelt

See also: **Thought.**

IDEAL

The attainment of an ideal is often the
beginning of a disillusion.

Stanley Baldwin

Idealists give invaluable service, the
give the distant view, which makes progress, as it makes a walk, exhilarating.

Samuel Augustus Barne

The life of the young man is his visions, hope of the future, plans of achievement and success for himself.

Arthur Brisbane

Absolute idealism [is] the last, boldest and most grandiose systematic defense of God, immortality and eternal values.

May Brodbeck

The "liberal" of our times has become all too often little more than a sentimentalist "with both feet planted firmly in mid-air."

Louis Bromfield

No ideal is as good as a fact.

Richard Clarke Cabot

Ideals were not archaic things, beautiful and impotent; they were the real sources of power among men.

Willa Sibert Cather

No folly is more costly than the folly of intolerant idealism.

Sir Winston Leonard Spencer Churchill

Ideality is only the avant-courier of the mind, and where that, in a healthy and normal state goes, I hold it to be a prophecy that realization can follow.

Horace Mann

Ideals are like the stars: we never reach them, but like the mariners of the sea, we chart our course by them.

Carl Schurz

We build statues of snow, and weep to see them melt.

Sir Walter Scott

Ideal beauty is a fugitive which is never located.

Marquise de Sévigné

See also: **Aim, Character, Desire, Morality**

IDLENESS

Prolonged idleness paralyzes initiative.

Anonymous

Lost time is never found again.

John Hill Aughey

If you are idle you are on the way to ruin, and there are few stopping places upon it. It is rather a precipice than a road.

Henry Ward Beecher

Idleness is the enemy of the soul.

Benedict of Nursia

In idleness there is perpetual despair.

Thomas Carlyle

Troubles spring from idleness, and grievous toils from needless ease: many without labor would live by their own wits only, but they break for want of stock.

Benjamin Franklin

The way to be nothing is to do nothing.

Nathaniel Howe

To be idle and to be poor have always been reproaches; and therefore every man endeavors with his utmost care to hide his poverty from others, and his idleness from himself.

Samuel Johnson

Not only is he idle who is doing nothing, but he that might be better employed.

Socrates

See also: **Indolence, Leisure**

IGNORANCE

To be ignorant of one's ignorance is the malady of ignorance.

Amos Bronson Alcott

Politicians, largely common men themselves, have never learned that it is impossible to underestimate the intelligence of the common man.

Anonymous

As if anything were so common as ignorance! The multitude of fools is a protection to the wise.

Cicero

Ignorance is the night of the mind, but a night without moon or star.

Confucius

The narrower the mind, the broader the statement.

Proctor Fyffe (Ted) Cook

Ignorance of communism, fascism, or any other police-state philosphy is far more dangerous than ignorance of the most virulent disease.

Dwight David Eisenhower

It is not wisdom but ignorance that teaches men presumption. Genius may sometimes be arrogant, but nothing is so diffident as knowledge.

Edward G. Bulwer-Lytton (Baron Lytton)

Ignorance deprives men of freedom because they do not know what alternatives there are. It is impossible to choose to do what one has never "heard of."

Ralph Barton Perry

Everybody is ignorant, only on different subjects.

Will (William Penn Adair) Rogers

So long as thou art ignorant be not ashamed to learn. Ignorance is the greatest of all infirmities, and, when justified, the chiefest of all follies.

Izaak Walton

See also: **Fool**

ILLUSION

A pleasant illusion is better than a harsh reality.

Christian Nestell Bovee

Nothing is more sad than the death of an illusion.

Arthur Koestler

The loss of our illusions is the only loss from which we never recover.

Marie Louise de la Ramée (Ouida)

In youth we feel richer for every new illusion; in maturer years, for every one we lose.

Anne Sophie Swetchine

See also: **Delusion, Imagination**

IMAGINATION

Lack of imagination causes cruelty.

Louis Dembitz Brandeis

We are all of us imaginative in some form or other, for images are the brood of desire.

George Eliot (Mary Ann Evans)

The imagination can be happy in places where the whole man is not.

Katharine Fullerton Gerould

Imagined woes pain none the less.

Heinrich Heine

No man will be found in whose mind airy notions do not sometimes tyrannize, and force him to hope or fear beyond the limits of sober probability.

Samuel Johnson

Whatever makes the past or future predominate over the present, exalts us in the scale of thinking beings.

Samuel Johnson

Solitude is as needful to the imagination as society is wholesome for the character.

James Russell Lowell

Imagination rules the world.
Napoleon I (Bonaparte)

The human race built most nobly when limitations were greatest and, therefore, when most was required of imagination in order to build at all. Limitations seem to have always been the best friends of architecture.

Frank Lloyd Wright

See also: **Creativity, Dream**

IMITATION

Was Christ a man like us?—Ah! let us try if we then, too, can be such men as he!

Matthew Arnold

Imitation belittles.
Christian Nestell Bovee

Imitators are a servile race.
Charles Fontaine

Imitation is the sincerest flattery.
Mohandas Karamchand (Mahatma) Gandhi

I hardly know so true a mark of a little mind as the servile imitation of others
Fulke Greville (First Baron Brooke)

When people are free to do as they please, they usually imitate each other.
Eric Hoffer

Man is an imitative creature, and whoever is foremost leads the herd
Johann Christoph Friedrich von Schiller

See also: **Conformity, Example**

IMMORTALITY

'Tis the divinity that stirs within us; 'tis heaven itself that points out an hereafter and intimates eternity to man.

Joseph Addison

Whatsoever that be within us that feels, thinks, desires, and animates, is something celestial, divine, and, consequently, imperishable.

Aristotle

Probably nobody completely repudiates a faith in immortality. A man may doubt it in his mind, but he still believes it in his faith.

George Arthur Buttrick

The old, old fashion—death! Oh, thank God, all who see it, for that older fashion yet—of immortality!

Charles John Huffam Dickens

One short sleep past, we wake eternally, and death shall be no more.

John Donne

We are much better believers in immortality than we can give grounds for. The real evidence is too subtle, or is higher than we can write down in propositions.

Ralph Waldo Emerson

We do not believe in immortality because we have proved it, but, we forever try to prove it because we believe it.

James Martineau

All men's souls are immortal, but the souls of the righteous are both immortal and divine.

Socrates

See also: **Eternity, Soul**

IMPOSSIBILITY

Most of the things worth doing in the world, had been declared impossible before they were done.

Louis Dembitz Brandies

It is not a lucky word, this same "impossible"; no good comes of those who have it so often in their mouth.

Thomas Carlyle

One great difference between a wise man and a fool is, the former only wishes for what he may possibly obtain; the latter desires impossibilities.

Democritus

Nothing is impossible; there are ways that lead to everything, and if we had sufficient will we should always have sufficient means. It is often merely for an excuse that we say things are impossible.

Duc François de La Rochefoucauld

"Impossible!" That is not good French.

Napoleon I (Bonaparte)

See also: **Absurdity, Perfection**

IMPROVEMENT

People seldom improve when they have no other model but themselves to copy after.

Oliver Goldsmith

If a better system is thine, impart it; if not, make use of mine.

Horace

The law of worthy life is fundamentally the law of strife; it is only through labor and painful effort, by grim energy and resolute courage that we move into better things.

Theodore Roosevelt

All of us, who are worth anything, spend our manhood in unlearning the follies, or expiating the mistakes of our youth.

Percy Bysshe Shelley

Much of the wisdom of one age, is the folly of the next.

Charles Simmons

See also: **Progress, Self-Improvement**

INCREDULITY

Nothing is so contemptible as that affectation of wisdom which some display by universal incredulity.

Oliver Goldsmith

Incredulity robs us of many pleasures, and gives us nothing in return.

James Russell Lowell

It is always well to accept your own shortcomings with candor but to regard those of your friends with polite incredulity.

(Joseph) Russell Lynes

The incredulous are of all men the most credulous; they believe the miracles of Vespasian, in order not to believe those of Moses.

Blaise Pascal

Some men will believe nothing but what they can comprehend: and there are but few things that such are able to comprehend.

Seigneur de Saint-Evremond

The amplest knowledge has the largest faith. Ignorance is always incredulous.

Robert Eldridge Aris Willmott

See also: **Agnosticism, Unbelief**

INDECISION

The wavering mind is but a base possession.

Euripides

There is no more miserable human being than one in whom nothing is habitual but indecision.

William James

When a man has not a good reason for doing a thing, he has one good reason for letting it alone.

Thomas Scott

See also: **Weakness**

INDEPENDENCE

Without moral and intellectual independence, there is no anchor for national independence.

David Ben-Gurion

The word independence is united to the ideas of dignity and virtue; the word dependence, to the ideas of inferiority and corruption.

Jeremy Bentham

No one can build his security upon the nobleness of another person.

Willa Sibert Cather

Happy the man to whom heaven has given a morsel of bread without laying him under the obligation of thanking any other for it than heaven itself.

Miguel de Cervantes Saavedra

It is not the greatness of a man's means that makes him independent, so much as the smallness of his wants.

William Cobbett

Let all your views in life be directed to a solid, however moderate, independence; without it no man can be happy, nor even honest.

Junius

The moral progression of a people can scarcely begin till they are independent.

James Martineau

Go to New England, and visit the domestic firesides, if you would see the secret of American Independence. Religion has made them what they are.

Tomás Cipriano de Mosquera

See also: **Freedom, Liberty**

INDIVIDUALITY

Have the courage to be different without being contrary—without flaunting your independence. The quality that makes us interesting, that makes us outstanding personalities, is the courage to be ourselves.

Anonymous

The American system of rugged individualism.

Herbert Clark Hoover

Delight is to him—a far, far upward, and inward delight—who against the proud gods and commodores of this earth, ever stands forth his own inexorable self.

Herman Melville

Individuality is everywhere to be spared and respected as the root of everything good.

Jean Paul Richter

We require individualism which does not wall man off from community; we require community which sustains but does not suffocate the individual.

Arthur Meier Schlesinger

See also: *Character*

INDOLENCE

I look upon indolence as a sort of suicide; for the man is efficiently destroyed, though the appetite of the brute may survive.

Cicero

Indolence is the sleep of the mind.
Luc de Clapiers (Marquis de Vauvenargues)

The darkest hour in the history of any young man is when he sits down to study how to get money without honestly earning it.

Horace Greeley

Nothing ages like laziness.
Edward G. Bulwer-Lytton (Baron Lytton)

By nature's laws, immutable and just, enjoyment stops where indolence begins.

Robert Pollok

I look upon indolence as a sort of suicide; for the man is effectually destroyed, though the appetite of the brute may survive.

Philip Dormer Stanhope (Lord Chesterfield)

See also: *Idleness*

INEQUALITY

No amount of artificial reinforcement can offset the natural inequalities of human individuals.

Henry Pratt Fairchild

There is always inequity in life. Some men are killed in a war, and some men are wounded, and some men are stationed in the Antarctic and some are stationed in San Francisco. It's very hard in military or personal life to assure complete equality. Life is unfair.

John Fitzgerald Kennedy

Some must follow, and some command, though all are made of clay.

Henry Wadsworth Longfellow

See also: *Equality, Injustice*

INFERIORITY

No man likes to have his intelligence or good faith questioned, especially if he has doubts about it himself.

Henry Brooks Adams

To be a human being means to possess a feeling of inferiority which constantly presses towards its own conquest. The paths to victory are as different in a thousand ways as the chosen goals of perfection. The greater the feeling of inferiority that has been experienced, the more powerful is the urge to conquest and the more violent the emotional agitation.

Alfred Adler

No one can make you feel inferior without your consent.

Anna Eleanor Roosevelt

See also: *Ignorance, Weakness*

INFLUENCE

No man should think himself a zero, and think he can do nothing about the state of the world.

Bernard Mannes Baruch

Not one false man but does unaccountable mischief.

> *Thomas Carlyle*

Men are won, not so much by being blamed, as by being encompassed with love.

> *William Ellery Channing*

Blessed is the influence of one true, loving human soul on another.

> *George Eliot (Mary Ann Evans)*

Every thought which genius and piety throw into the world alters the world.

> *Ralph Waldo Emerson*

A good man does good merely by living.

> *Edward G. Bulwer-Lytton (Baron Lytton)*

A word or a nod from the good, has more weight than the eloquent speeches of others.

> *Plutarch*

The words that a father speaks to his children in the privacy of home are not heard by the world, but, as in whispering galleries, they are clearly heard at the end, and by posterity.

> *Jean Paul Richter*

Let him that would move the world, first move himself.

> *Socrates*

INGRATITUDE

He that forgets his friend is ungrateful to him; but he that forgets his Saviour is unmerciful to himself.

> *John Bunyan*

We seldom find people ungrateful so long as it is thought we can serve them.

> *Duc François de La Rochefoucauld*

If you pick up a starving dog and make him prosperous, he will not bite you. That is the principal difference between a dog and a man.

> *Samuel Langhorne Clemens (Mark Twain)*

One great cause of our insensibility to the goodness of our Creator is the very extensiveness of his bounty.

> *William Paley*

He that calls a man ungrateful, sums up all the evil of which one can be guilty.

> *Jonathan Swift*

See also: **Gratitude, Selfishness**

INHERITANCE

What madness it is for a man to starve himself to enrich his heir, and so turn a friend into an enemy! For his joy at your death will be proportioned to what you leave him.

> *Seneca*

They who provide much wealth for their children but neglect to improve them in virtue, do like those who feed their horses high, but never train them to be useful.

> *Socrates*

Who comes for the inheritance is often made to pay for the funeral.

> *Yiddish Proverb*

See also: **Death**

INJURY

Nothing can work me damage except myself. The harm that I sustain I carry about with me, and am never a real sufferer but by my own fault.

> *Bernard of Clairvaux*

No man is hurt but by himself.

Diogenes

Christianity commands us to pass by injuries; policy, to let them pass by us

Benjamin Franklin

Slight small injuries, and they will become none at all.

Thomas Fuller

The purpose of an injury is to vex and trouble me. Now, nothing can do that to him that is truly valiant.

Samuel Johnson

He who has injured thee was either stronger or weaker than thee. If weaker, spare him; if stronger, spare thyself.

Seneca

The injuries we do, and those we suffer, are seldom weighed in the same balance.

Charles Simmons

See also: Abuse, Cruelty, Slander

INJUSTICE

No one will dare maintain that it is better to do injustice than to bear it.

Aristotle

If thou suffer injustice, console thyself; the true unhappiness is in doing it.

Democritus

Anyone entrusted with power will abuse it if not also animated with the love of truth and virtue, no matter whether he be a prince, or one of the people.

Jean de La Fontaine

Of all injustice, that is the greatest which goes under the name of law; and of all sorts of tyranny the forcing of the letter of the law against the equity, is the most insupportable.

Sir Roger L'Estrange

Did the mass of men know the actual selfishness and injustice of their rulers, not a government would stand a year. The world would foment with revolution.

Theodore Parker

He who commits injustice is ever made more wretched than he who suffers it.

Plato

See also: Inequality, Justice, Tyranny

INNOCENCE

Innocence, most often, is a good fortune and not a virtue.

Anatole France

He is armed without who is innocent within, be this thy screen, and this thy wall of brass.

Horace

Against the head which innocence secures, insidious malice aims her darts in vain; turned backward by the powerful breath of heaven.

Samuel Johnson

They that know no evil will suspect none.

Ben (Benjamin) Jonson

Innocence is but a poor substitute for experience.

Edward G. Bulwer Lytton (Baron Lytton)

To be innocent is to be not guilty; but to be virtuous is to overcome our evil inclinations.

William Penn

Innocence is like polished armor; it adorns and defends.

Robert South

There is no courage but in innocence; no constancy but in an honest cause.

Thomas Southerne

See also: **Guilt, Ignorance, Justice, Virtue**

INSANITY

Every sense hath been o'erstrung, and each frail fibre of the brain sent forth her thoughts all wild and wide.

George Gordon Byron (Lord Byron)

Great wits are sure to madness near allied,
And thin partitions do their bounds
    divide.

John Dryden

Insanity destroys reason, but not wit.

Nathaniel Emmons

Insane people easily detect the nonsense of other people.

John Hallam

INSINCERITY

Nothing is more disgraceful than insincerity.

Cicero

Of all the evil spirits abroad at this hour in the world, insincerity is the most dangerous.

James Anthony Froude

Insincerity in a man's own heart must make all his enjoyments—all that concerns him, unreal; so that his whole life must seem like a merely dramatic representation.

Nathaniel Hawthorne

It is a shameful and unseemly thing to think one thing and speak another, but how odious to write one thing and think another.

Seneca

See also: **Deceit, Dishonesty, Hypocrisy, Pretension**

INSTABILITY

Everything by starts, and nothing long.

John Dryden

    Some have at first for wits, then poets passed;
    Turned critics next, and proved plain fools at last.

Alexander Pope

A rolling stone can gather no moss.

Publilius Syrus

It will be found that they are the weakest-minded and the hardest-hearted men, that most love change.

John Ruskin

He who begins many things finishes nothing.

Charles Simmons

See also: **Chance, Indecision**

INSTINCT

There is not, in my opinion, anything more mysterious in nature than this instinct in animals, which thus rise above reason, and yet fall infinitely short of it.

Joseph Addison

Though reason is progressive, instinct is stationary. Five thousand years have added no improvement to the hive of the bee, or the house of the beaver.

Charles Caleb Colton

A goose flies by a chart which the Royal Geographical Society could not mend.

Oliver Wendell Holmes

See also: *Common Sense*

INSTRUCTION

The wise are instructed by reason; ordinary minds, by experience; the stupid, by necessity; and brutes by instinct.

Cicero

In moral lessons the understanding must be addressed before the conscience, and the conscience before the heart, if we would make the deepest impressions.

Nathaniel Emmons

A good newspaper and Bible in every house, a good schoolhouse in every district, and a church in every neighborhood, all appreciated as they deserve, are the chief support of virtue, morality, civil liberty, and religion.

Benjamin Franklin

See also: *Education, Guidance, Teaching*

INSULT

I once met a man who had forgiven an injury. I hope some day to meet the man who has forgiven an insult.

Sir Thomas Fowell Buxton

Whatever be the motive of an insult it is always best to overlook it; for folly scarcely can deserve resentment, and malice is punished by neglect.

Samuel Johnson

Oppression is more easily borne than insult.

Junius

There are two insults which no human will endure: the assertion that he hasn't a sense of humor, and the doubly impertinent assertion that he has never known trouble.

Sinclair Lewis

He who puts up with insult invites injury.

Proverb

It is often better not to see an insult than avenge it.

Seneca

INTEGRITY

Nothing more completely baffles one who is full of trick and duplicity, than straightforward and simple integrity in another.

Charles Caleb Colton

A man of integrity will never listen to any plea against conscience.

Henry Home

Undoubtedly, there is little integration or integrity in most men's characters; there is only habit and a plodding limitation in life and mind; and if social pressure were not added to lack of opportunity, disorderly lives would be more common than they are.

George Santayana

See also: **Honesty, Honor**

INTELLIGENCE

It is impossible to underrate human intelligence—beginning with one's own.

Henry Brooks Adams

A Negro cook told her children, "When you don't have an education, you've got to use your brains."

Anonymous

Intelligence increases mere physical ability one half. The use of the head abridges the labor of the hands.

Henry Ward Beecher

I think America is richer in intelligence than any other country in the world; and that its intelligence is more scattered than in any country of the world.

Will (William James) Durant

The test of a first-rate intelligence is the ability to hold two opposed ideas in the mind, at the same time, and still retain the ability to function.

Francis Scott Key Fitzgerald

The difference between intelligence and an education is this—that intelligence will make you a good living.

Charles Franklin Kettering

See also: **Common Sense, Discretion, Judgement, Knowledge, Prudence**

INTEREST

Interest makes some people blind, and others quick-sighted.

Francis Beaumont

There are no uninteresting things, there are only uninterested people.

Gilbert Keith Chesterson

It is more than possible, that those who have neither character nor honor, may be wounded in a very tender part, their interest.

Junius

Interest speaks all languages, and acts all parts, even that of disinterestedness itself.

Duc François de La Rochefoucauld

The behavior of nations over a long period of time is the most reliable, though not the only, index of their national interest.

Walter Lippmann

Interest has the security, though not the virtue of a principle. As the world goes, it is the surest side; for men daily leave both relations and religion to follow it.

William Penn

See also: **Attention**

INTOLERANCE

Nothing dies so hard, or rallies so often as intolerance.

Henry Ward Beecher

Intolerance has been the curse of every age and state.

Samuel Davies

In the blood of the Martyrs to intolerance are the seeds of unbelief.

Walter Lippmann

The devil loves nothing better than the intolerance of reformers, and dreads nothing so much as their charity and patience.

James Russell Lowell

The intolerant man is the real pedant.

Jean Paul Richter

See also: Fanaticism, Tyranny, Zeal

JAZZ

The chief trouble with jazz is that there is not enough of it; some of it we have to listen to twice.

Don Herold

Jazz will endure as long as people hear it through their feet instead of their brains.

John Philip Sousa

See also: Music

JEALOUSY

Jealousy is . . . a tiger that tears not only its prey but also its own raging heart.

Michael Beer

Jealousy sees things always with magnifying glasses which make little things large, of dwarfs giants, of suspicions truths.

Miguel de Cervantes Saavedra

. . . jealous rather in the manner of a miser who underpays his servant and therefore suspects his honesty.

John Collier

In jealousy there is more of self-love, than of love to another.

Duc François de La Rochefoucauld

He who is next heir to supreme power, is always suspected and hated by him who actually wields it.

Tacitus

See also: Rivalry

JESTING

Men ought to find the difference between saltness and bitterness. Certainly, he that hath a satirical vein, as he maketh others afraid of his wit, so he had need be afraid of others' memory.

Francis Bacon

Many a true word is spoken in jest.

English Proverb

Judge of a jest when you have done laughing.

William Lloyd

The jest loses its point when he who makes it is the first to laugh.

Johann Christoph Friedrich von Schiller

A joker is near akin to a buffoon; and neither of them is the least related to wit.

Philip Dormer Stanhope (Lord Chesterfield)

See also: Humor, Levity, Wit.

JOURNALISM

I would sooner call myself a journalist than an author, for a journalist is a journeyman.

Gilbert Keith Chesterton

Get your facts first, and then you can distort 'em as you please.

Samuel Langhorne Clemens (Mark Twain)

A journalist is a grumbler, a censurer, a giver of advice, a regent of sovereigns, a tutor of nations. Four hostile newspapers are more to be feared than a thousand bayonets.

Napoleon I (Bonaparte)

All journalists are, by virtue of their handicraft, alarmists; this is their way of making themselves interesting.

George Allardice Riddell

The journalist holds up an umbrella, protecting society from the fiery hail of conscience.

George William Russell

See also; **Newspaper**

JOY

Man is the merriest, the most joyous of all the species of creation. Above and below him all are serious.

Joseph Addison

Joy is more divine than sorrow, for joy is bread and sorrow is medicine.

Henry Ward Beecher

Grief can take care of itself, but to get full value of a joy you must have somebody to divide it with.

Samuel Langhorne Clemens (Mark Twain)

We lose the peace of years when we hunt after the rapture of moments.

Edward G. Bulwer-Lytton (Baron Lytton)

There are some people who have the quality of richness and joy in them and they communicate it to everything they touch. It is first of all a physical quality; then it is quality of the spirit.

Thomas Clayton Wolfe

The most profound joy has more of gravity than of gaiety in it.

Michel Eyquem de Montaigne

See also: **Happiness, Smile.**

JUDAISM

Judaism lives not in an abstract creed, but in its institutions.

Jacob Auerbach

Jesus was so much filled with the last and deepest thoughts of his people that he appears to us as the incarnation of the genius of Judaism.

Kurt Breysig

The religion of the Jews is, indeed, a light; but it is as the light of the glow-worm, which gives no heat, and illumines nothing but itself.

Samuel Taylor Coleridge

The history of the Jewish religion was the profoundest and richest that any nation had, and indeed was . . . the religious history of the human race.

Adolf von Harnack

Jesus was not a Christian, he was a Jew. He did not proclaim a new faith, but taught men to do the will of God. According to Jesus, as to the Jews generally, this will of God is to be found in the Law and the other canonical Scriptures.

Julius Wellhausen

See also: **Religion**

JUDGMENT

To judge by the event, is an error all abuse and all commit; for in every instance, courage, if crowned with success, is heroism; if clouded by defeat, temerity.

Charles Caleb Colton

You shall judge of a man by his foes as well as by his friends.

Joseph Conrad

The seat of knowledge is in the head; of wisdom, in the heart. We are sure to judge wrong if we do not feel right.

William Hazlitt

Judgment is forced upon us by experience.

Samuel Johnson

Everyone complains of the badness of his memory, but nobody of his judgment.

Duc François de La Rochefoucauld

The greater part of people judge of men either by the company with whom they live, or by their fortune.

Duc François de La Rochefoucauld

We judge ourselves by what we feel capable of doing; others judge us by what we have done.

Henry Wadsworth Longfellow

It is with our judgments as with our watches: no two go just alike, yet each believes his own.

Alexander Pope

I mistrust the judgment of every man in a case in which his own wishes are concerned.

Arthur Wellesley (Duke of Wellington)

One cool judgment is worth a thousand hasty councils. The thing to do is to supply light and not heat.

(Thomas) Woodrow Wilson

See also: Prudence, Understanding, Wisdom

JUSTICE

Justice discards party, friendship, and kindred, and is therefore represented as blind.

Joseph Addison

To be perfectly just is an attribute of the divine nature; to be so to the utmost of our abilities, is the glory of man.

Joseph Addison

Justice is to give to every man his own.

Aristotle

He who goes no further than bare justice, stops at the beginning of virtue.

Hugh Blair

Though force can protect in emergency, only justice, fairness, consideration and cooperation can finally lead men to the dawn of eternal peace.

Dwight David Eisenhower

Justice is as strictly due between neighbor nations, as between neighbor citizens. A highwayman is as much a robber when he plunders in a gang, as when single; and a nation that makes an unjust war is only a great gang of robbers.

Benjamin Franklin

The achievement of justice is an endless process.

John Fitzgerald Kennedy

Man is unjust, but God is just; and finally justice triumphs.

Henry Wadsworth Longfellow

Justice is the insurance we have on our lives and property, and obedience is the premium we pay for it.

William Penn

What is in conformity with justice should also be in conformity to the laws.

Socrates

See also: **Equality, Law, Rights**

KINDNESS

Win hearts, and you have all men's hands and purses.

William Henry Burleigh

We cannot be just unless we are kind-hearted.

Luc de Clapiers (Marquis de Vauvenargues)

What do we live for, if it is not to make life less difficult to each other?

George Eliot (Mary Ann Evans)

When death, the great reconciler, has come, it is never our tenderness that we repent of, but our severity.

George Eliot (Mary Ann Evans)

A kind heart is a fountain of gladness, making everything in its vicinity freshen into smiles.

Washington Irving

To cultivate kindness is a valuable part of the business of life.

Samuel Johnson

Kind words prevent a good deal of that perverseness which rough and imperious usage often produces in generous minds.

John Locke

Frankness and complete trust in the natural kindness of human nature will seldom fail, perhaps because it gives one even greater satisfaction to be helpful than helped.

Fulton Oursler

I expect to pass through life but once. If therefore, there be any kindness I can show, or any good thing I can do to any fellowbeing, let me do it now, and not defer or neglect it, as I shall not pass this way again.

William Penn

Human kindness has never weakened the stamina or softened the fiber of a free people. A nation does not have to be cruel in order to be tough.

Franklin Delano Roosevelt

I had rather never receive a kindness, than never bestow one. Not to return a benefit is the greater sin, but not to confer it, is the earlier.

Seneca

See also: **Help**

KING

All precepts concerning kings are comprehended in these: remember thou art a man; remember thou art God's vice-regent.

Francis Bacon

Wise kings generally have wise counselors; and he must be a wise man himself who is capable of distinguishing one.

Diogenes

Kings' titles commonly begin by force, which time wears off and mellows into right; and power which in one age is tyranny is ripened in the next to true succession.

John Dryden

Implements of war and subjugation are the last arguments to which kings resort.

Patrick Henry

In sovereignty it is a most happy thing not to be compelled, but so it is a most miserable thing not to be counselled.

Ben (Benjamin) Jonson

One of the strongest natural proofs of the folly of hereditary right in kings is, that nature disapproves it; otherwise she would not so frequently turn it into ridicule by giving mankind an ass in place of a lion.

Thomas Paine

Kings, in this chiefly, should imitate God; their mercy should be above all their works.

William Penn

See also: **Government, Power**

KISS

A kiss is a lovely trick designed by nature to stop speech when words become superfluous.

Ingrid Bergman

Eden revives in the first kiss of love.
George Gordon Byron (Lord Byron)

A long, long kiss—the kiss of youth and love.

George Gordon Byron (Lord Byron)

That farewell kiss which resembles greeting, that last glance of love which becomes the sharpest pang of sorrow.
George Eliot (Mary Ann Evans)

Leave but a kiss in the cup, and I'll not look for wine.

Ben (Benjamin) Jonson

I clasp thy waist; I feel thy bosom's beat. O, kiss me into faintness, sweet and dim.

Alexander Smith

Dear as remembered kisses after death.
Alfred Lord Tennyson

Once he drew, with one long kiss, my whole soul through my lips.
Alfred Lord Tennyson

I kissed my first woman and smoked my first cigarette on the same day; I have never had time for tobacco since.
Arturo Toscanini

A kiss from my mother made me a painter.

Benjamin West

See also: **Love, Romance**

KNOWLEDGE

What one knows is, in youth, of little moment; they know enough who know how to learn.

Henry Brooks Adam

A great deal of knowledge, which is not capable of making a man wise, has a natural tendency to make him vain and arrogant.

Joseph Addison

All knowledge and wonder (which is the seed of knowledge) is an impression of pleasure in itself.

Francis Bacon

Knowledge itself is power.

Francis Bacon

The first step to knowledge is to know that we are ignorant.

Richard Cecil

The essence of knowledge is, having it, to apply it; not having it, to confess your ignorance.

Confucius

Knowledge dwells in heads replete with thoughts of other men; wisdom, in minds attentive to their own.

William Cowper

The more extensive a man's knowledge of what has been done, the greater will be his power of knowing what to do.

Benjamin Disraeli

Knowledge is the eye of desire and can become the pilot of the soul.

Will (William James) Durant

What novelty is worth the sweet monotony where everything is known, and loved because it is known?

George Eliot (Mary Ann Evans)

Knowledge of our duties is the most essential part of the philosophy of life. if you escape duty you avoid action. The world demands results.

George Washington Goethals

Knowledge and timber should not be much used until they are seasoned.

Oliver Wendell Holmes

The best part of our knowledge is that which teaches us where knowledge leaves off and ignorance begins.

Oliver Wendell Holmes

If a little knowledge is dangerous, where is the man who has so much as to be out of danger?

Thomas Henry Huxley

All I know is what I read in the papers.

Will (William Penn Adair) Rogers

The end of all knowledge should be in virtuous action.

Sir Philip Sidney

Base-minded they that lack intelligence; for God himself for wisdom most is praised, and men to God thereby are highest raised.

Edmund Spenser

Knowledge is a comfortable and necessary retreat and shelter for us in advanced age, and if we do not plant it while young, it will give us no shade when we grow old.

Philip Dormer Stanhope (Lord Chesterfield)

Knowledge, like religion, must be "experienced" in order to be known.

Edwin Percy Whipple

See also: **Discovery, Science, Understanding**

LABOR

If we would have anything of benefit, we must earn it, and earning it become shrewd, inventive, ingenious, active, enterprising.

Henry Ward Beecher

The true epic of our times is not "arms and the man," but "tools and the man," an infinitely wider kind of epic.

Thomas Carlyle

A truly American sentiment recognises the dignity of labor and the fact that honor lies in honest toil.

(Stephen) Grover Cleveland

A man's best friends are his ten fingers.

Robert Collyer

No way has been found for making heroism easy, even for the scholar. Labor, iron labor, is for him. The world was created as an audience for him; the atoms of which it is made are opportunities.

Ralph Waldo Emerson

Excellence in any department can be attained only by the labor of a lifetime; it is not to be purchased at a lesser price.

Samuel Johnson

The labor of the body relieves us from the fatigues of the mind; and this it is which forms the happiness of the poor.

Duc François La Rochefoucauld

Love, therefore, labor; if thou shouldst not want it for food, thou mayest for physic. It is wholesome to the body and good for the mind; it prevents the fruit of idleness.

William Penn

I believe in the dignity of labor, whether with head or hand; that the world owes every man an opportunity to make a living.

John Davison Rockefeller, Jr.

No race can prosper 'til it learns that there is as much dignity in tilling the field, as in writing a poem.

Booker Taliaferro Washington

Labor is the great producer of wealth; it moves all other causes.

Daniel Webster

See also: Capitalism, Effort, Employment, Work

LANGUAGE

Slovenly language corrodes the mind.

James Truslow Adams

A man's language is an unerring index of his nature.

Laurence Binyon

The language denotes the man; a coarse or refined character finds its expression naturally in a coarse or refined phraseology.

Christian Nestell Bovee

Language is the armory of the human mind, and at once contains the trophies of its past and the weapons of its future conquests.

Samuel Taylor Coleridge

Language is a solemn thing: it grows out of life—out of its agonies and ecstasies, its wants and its weariness. Every language is a temple in which the soul of those who speak it is enshrined.

Oliver Wendell Holmes

The function of language is twofold: to communicate emotion and to give information.

Aldous Leonard Huxley

Language is only the instrument of science, and words are but the signs of ideas.

Samuel Johnson

Language most shows a man; speak that I may see thee; it springs out of the most retired and inmost part of us.

Ben (Benjamin) Jonson

England and America are two countries separated by the same language.

George Bernard Shaw

Language as well as the faculty of speech, was the immediate gift of God.

Noah Webster

See also: **Accent, Literature, Speech, Word, Writing**

LAUGHTER

You grow up the day you have the first real laugh—at yourself.

Ethel Barrymore

A laugh, to be joyous, must flow from a joyous heart, for without kindness there can be no true joy.

Thomas Carlyle

No man who has once heartily and wholly laughed can be altogether and irreclaimably depraved.

Thomas Carlyle

Laughter is the tonic, the relief, the surcease for pain.

Charles Spencer (Charlie) Chaplin

People who believe in little laugh at little.

Leonard Feeney

The loud laugh, that speaks the vacant mind.

Oliver Goldsmith

Alas for the worn and heavy soul, if, whether in youth or in age, it has outlived its privilege of spring time and sprightliness.

Nathaniel Hawthorne

Laughing is the sensation of feeling good all over, and showing it principally in one spot.

Bob (Leslie Townes) Hope

Excellent authority tells us that the right laughter is medicine to weary bones.

Carl Sandburg

See also: **Mirth, Smile.**

LAW

In the search for ways to maintain our values and pursue them in an orderly way, we must look beyond the resources of law.

Dean Gooderham Acheson

They are the best laws, by which the king has the greatest prerogative, and the people the best liberty.

Francis Bacon

A law is valuable not because it is law, but because there is right in it.

Henry Ward Beecher

Law is the embodiment of the moral sentiment of the people.

Sir William Blackstone

In all forms of Government the people is the true legislator.

Edmund Burke

In law nothing is certain but the expense.

Samuel Butler

Law and equity are two things that God hath joined together, but which man has put asunder.

Charles Caleb Colton

Men do not make laws. They do but discover them.

(John) Calvin Coolidge

Laws should be like clothes. They should be made to fit the people they are meant to serve.

Clarence Seward Darrow

When men are pure, laws are useless;
when men are corrupt, laws are broken.
Benjamin Disraeli

The clearest way to show what the rule
of law means to us in everyday life is to
recall what has happened when there is
no rule of law. The dread knock on the
door in the middle of the night.
Dwight David Eisenhower

Law never does anything constructive.
We have had enough of legislators
promising to do that which laws can not
do.
Henry Ford

Ours is an accusatorial and not an in-
quisitorial system—a system in which
the state must establish guilt by evidence independently and freely secured
and may not by coercion prove its
charge against an accused out of his
own mouth.
Felix Frankfurter

See also: **Government, Justice, Order,
Politics**

LEADERSHIP

And when we think we lead, we are
most led.
George Gordon Byron (Lord Byron)

A platoon leader doesn't get his platoon
to go by getting up and shouting and
saying, "I am smarter, I am bigger. I am
stronger. I am the leader." He gets men
to go along with him because they want
to do it for him and they believe in him.
Dwight David Eisenhower

Leadership and learning are indispensable to each other.
John Fitzgerald Kennedy

The leader must know, must know that
he knows, and must be able to make it
abundantly clear to those about him that
he knows.
Clarence Belden Randall

It [leadership in a democratic society] is
the task of persuading people to sacrifice their short-run individual gratifications in order to achieve long-run community interests.
George F. Will

See also: **Courage, Guidance, Hero**

LEARNING

That learning is most requisite which
unlearns evil.
Antisthenes

Learning teaches how to carry things in
suspense, without prejudice, till you resolve.
Francis Bacon

Some will never learn anything because
they understand everything too soon.
Sir Thomas Pope Blount

Acquire new knowledge whilst thinking
over the old, and you may become a
teacher of others.
Confucius

Seeing much, suffering much, and
studying much, are the three pillars of
learning.
Benjamin Disraeli

We cannot learn men from books.
Benjamin Disraeli

The trouble about man is twofold. He
cannot learn truths which are too complicated; he forgets truths which are too
simple.
Dame Rebecca West

Learning makes a man fit company for himself.

Edward Young

See also: *Education, Instruction, Knowledge, Study, Teaching, University*

LEISURE

Leisure is a beautiful garment, but it will not do for constant wear.

Anonymous

The aim of education is the wise use of leisure.

Aristotle

The end of labor is to gain leisure.

Aristotle

He does not seem to me to be a free man who does not sometimes do nothing.

Cicero

Employ thy time well if thou meanest to gain leisure; and since thou art not sure of a minute, throw not away an hour. Leisure is time for doing something useful and this leisure the diligent man will obtain, but the lazy man never, for a life of leisure and a life of laziness are two things.

Benjamin Franklin

You cannot give an instance of any man who is permitted to lay out his own time, contriving not to have tedious hours.

Samuel Johnson

See also: *Idleness, Rest*

LENIENCY

It is only necessary to grow old to become more indulgent. I see no fault committed that I have not committed myself.

Johann Wolfgang von Goethe

Lenity is a part of mercy, but she must not speak too loud for fear of waking justice.

Joseph Joubert

Lenity will operate with greater force in some instances than rigor. It is, therefore, my first wish to have all my conduct distinguished by it.

George Washington

See also: *Clemency, Compassion, Mercy*

LEVITY

In infants, levity is a prettiness; in men, shameful defect; in old age, a monstrous folly.

Duc François de La Rochefoucauld

Levity of behavior is the bane of all that is good and virtuous.

Seneca

Nothing like a little judicious levity.

Robert Louis Balfour Stevenson

See also: *Humor, Jesting, Laughter, Mirth*

LIAR: See LYING

LIBERTY

Absolute liberty is absence of restraint; responsibility is restraint; therefore, the ideally free individual is responsible to himself.

Henry Brooks Adams

A day, an hour of virtuous liberty is worth a whole eternity of bondage.
Joseph Addison

Liberty in itself is not government.
Bernard Mannes Baruch

The people never give up their liberties but under some delusion.
Edmund Burke

What is liberty without wisdom and without virtue? It is the greatest of all possible evils, for it is folly, vice, and madness, without tuition or restraint.
Edmund Burke

Liberty in the most literal sense is the negation of law, for law is restraint, and the absence of restraint is anarchy.
Benjamin Nathan Cardozo

Oh, give me liberty! for even were paradise my prison, still I should long to leap the crystal walls.
John Dryden

When liberty destroys order, the hunger for order will destroy liberty.
Will (William James) Durant

A Bible and a newspaper in every house, a good school in every district,—all studied and appreciated as they merit,—are the principal support of virtue, morality, and civil liberty.
Benjamin Franklin

Is life so dear, or peace so sweet as to be purchased at the price of chains and slavery? Forbid it, Almighty God! I know not what course others may take, but, as for me, give me liberty or give me death.
Patrick Henry

The spark of liberty in the mind and spirit of man cannot be long extinguished; it will break into flames that will destroy every coercion which seems to limit it.
Herbert Clark Hoover

We hold these truths to be self-evident, that all men are created equal; that they are endowed by their Creator with inalienable rights; and that among these are life, liberty, and the pursuit of happiness.
Thomas Jefferson

Let every nation know, whether it wishes us well or ill, that we shall pay any price, bear any burden, meet any hardship, support any friend, oppose any foe to assure the survival and the success of liberty.
John Fitzgerald Kennedy

Unless liberty flourishes in all lands, it cannot flourish in one.
John Fitzgerald Kennedy

Where liberty dwells, there is my country.
John Milton

See also: **Democracy, Freedom, Rights**

LIFE

Life is activity, hence the deep-seated objections to negations.
James Truslow Adams

I don't want to own anything that won't fit into my coffin.
Fred Allen

Every man's life is a fairy tale, written by God's fingers.
Hans Christian Andersen

Age and youth look upon life from the opposite ends of the telescope; to the one it is exceedingly long, to the other exceedingly short.

Henry Ward Beecher

All of the animals, excepting man, know that the principal business of life is to enjoy it.

Samuel Butler

One life; a little gleam of time between two eternities; no second chance for us forever more.

Thomas Carlyle

One of the most tragic things I know about human nature is that all of us tend to put off living. We are all dreaming of some magical rose garden over the horizon—instead of enjoying the roses that are blooming outside our windows today.

Dale Carnegie

Let us so live that when we come to die even the undertaker will be sorry.

Samuel Langhorne Clemens (Mark Twain)

LIGHT

The first creation of God, in the works of the days was the light of sense; the last was the light of reason; and his Sabbath work, ever since, is the illumination of the spirit.

Francis Bacon

Light is the symbol of truth,
James Russell Lowell

Hail! holy light, offspring of heaven, first born!

John Milton

Light is the shadow of God.

Plato

The eye's light is a noble gift of heaven! All beings live from light; each fair created thing, the very plants, turn with a joyful transport to the light.

Johann Christoph Friedrich von Schiller

LITERATURE

If I might control the literature of the household, I would guarantee the well-being of the church and state.

Francis Bacon

A country which has no national literature, or a literature too insignificant to force its way abroad, must always be, to its neighbors at least, in every important spiritual respect, an unknown and unestimated country.

Thomas Carlyle

Literature is but language; it is only a rare and amazing miracle by which a man really says what he means.

Gilbert Keith Chesterton

Literature has now become a game in which the booksellers are the kings; the critics, the knaves; the public, the pack; and the poor author, the mere table or thing played upon.

Charles Caleb Colton

There is such a thing as literary fashion, and prose and verse have been regulated by the same caprice that cuts our coats and cocks our hats.

Benjamin Disraeli

The decline of literature indicates the decline of a nation; the two keep pace in their downward tendency.

Johann Wolfgang von Gothe

Let your literary compositions be kept from the public eye for nine years at least.

Horace

In science, read, by preference, the newest works; in literature, the oldest. The classic literature is always modern.

Edward G. Bulwer-Lytton (Baron Lytton)

Great literature is simply language charged with meaning to the utmost possible degree.

Ezra Loomis Pound

The literature of a people must spring from the sense of its nationality; and nationality is impossible without self-respect, and self-respect is impossible without liberty.

Harriet Elizabeth Beecher Stowe

See also: **Book, Reading**

LITTLE THINGS. *See* TRIFLES

LOGIC

Logic and rhetoric make men able to contend. Logic differeth from rhetoric as the fist from the palm; the one close, the other at large.

Francis Bacon

A paradox is a contradiction in which you take sides—both sides.

Gregory Bateson

Logic and metaphysics make use of more tools than all the rest of the sciences put together, and they do the least work.

Charles Caleb Colton

Ethics make one's soul mannerly and wise, but logic is the armory of reason, furnished with all offensive and defensive weapons.

Thomas Fuller

It may be that dialectical theory finds its present truth in its own hopelessness.

Ronald David Laing

Syllogism is of necessary use, even to the lovers of truth, to show them the fallacies that are often concealed in florid, witty or involved discourses.

John Locke

It was a saying of the ancients, that "truth lies in a well"; and to carry on the metaphor, we may justly say, that logic supplies us with steps whereby we may go down to reach the water.

Isaac Watts

See also: **Philosophy, Reason, Science, Truth**

LONELINESS

The whole world has always been full of that loneliness. The Loneliness does not come from the War. The War did not make it. It was the loneliness that made the War. It was the despair in all things for no longer having in them the grace of God.

William Saroyan

All this hideous doubt, despair, and dark confusion of the soul a lonely man must know, for he is united to no image save that which he creates himself.

Thomas Clayton Wolfe

See also: **Absence, Quiet, Solitude**

LOOKS

'Tis not my talent to conceal my thought, or carry smiles and sunshine in my face, when discontent sits heavy at my heart.

Joseph Addison

Features—the great soul's apparent seat.
William Cullen Bryant

What brutal mischief sits upon his brow! He may be honest, but he looks damnation.

John Dryden

Looks are more expressive and reliable than words; they have a language which all understand, and language itself is to be interpreted by the look as well as tone with which it is uttered.

Tryon Edwards

A good face is a letter of recommendation, a good heart is a letter of credit.
Edward G. Bulwer-Lytton (Baron Lytton)

See also: **Appearance, Face**

LOQUACITY

He who talks much cannot always talk well.

Carlo Goldoni

Every absurdity has a champion to defend it, for error is always talkative.
Oliver Goldsmith

They always talk who never think, and who have the least to say.
Matthew (Matt) Prior

Speaking much is a sign of vanity, for he that is lavish in words is a niggard in deed.

Sir Walter Raleigh

Nature has given us two ears, two eyes, and but one tongue, to the end that we should hear and see more than we speak.

Socrates

No fool can be silent at a feast.

Solon

See also: **Babble**

LOSS

Losing is like dying.

George Allen

Show me a good loser and I'll show you a loser.

Vince Lombardi

When wealth is lost, nothing is lost; when health is lost, something is lost; when character is lost, all is lost.

German Motto

See also: **Adversity, Gain**

LOVE

If there is anything better than to be loved, it is loving.

Anonymous

True love is eternal, infinite, and always like itself. It is equal and pure, without violent demonstrations: it is seen with white hairs and is always young in the heart.

Honoré de Balzac

Let no one who loves be called altogether unhappy.

Sir James Matthew Barrie

Of all the paths leading to a woman's love, pity is the straightest.

Francis Beaumont

Young love is a flame; very pretty, often very hot and fierce, but still only light and flickering. The love of the older and disciplined heart is as coals, deep-burning, unquenchable.

Henry Ward Beecher

It is good that men should think; but it is indispensable that men should love.

Bernard Iddings Bell

Love cannot be forced, love cannot be coaxed and teased. It comes out of Heaven, unasked and unsought.

Pearl Sydenstricker Buck

'Tis better to have loved and lost, than never to have lost at all.

Samuel Butler

Man's love is of man's life a part; it is woman's whole existence.

George Gordon Byron (Lord Byron)

Love, and you shall be loved. All love is mathematically just, as much as the two sides of an algebraic equation.

Ralph Waldo Emerson

A man nearly always loves for other reasons than he thinks. A lover is apt to be as full of secrets from himself as is the object of his love from him.

Ben Hecht

There comes a time when the souls of human beings, women more even than men, begin to faint for the atmosphere of the affections they are made to breathe.

Oliver Wendell Holmes

Love, we say, is life; but love without hope and faith is agonizing death.

Elbert Green Hubbard

The first symptom of love in a young man, is timidity; in a girl, it is boldness. The two sexes have a tendency to approach, and each assumes the qualities of the other.

Victor Marie Hugo

A women is more considerate in affairs of love than a man; because love is more the study and business of her life.

Washington Irving

Love . . . is like a beautiful flower which I may not touch, but whose fragrance makes the garden a place of delight just the same.

Helen Adams Keller

The reason why lovers are never weary of one another is this—they are always talking of themselves.

Duc François de La Rochefoucauld

Love is often a fruit of marriage.

Molière (Jean Baptiste Poquelin)

Love is indeed heaven upon earth; since heaven above would not be heaven without it; for where there is not love, there is fear; but, "Perfect love casteth out fear." And yet we naturally fear most to offend what we most love.

William Penn

It is better to have loved and lost, than not to love at all.

Alfred Lord Tennyson

I never could explain why I love anybody, or anything.

Walt (Walter) Whitman

*See also: **Affection, Desire, Esteem, Marriage, Romance, Sex***

LOYALTY

We must announce our loyalty . . . to those religious, political and humanitarian principles which seem best calculated to see a man or a nation through a period of darkness.

James Albert Michener

Unless you can find some sort of loyalty, you cannot find unity and peace in your active living.

Josiah Royce

Loyalty means nothing unless it has at its heart the absolute principle of self-sacrifice.

(Thomas) Woodrow Wilson

See also: **Fidelity**

LUCK

A pound of pluck is worth a ton of luck.
James Abram Garfield

There are no chances so unlucky from which clever people are not able to reap some advantage, and none so lucky that the foolish are not able to turn to their own disadvantage.

Duc François de La Rochefoucauld

The only sure thing about luck is that it will change.

Wilson Mizner

Most people know that there is no such thing as luck, but it is difficult to find anyone who does not believe in it.

Raoul de Sales

Better an ounce of luck than a pound of gold.

Yiddish Proverb

Intelligence is not needed for luck, but luck is needed for intelligence.

Yiddish Proverb

See also: **Accident, Chance, Destiny, Fate, Fortune**

LYING

Never chase a lie. Let it alone, and it will run itself to death. I can work out a good character much faster than any one can lie me out of it.

Lyman Beecher

With a man, a lie is a last resort; with women, it's First Aid.

Frank Gelett Burgess

I do not mind lying, but I hate inaccuracy.

Samuel Butler

A lie should be trampled on and extinguished wherever found. I am for fumigating the atmosphere when I suspect that falsehood, like pestilence, breathes around me.

Thomas Carlyle

One of the striking differences between a cat and a lie is that a cat has only nine lives.

Samuel Langhorne Clemens (Mark Twain)

We lie loudest when we lie to ourselves.
Eric Hoffer

Sin has many tools, but a lie is the handle that fits them all.

Oliver Wendell Holmes

When thou art obliged to speak, be sure to speak the truth; for equivocation is half way to lying, and lying is whole way to hell.

William Penn

The liar's punishment is not in the least that he is not believed, but that he cannot believe anyone else.

George Bernard Shaw

Although the devil be the father of lies, he seems, like other great inventors, to have lost much of his reputation by the continual improvements that have been made upon him.

Jonathan Swift

No man lies consistently, and he cannot lie about everything if he talks to you long.

(Thomas) Woodrow Wilson

See also: **Deceit, Dishonesty, Fraud, Hypocrisy**

MAJORITY

One with the law is a majority.
(John) Calvin Coolidge

One and God make a majority.
Frederick Douglass

We go by the major vote, and if the majority are insane, the sane must go to the hospital.

Horace Mann

The voice of the majority is no proof of justice.
Johann Christoph Friedrich von Schiller

The thing we have to fear in this country, to my way of thinking, is the influence of the organized minorities, because somehow or other the great majority does not seem to organize. They seem to feel that they are going to be effective because of their known strength, but they give no expression of it.

Alfred Emanuel Smith

There is one body that knows more than anybody, and that is everybody.
Alexandre de Talleyrand-Périgord

It never troubles the wolf how many the sheep may be.

Virgil

See also: **Democracy, Minority, Politics**

MAN

It is not what he has, or even what he does which expresses the worth of a man, but what he is.
Henri Frédéric Amiel

Man perfected by society is the best of all animals; he is the most terrible of all when he lives without law, and without justice.

Aristotle

Man is an animal and until his immediate material and economic needs are satisfied, he cannot develop further.
Wystan Hugh Auden

Man is an animal which alone among the animals refuses to be satisfied by the fulfillment of animal desires.
Alexander Graham Bell

Man is a wealth grubber, man is a pleasure seeker; man is a power wielder; man is a thinker, and man is a creative lover.

Alexander Graham Bell

Indisputably a great, good, handsome man is the first of created things.
Charlotte Brontë

Show me the man you honor, and I will know what kind of a man you are, for it shows me what your ideal of manhood is, and what kind of a man you long to be.

Thomas Carlyle

What God hath joined together no man shall put asunder: God will take care of that.

George Bernard Shaw

Marriage is one long conversation chequered by disputes.

Robert Louis Balfour Stevenson

The reason why so few marriages are happy is because young ladies spend their time, in making nets, not in making cages.

Jonathan Swift

There is more of good nature than of good sense at the bottom of most marriages.

Henry David Thoreau

What a holler would ensue, if people had to pay the minister as much to marry them as they have to pay a lawyer to get them a divorce.

Claire Trevor

See also: **Bachelor, Daughter, Family, Father, Home, Husband, Love, Mother, Wife**

MARTYR

I think the most uncomfortable thing about martyrs is that they look down on people who aren't.

Samuel Nathaniel Behrman

Fools love the martyrdom of fame.

George Gordon Byron (Lord Byron)

The way of the world is, to praise dead saints, and persecute living ones.

Nathaniel Howe

It is the cause and not merely the death that makes the martyr.

Napoleon I (Bonaparte)

Even in this world they will have their judgment-day; and their names, which went down in the dust like a gallant banner trodden in the mire, shall rise again all glorious in the sight of nations.

Harriet Elizabeth Beecher Stowe

See also: **Faith**

MATURITY

By education most have been misled;
So they believe, because they were so
   bred.
The priest continues what the nurse
   began,
And thus the child imposes on the man.

John Dryden

By the age of twenty, any young man should know whether or not he is to be a specialist and just where his tastes lie. By postponing the question we have set on immaturity a premium which controls most American personality to its deathbed.

Robert Silliman Hillyer

To be mature means to face, and not evade, every fresh crisis that comes.

Fritz Künkel

Men come to their meridian at various periods of their lives.

John Henry Newman

See also: **Age, Wisdom**

MAXIM

It is more trouble to make a maxim than it is to do right.

Samuel Langhorne Clemens (Mark Twain)

A maxim is a conclusion from observation of matters of fact, and is merely speculative; a principle carries knowledge within itself, and is prospective.

Samuel Taylor Coleridge

A man of maxims only, is like a cyclops with one eye, and that in the back of his head.

Samuel Taylor Coleridge

Pithy sentences are like sharp nails which force truth upon our memory.

Denis Diderot

Maxims are the condensed good sense of nations.

Sir James Mackintosh

Precepts or maxims are of great weight; and a few useful ones at hand do more toward a happy life than whole volumes that we know not where to find.

Seneca

MEDICINE

Cure the disease and kill the patient.
Francis Bacon

Nature, time, and patience are the three great physicians.

Henry George Bohn

Medicine is the only profession that labors incessantly to destroy the reason for its own existence.

James Bryce

The best of all medicines are rest and fasting.

Benjamin Franklin

Twentieth century medical care cannot be given in 19th century hospitals. It is necessary that we proceed with a hospital modernization program without delay, not only in the interests of providing urgently needed health care, but also in the interest of economy.

Jacob K. Javits

We have not only multiplied diseases, but we have made them more fatal.

Richard Rush

The strain on existing hospitals, urban and rural, and public and private, has continued to worsen. The advent of medicare and medicaid have accentuated the trend.

William F. Ryan

See also: **Disease, Health**

MEMORY

Memory can gleam, but never renew. It brings us joys faint as in the perfume of the flowers, faded and dried, of the summer that is gone.

Henry Ward Beecher

A memory without blot of contamination must be an exquisite treasure, an inexhaustible source of pure refreshment.

Charlotte Brontë

Joy's recollection is no longer joy, while sorrow's memory is sorrow still.

George Gordon Byron (Lord Byron)

Memory is the receptacle and sheath of all knowledge.

Cicero

Of all the faculties of the mind, memory is the first that flourishes, and the first that dies.

Charles Caleb Colton

The joys I have possessed are ever mine;
out of thy reach, behind eternity, hid in
the sacred treasure of the past, but blest
remembrance brings them hourly back.
John Dryden

There is a remembrance of the dead, to
which we turn even from the charms of
the living. These we would not exchange for the song of pleasure or the
bursts of revelry.
Washington Irving

The true art of memory is the art of attention.
Samuel Johnson

We consider ourselves as defective in
memory, either because we remember
less than we desire, or less than we suppose others to remember.
Samuel Johnson

Women and elephants never forget.
Dorothy Parker

MEN

If a woman wears gay colors, rouge and
a startling hat, a man hesitates to take
her out. If she wears a little turban and a
tailored suit he takes her out and stares
all evening at a woman in gay colors,
rouge and a startling hat.
Baltimore Beacon

All great men are in some degree inspired.
Cicero

The real difference between men is energy. A strong will, a settled purpose, an
invincible determination, can accomplish almost anything; and in this lies
the distinction between great men and
little men.
Thomas Fuller

It is far easier to know men than to
know man
Due François de La Rochefoucauld

Lives of great men all remind us, we can
make our lives sublime.
Henry Wadsworth Longfellow

God divided man into men, that they
might help each other.
Seneca

Men are but children, too, though they
have gray hairs; they are only of a larger
size.
Seneca

It is a folly to expect men to do all that
they may reasonably be expected to do.
Richard Whately

See also: **Bachelor, Father, Husband,
Man**

MERCY

Among the attributes of God, although
they are all equal, mercy shines with
even more brilliancy than justice.
Miguel de Cervantes Saavedra

Mercifulness makes us equal to the
gods.
Claudian

Mercy to him that shows it, is the rule.
William Cowper

Mercy more becomes a magistrate than
the vindictive wrath which men call justice.
Henry Wadsworth Longfellow

The oils and herbs of mercy are so few.
Edna St. Vincent Millay

Mercy turns her back to the unmerciful.
Francis Quarles

Who will not mercy unto others show,
How can he mercy ever hope to have?

Edmund Spenser

Hate shuts her soul when dove-eyed
mercy pleads.

Charles Sprague

Mercy is like the rainbow, which God
hath set in the clouds; it never shines
after it is right. If we refuse mercy here,
we shall have justice in eternity.

Jeremy Taylor

See also: **Clemency, Compassion, Forgiveness, Pardon, Pity**

MERIT

The sufficiency of my merit, is to know
that my merit is not sufficient.

Augustine of Hippo

Contemporaries appreciate the man
rather than his merit; posterity will regard the merit rather than the man.

Charles Caleb Colton

I will not be concerned at other men's
not knowing me; I will be concerned at
my own want of ability.

Confucius

There's a proud modesty in merit;
averse from asking, and resolved to pay
ten times the gifts it asks.

John Dryden

True merit, like a river, the deeper it is,
the less noise it makes.

Charles Montagu (1st Earl of Halifax)

If you wish your merit to be known, acknowledge that of other people.

Oriental Proverb

Charms strike the sight, but merit wins
the soul.

Alexander Pope

See also: **Excellence, Virtue, Worth**

MIND

Old minds are like old horses; you must
exercise them if you wish to keep them
in working order.

John Quincy Adams

He who cannot contract the sight of his
mind, as well as dilate it, wants a great
talent in life.

Francis Bacon

All the choir of heaven and furniture of
earth—in a word, all those bodies which
compose the mighty frame of the world
—have not any subsistence without a
mind.

George Berkeley

Few minds wear out; more rust out.

Christian Nestell Bovee

Mind unemployed is mind unenjoyed.

Christian Nestell Bovee

To pass from a mirror-mind to a mind
with windows is an essential element in
the development of real personality.

Harry Emerson Fosdick

As the mind must govern the hands, so
in every society the man of intelligence
must direct the man of labor.

Samuel Johnson

The human mind is our fundamental
resource.

John Fitzgerald Kennedy

As the soil, however rich it may be, cannot be productive without culture, so the mind without cultivation can never produce good fruit.

Seneca

It is the mind that maketh good or ill, that maketh wretch or happy, rich or poor.

Edmund Spenser

Sublime is the dominion of the mind over the body, that for a time can make flesh and nerve impregnable, and string the sinews like steel, so that the weak become so mighty.

Harriet Elizabeth Beecher Stowe

If we work marble, it will perish; if we work upon brass, time will efface it; if we rear temples, they will crumble into dust; but if we work upon immortal minds and instill into them just principles, we are then engraving that upon tablets which no time will efface, but will brighten and brighten to all eternity.

Daniel Webster

I not only use all the brains I have, but all I can borrow.

(Thomas) Woodrow Wilson

See also: **Intelligence, Psychology, Reason, Understanding**

MINORITY

Every new opinion, at its starting, is precisely in a minority of one.

Thomas Carlyle

Governments exist to protect the rights of minorities. The loved and the rich need no protection,—they have many friends and few enemies.

Wendell Phillips

Votes should be weighed, not counted.

Johann Christoph Frederich von Schiller

The smallest number, with God and truth on their side, are weightier than thousands.

Charles Simmons

See also: **Democracy, Government, Politics**

MIRTH

Man is the merriest species of the creation; all above or below him are serious.

Joseph Addison

An ounce of mirth is worth a pound of sorrow.

Richard Baxter

Unseasonable mirth always turns to sorrow.

Miguel de Cervantes Saavedra

Fun gives you a forcible hug, and shakes laughter out of you, whether you will or no.

David Garrick

Merriment is always the effect of a sudden impression. The jest which is expected is already destroyed.

Samuel Johnson

Nothing is more hopeless than a scheme of merriment.

Samuel Johnson

Care to our coffin adds a nail, no doubt; and every grin, so merry, draws one out.

John Wolcot (Peter Pindar)

See also: **Happiness, Joy, Laughter**

MISER

There is not in nature anything so remotely distant from God, or so extremely opposite to him, as a greedy and griping niggard.

Isaac Barrow

A mere madness—to live like a wretch that he may die rich.

Richard Eugene Burton

Misers mistake gold for good, whereas it is only a means of obtaining it.

Duc François de La Rochefoucauld

The miser, starving his brother's body, starves also his own soul, and at death shall creep out of his great estate of injustice, poor and naked and miserable.

Theodore Parker

How vilely he has lost himself who becomes a slave to his servant, and exalts him to the dignity of his Maker! Gold is the God, the wife, the friend of the money-monger of the world.

William Penn

A miser grows rich by seeming poor; an extravagant man grows poor by seeming rich.

William Shenstone

Groan under gold, yet weep for want of bread.

Edward Young

See also: **Avarice, Frugality, Money, Selfishness**

MISERY

A misery is not to be measured from the nature of the evil, but from the temper of the sufferer.

Joseph Addison

There are a good many real miseries in life that we cannot help smiling at, but they are the smiles that make wrinkles and not dimples.

Oliver Wendell Holmes

We should pass on from crime to crime, heedless and remorseless, if misery did not stand in our way, and our own pains admonish us of our folly.

Samuel Johnson

No scene of life but teems with mortal woe.

Sir Walter Scott

Half the misery in the world comes of want of courage to speak and to hear the truth plainly, and in a spirit of love.

Harriet Beecher Stowe

See also: **Adversity, Affliction, Pain**

MOB

A crowd always thinks with its sympathy, never with its reason.

William·Rounseville Alger

It is an easy and vulgar thing to please the mob, and not a very arduous task to astonish them; but to benefit and improve them is a work fraught with difficulty, and teeming with danger.

Charles Caleb Colton

A mob is the scum that rises upmost when the nation boils.

John Dryden

A mob is a society of bodies, voluntarily bereaving themselves of reason, and traversing its work. The mob is man, voluntarily descending to the nature of the beast. Its fit hour of activity is night; its actions are insane, like its whole constitution.

Ralph Waldo Emerson

Every numerous assembly is a mob; everything there depends on instantaneous turns.

Jean de Gondi (Cardinal de Retz)

Get together a hundred or two men, however sensible they may be, and you are very likely to have a mob.

Samuel Johnson

Let there be an entire abstinence from intoxicating drinks throughout this country during the period of a single generation, and a mob would be as impossible as combustion without oxygen.

Horace Mann

A mob is a sort of bear; while your ring is through its nose, it will even dance under your cudgel; but should the ring slip, and you lose your hold, the brute will turn and rend you.

Jane Porter

Human affairs are not so happily arranged that the best things please the most men. It is the proof of a bad cause when it is applauded by the mob.

Seneca

MODERATION

I knew a wise man who had for a byword, when he saw men hasten to a conclusion, "stay a little, that we may come to the end sooner."

Francis Bacon

There is a German proverb which says that "Take it easy," and "Live long," are brothers.

Christian Nestell Bovee

The pursuit, even of the best things, ought to be calm and tranquil.

Cicero

Moderation is the inseparable companion of wisdom, but with it genius has not even nodding acquaintance.

Charles Caleb Colton

The superior man wishes to be slow in his words, and earnest in his conduct.

Confucius

Everything that exceeds the bounds of moderation, has an unstable foundation.

Seneca

See also: **Self-Control**

MODESTY

Modesty is not only an ornament, but also a guard to virtue.

Joseph Addison

Modesty is the conscience of the body.

Honoré de Balzac

Modesty is the citadel of beauty and virtue.

Demades

Modesty is the color of virtue.

Diogenes

A false modesty is the meanest species of pride.

Edward Gibbon

Modesty seldom resides in a breast that is not enriched with nobler virtues.

Oliver *Goldsmith*

See also: **Blush, Decency, Humility**

MONEY

Money is like manure, of very little use except to be spread.

Francis Bacon

Money speaks sense in a language all nations understand.

Aphra Behn

Money is a good servant, but a poor master.

Dominique Bouhours

For money has a power above
The stars and fate, to manage love.

Samuel Butler

Our incomes are like our shoes; if too small, they gall and pinch us; but if too large, they cause us to stumble and to trip.

Charles Caleb Colton

The use of money is all the advantage there is in having it.

Benjamin Franklin

It is my opinion that a man's soul may be buried and perish under a dung-heap, or in a furrow of the field, just as well as under a pile of money.

Nathaniel Hawthorne

The first panacea for a mismanaged nation is inflation of the currency.

Ernest Hemingway

Put not your trust in money, but put your money in trust.

Oliver Wendell Holmes

Money is a handmaiden, if thou knowest how to use it; a mistress, if thou knowest not.

Horace

Money is like a sixth sense—and you can't make use of the other five without it.

(William) Somerset Maugham

Money is not required to buy one necessity of the soul.

Henry David Thoreau

See also: **Wealth**

MONUMENT

Tombs are the clothes of the dead; a grave is but a plain suit; a rich monument is an embroidered one.

Thomas Fuller

No man who needs a monument ever ought to have one.

Nathaniel Hawthorne

They only deserve a monument who do not need one; that is, who have raised themselves a monument in the minds and memories of men.

William Hazlitt

Monuments are the grappling-irons that bind one generation to another.

Joseph Joubert

Virtue alone outbuilds the pyramids; her monument shall last when Egypts fall.

Edward Young

See also: **Art, Civilization, Culture,
Death, Grave, History**

MORALITY

People committing acts in obedience to law or habit are not being moral.

Wystan Hugh Auden

Some would divorce morality from religion; but religion is the root without which morality would die.

Cyrus Augustus Bartol

Every young man would do well to remember that all successful business stands on the foundation of morality.
Henry Ward Beecher

The divorcement of morals and piety is characteristic of all pagan religions.
David James Burrell

Morality is the vestibule of religion.
Edwin Hubbel Chapin

Too many moralists begin with a dislike of reality: a dislike of men as they are.
Clarence Shepard Day, Jr.

Moral vanity is the snare of good people.
Margaret Deland

Conventional morality is a drab morality, in which the only fatal thing is to be conspicuous.
John Dewey

Two points of danger beset mankind; namely, making sin seem either too large or too small.
Mary Baker Eddy

There can by no high civility without a deep morality.
Ralph Waldo Emerson

What is moral is what you feel good after and what is immoral is what you feel bad after.
Ernest Hemingway

The moral experience of men has everywhere and in all ages been the same.
John Haynes Holmes

Turning the other cheek is a kind of moral jiu-jitsu.
Gerald Stanley Lee

To give a man a full knowledge of true morality, I would send him to no other book than the New Testament.
John Locke

I restrict myself within bounds in saying, that, so far as I have observed in this life, ten men have failed from defect in morals where one has failed from defect in intellect.
Horace Mann

See also: **Behavior, Honesty, Virtue**

MOTHER

All that I am my mother made me.
John Quincy Addams

The future of society is in the hands of the mothers. If the world was lost through woman, she alone can save it.
Louis de Beaufort

The mother's heart is the child's schoolroom.
Henry Ward Beecher

I think it must somewhere be written, that the virtues of mothers shall be visited on their children, as well as the sins of the fathers.
Charles John Huffam Dickens

There is in all this cold and hollow world no fount of deep, strong, deathless love, save that within a mother's heart.
Felicia Dorothea Browne Hemans

What are Raphael's Madonnas but the shadow of a mother's love, fixed in permanent outline forever?
Thomas Wentworth Storrow Higginson

A man never sees all that his mother has been to him till it's too late to let her know that he sees it.

William Dean Howells

God could not be everywhere, and therefore he made mothers.

Jewish Proverb

See also: **Family, Wife, Woman**

MURDER

Blood, though it sleep a time, yet never dies.

George Chapman

Nor cell, nor chain, nor dungeon speaks to the murderer like the voice of solitude.

Charles Robert Maturin

One murder made the villain; millions the hero. Princes were privileged to kill, and numbers sanctified the crime.

Beilby Porteus

Every unpunished murder takes away something from the security of every man's life.

Daniel Webster

See also: **Crime**

MUSIC

Music is the only sensual gratification in which mankind may indulge to excess without injury to their moral or religious feelings.

Joseph Addison

Music washes away from the soul the dust of every-day life.

Berthold Auerbach

All human activity must pass through its periods of rise, ripeness, and decline, and music has been, to a certain extent, fortunate in that it is the last of the great arts to suffer this general experience.

Sir Thomas Beecham

Composers should write tunes that chauffeurs and errand boys can whistle.

Sir Thomas Beecham

Music is the mediator between the spiritual and the sensual life. Although the spirit be not master of that which it creates through music, yet it is blessed in this creation, which, like every creation of art, is mightier than the artist.

Ludwig van Beethoven

In the germ, when the first trace of life begins to stir, music is the nurse of the soul; it murmurs in the ear, and the child sleeps; the tones are companions of his dreams, they are the world in which he lives.

Antoine Bettini

Music is well said to be the speech of angels.

Thomas Carlyle

O Music! miraculous art! . . . A blast of thy trumpet, and millions rush forward to die; a peal of thy organ, and uncounted nations sink down to pray.

Benjamin Disraeli

There is no feeling, except the extremes of fear and grief, that does not find relief in music.

George Eliot (Mary Ann Evans)

Music itself is the purest expression of emotion. To me, emotion is the guts of theater. With music you can say in one moment what an author would take a whole scene to tell you in a drama.

Joshua Logan

It is not necessary to understand music; it is only necessary that one enjoy it.

Leopold Antoni Stanislaw Stokowski

The trouble with music appreciation in general is that people are taught to have too much respect for music; they should be taught to love it instead.

Igor Fedorovich Stravinsky

See also: **Art, Jazz, Poetry, Voice**

MYSTERY

A good parson once said, that where mystery begins, religion ends. Cannot I say, as truly at least, of human laws, that where mystery begins, justice ends?

Edmund Burke

A mystery is something of which we know that it is, though we do not know how it is.

Joseph Cook

He had lived long enough to know that it is unwise to wish everything explained.

Benjamin Disraeli

All is mystery; but he is a slave who will not struggle to penetrate the dark veil.

Benjamin Disraeli

Mystery is but another name for our ignorance; if we were omniscient, all would be perfectly plain.

Tryon Edwards

The most beautiful experience we can have is the mysterious. It is the fundamental emotion which stands at the cradle of true art and true science.

Albert Einstein

As defect of strength in us makes some weights to be immovable, so likewise, defect of understanding makes some truths to be mysterious.

Thomas Sherlock

See also: **Doubt, Faith, Question**

NAME

Some to the fascination of a name surrender judgment hoodwinked.

William Cowper

Favor or disappointment has been often conceded, as the name of the claimant has affected us; and the accidental affinity or coincidence of a name, connected with ridicule or hatred, with pleasure or disgust, has operated like magic.

Benjamin Disraeli

A name is a kind of face whereby one is known.

Thomas Fuller

Some men do as much begrudge others a good name, as they want one themselves; and perhaps that is the reason of it.

William Penn

A person with a bad name is already half-hanged.

Proverb

See also: **Honor**

NATION

In the youth of a state, arms do flourish; in the middle age, learning; and then both of them together for a time; in the declining age, mechanical arts and merchandise.

Francis Bacon

A nation is a totality of men united through community of fate into a community of character.

Otto Bauer

A day of small nations has long passed away. The day of Empires has come.

Joseph Chamberlain

A nation's character is the sum of its splendid deeds; they constitute one common patrimony, the nation's inheritance. They awe foreign powers, they arouse and animate our own people.

Henry Clay

Individuals may form communities, but it is institutions alone that can create a nation.

Benjamin Disraeli

A nation is a work of art and a work of time.

Benjamin Disraeli

The basic resource of a nation is its people. Its strength can be no greater than the health and vitality of its population. Preventable sickness, disability and physical or mental incapacity are matters of both individual and national concern.

John Fitzgerald Kennedy

A nation, like a person, has a mind—a mind that must be kept informed and alert, that must know itself, that understands the hopes and the needs of its neighbors—all the other nations that live within the narrowing circle of the world.

Franklin Delano Roosevelt

See also: **America**

NATIONALISM

The root problem is very simply stated: if there were no sovereign independent states, if the states of the civilized world were organized in some sort of federalism, as the states of the American Union, for instance, are organized, there would be no international war as we know it.... The main obstacle is nationalism.

Sir Norman Angell

Nationalism is an infantile disease. It is the measles of mankind.

Albert Einstein

National memories lie deeper in man's heart than we generally imagine.

Heinrich Heine

We are in the midst of a great transition from narrow nationalism to international partnership.

Lyndon Baines Johnson

See also: **Patriotism**

NATURE

Nature is commanded by obeying her.

Francis Bacon

In nature things move violently to their place, and calmly in their place.

Francis Bacon

Nature's laws affirm instead of prohibiting. If you violate her laws you are your own prosecuting attorney, judge, jury, and hangman.

Luther Burbank

Nature is the time-vesture of God that reveals him to the wise, and hides him from the foolish.

Thomas Carlyle

I follow nature as the surest guide, and resign myself, with implicit obedience, to her sacred ordinances.

Cicero

Nature is too thin a screen; the glory of the One breaks in everywhere.

Ralph Waldo Emerson

Nature does not complete things. She is chaotic. Man must finish, and he does so by making a garden and building a wall.

Robert Lee Frost

It were happy if we studied nature more in natural things; and acted according to nature, whose rules are few, plain, and most reasonable.

William Penn

Everything made by man may be destroyed by man: there are no ineffaccable characters except those engraved by nature; and nature makes neither princes, nor rich men, nor great lords.

Jean Jacques Rousseau

See also: **Earth, Life, Rain, Twilight, World**

NECESSITY

Necessity is the mother of invention.

George Farquhar

Necessity never made a good bargain.

Benjamin Franklin

Necessity may render a doubtful act innocent, but it cannot make it praiseworthy.

Joseph Joubert

We cannot conquer fate and necessity, yet we can yield to them in such a manner as to be greater than if we could.

Walter Savage Landor

And with necessity, the tyrant's plea, excused his devilish deeds.

John Milton

Necessity is the argument of tyrants: it is the creed of slaves.

William Pitt

Necessity of action takes away the fear of the act, and makes bold resolution the favorite of fortune.

Francis Quarles

Our necessities are few but our wants are endless.

Henry Wheeler Shaw (Josh Billings)

What was once to me mere matter of the fancy, now have grown to be the necessity of heart and life.

Alfred, Lord Tennyson

The argument of necessity is not only the tyrant's plea, but the patriot's defense, and the safety of the state.

James Wilson

See also: **Destiny, Fate, Obligation**

NEGLECT

A wise and salutary neglect.

Edmund Burke

Negligence is the rust of the soul, that corrodes through all her best resolves.

Owen Felltham

A little neglect may breed great mischief; for want of a nail the shoe was lost; for want of a shoe the horse was lost, and for want of a horse the rider was lost, being overtaken and slain by an enemy, all for want of a little care about a horse-shoe nail.

Benjamin Franklin

He that thinks he can afford to be negligent, is not far from being poor.

Samuel Johnson

See also: **Idleness, Procrastination**

NEWSPAPER

From the American newspapers you'd think America was populated solely by naked women and cinema stars.

Viscountess Nancy Langhorne Astor

A newspaper is a circulating library with high blood pressure.

Arthur (Bugs) Baer

Newspapers are the schoolmasters of the common people—a greater treasure to them than uncounted millions of gold.

Henry Ward Beecher

The paper which obtains a reputation for publishing authentic news and only that which is fit to print, . . . will steadily increase its influence.

Andrew Carnegie

Newspapers are the world's mirrors.

James Ellis

A ration of one newspaper a day ought to be enough for anyone who still prefers to retain a little mental balance.

Clifton Fadiman

In these times we fight for ideas, and newspapers are our fortresses.

Heinrich Heine

While news is important, news interpretation is far more important.

H. V. Kaltenborn (Hans von Kaltenborn)

A good newspaper, I suppose, is a nation talking to itself.

Arthur Miller

I fear three newspapers more than a hundred thousand bayonets.

Napoleon I (Bonaparte)

I prefer to be loved rather than disliked. But I don't think you can really write news in Washington and be loved.

Drew Pearson

NOVELTY

There is nothing new under the sun.

George Michael Cohan

The earth was made so various, that the mind of desultory man, studious of change, and pleased with novelty, might be indulged.

William Cowper

Such is the nature of novelty that where anything pleases it becomes doubly agreeable if new; but if it displeases, it is doubly displeasing on that very account.

David Hume

It is not only old and early impressions that deceive us; the charms of novelty have the same power.

Blaise Pascal

Novelty is the great parent of pleasure.

Robert South

See also: **Discovery, Originality, Variety**

NUCLEAR ENERGY

We are convinced that parallel to the formation of a regional common market we must take concrete steps to begin a process of inter-American integration built around the utilization of atomic energy.

Arthur Costa e Silva

The discovery of nuclear chain reaction need not bring about the destruction of mankind any more than the discovery of matches.

Albert Einstein

The real vision of the atomic future rests not in the material abundance which it should eventually bring for man's convenience and comfort in living. It lies in finding at last, through the common use of such abundance, a way to make the nations of the world friendly neighbors on the same street.

Dwight David Eisenhower

The powers of the atom unleashed by science are too startling, too intoxicating, and at the same time too useful as human tools for any of us to wish to abandon the astonishing new technology. But, if we will not abandon it we must master it.

Adlai Ewing Stevenson

See also: **Nuclear Warfare, Science**

NUCLEAR WARFARE

We develop weapons, not to wage war, but to prevent war. Only in the clear light of this greater truth can we properly examine the lesser matter of the testing of our nuclear weapons.

Dwight David Eisenhower

People who talk of outlawing the atomic bomb are mistaken—what needs to be outlawed is war.

Leslie Richard Groves

With a 3-minute warning, 15-minute warning or no warning at all, we could still absorb a surprise [nuclear] attack and strike back with sufficient power to destroy the attacker.

Robert Strange McNamara

See also: **Nuclear Energy, War**

OATH

Of all men, a philosopher should be no swearer; for an oath, which is the end of controversies in law, cannot determine any here, where reason only must decide.

Sir Thomas Browne

Oaths are but words, and words but wind.

Samuel Butler

Rash oaths, whether kept or broken, frequently lead to guilt.

Samuel Johnson

See also: **Assertion**

OBEDIENCE

Obedience is the mother of success and is wedded to safety.

Aeschylus

Wicked men obey from fear; good men, from love.

Aristotle

"Theirs not to make reply, theirs not to reason why," may be a good enough motto for men who are on their way to be shot. But from such men expect no empires to be built, no inventions made, no great discoveries brought to light.

Bruce Barton

The best way to insure implicit obedience is to commence tyranny in the nursery.

Benjamin Disraeli

It is vain thought to flee from the work that God appoints us, for the sake of finding a greater blessing, instead of seeking it where alone it is to be found—in loving obedience.

George Eliot (Mary Ann Evans)

The only safe ruler is he who has learned to obey willingly.

Thomas à Kempis

See also: **Duty, Humility**

OBJECTIVE

We succeed only as we identify in life, or in war, or in anything else, a single overriding objective, and make all other considerations bend to that one objective.

Dwight David Eisenhower

No wind makes for him that hath no intended port to sail unto.

Michel Eyquem de Montaigne

See also: **Aim, End, Purpose**

OBLIGATION

To owe an obligation to a worthy friend, is a happiness, and can be no disparagement.

Pierre Charron

When some men discharge an obligation you can hear the report for miles around.

Samuel Langhorne Clemens (Mark Twain)

Obligation is thraldom, and thraldom is hateful.

Thomas Hobbes

In some there is a kind of graceless modesty that makes a man ashamed of requiting an obligation, because it is a confession that he has received one.

Seneca

See also: **Borrowing, Debt, Duty, Necessity, Responsibility**

OBLIVION

Fame is a vapor; popularity an accident; riches take wings; the only certainty is oblivion.

Horace Greeley

Oblivion is the rule, and fame the exception of humanity.

Antoine Rivarol

Oblivion is the flower that grows best on graves.

George Sand

See also: **Death, Grave, Obscurity**

OBSCURITY

There is no defence against reproach but obscurity; it is a kind of concomitant to greatness, as satires and invectives were an essential part of a Roman triumph.

Joseph Addison

The obscure is the principal ingredient of the sublime.

Benjamin Disraeli

How many wonderful men, and who possessed the noblest genius, have died without ever being spoken of! How many live at the present moment of whom men do not speak, and of whom they will never speak!

Jean de La Bruyère

Thus let me live, unseen, unknown;
  Thus unlamented let me die,
Steal from the world, and not a stone
  Tell where I lie.
Alexander Pope

Who is the Forgotten Man? He is the clean, quiet, virtuous, domestic citizen, who pays his debts and his taxes and is never heard of out of his little circle.
William Graham Sumner

See also: **Mystery, Oblivion, Secrecy**

OBSERVATION

Each one sees what he carries in his heart.
Johann Wolfgang von Goethe

Objects imperfectly discerned take forms from the hope or fear of the beholder.
Samuel Johnson

General observations drawn from particulars are the jewels of knowledge, comprehending great store in a little room.
John Locke

See also: **Attention, Experience, Eye,
    Science**

OPINION

He who is master of all opinions can never be the bigot of any.
William Rounseville Alger

An obstinate man does not hold opinions—they hold him.
Joseph Butler

It is not only arrogant, but profligate, for a man to disregard the world's opinion of himself.
Cicero

It were not best that we should all think alike; it is difference of opinion that makes horse races.
Samuel Langhorne Clemens (Mark Twain)

The masses procure their opinions ready made in open market.
Charles Caleb Colton

Predominant opinions are generally the opinions of the generation that is vanishing.
Benjamin Disraeli

The eyes of other people are the eyes that ruin us. If all but myself were blind, I should want neither fine clothes, fine houses, nor fine furniture.
Benjamin Franklin

A man's opinions are generally of much more value than his arguments.
Oliver Wendell Holmes

All power, even the most despotic, rests ultimately on opinion.
David Hume

Error of opinion may be tolerated where reason it left free to combat it.
Thomas Jefferson

Those who never retract their opinions love themselves more than they love truth.
Joseph Joubert

See also: **Idea, Judgment, Philosophy,
    Prejudice, Sentiment**

OPPORTUNITY

A wise man will make more opportunities than he finds.
Francis Bacon

You will never "find" time for anything. If you want time you must make it.
Charles Buxton

A word spoken in season, at the right moment, is the matter of ages.

Thomas Carlyle

Next to knowing when to seize an opportunity, the most important thing in life is to know when to forego an advantage.

Benjamin Disraeli

All that is valuable in human society depends upon the opportunity for development accorded the individual.

Albert Einstein

The very essence of equality of opportunity and of American individualism ... demands economic justice as well as political and social justice. It is no system of laissez faire.

Herbert Clark Hoover

To improve the golden moment of opportunity and catch the good that is within our reach, is the great art of life.

Samuel Johnson

If you can fill the unforgiving minute
With sixty seconds' worth of distance run,
Yours is the Earth and everything that's in it,
And—which is more—you'll be a man, my son!

Rudyard Kipling

What passes for optimism is most often the effect of an intellectual error.

Raymond Aron

Optimism is the content of small men in high places.

Francis Scott Key Fitzgerald

Two men look out through the same bars: One sees the mud, and one the stars.

Frederick Langbridge

Every cloud has its silver lining but it is sometimes a little difficult to get it to the mint.

Donald Robert Perry (Don) Marquis

An optimist is a guy that has never had much experience.

Donald Robert Perry (Don) Marquis

In these times you have to be an optimist to open your eyes when you awake in the morning.

Carl Sandburg

An optimist is a person who sees a green light everywhere, while the pessimist sees only the red stop light ... But the truly wise person is color-blind.

Albert Schweitzer

See also: **Pessimism**

ORDER

Good order is the foundation of all good things.

Edmund Burke

Set all things in their own peculiar place
And know that order is the greatest grace.

John Dryden

A place for everything, everything in its place.

Benjamin Franklin

He who has no taste for order, will be often wrong in his judgment, and seldom considerate or conscientious in his actions.

Johann Kaspar Lavater

Order is heav'n's first law.

Alexander Pope

See also: **Discipline, Efficiency, Law**

ORIGINALITY

The merit of originality is not novelty, it is sincerity. The believing man is the original man; he believes for himself, not another.

Thomas Carlyle

Every human being is intended to have a character of his own; to be what no other is, and to do what no other can do.

William Ellery Channing

What a good thing Adam had—when he said a good thing, he knew nobody had said it before.

Samuel Langhorne Clemens (Mark Twain)

The originality of a subject is in its treatment.

Benjamin Disraeli

See also. **Creativity, Discovery, Fashion, Novelty**

OSTENTATION

An ostentatious man will rather relate a blunder or an absurdity he has committed, than be debarred from talking of his own dear person.

Joseph Addison

Ostentation is the signal flag of hypocrisy. The charlatan is verbose and assumptive; the Pharisee is ostentatious, because he is a hypocrite. Pride is the master sin of the devil, and the devil is the father of lies.

Edwin Hubbel Chapin

Do what good thou canst unknown, and be not vain of what ought rather to be felt than seen.

William Penn

See also: **Pretension, Pride**

PAIN

Pain is the outcome of sin.

Buddha

Pain is the deepest thing we have in our nature, and union through pain and suffering has always seemed more real and holy than any other.

Arthur Henry Hallam

Pain spiritualizes even beasts.

Heinrich Heine

The same refinement which brings us new pleasures, exposes us to new pains.

Edward G. Bulwer-Lytton (Baron Lytton)

Pain itself is not without its alleviations. It is seldom both violent and long-continued; and its pauses and intermissions become positive pleasures. It has the power of shedding a satisfaction over intervals of ease, which few enjoyments exceed.

William Paley

The only folks who give us pain are those we love the best.

Ella Wheeler Wilcox

The greatest pain is that which you can't tell others.

Yiddish Proverb

See also: **Affliction, Disease, Grief, Misery, Sorrow, Suffering**

PARDON

They never pardon who commit the wrong.

John Dryden

God will pardon: that's His business.

Heinrich Heine

We pardon as long as we love.

Duc François de La Rochefoucauld

Pardon is the virtue of victory.

Giuseppe Mazzini

To pardon those absurdities in ourselves which we cannot suffer in others, is neither better nor worse than to be more willing to be fools ourselves than to have others so.

Alexander Pope

See also: **Clemency, Forgiveness, Mercy, Parent**

PARENT

The joys of parents are secret, and so are their griefs and fears.

Francis Bacon

It is the intimations of mortality, not immortality, that devastate parents in the presence of their young.

John Mason Brown

The thing that impresses me most about America is the way parents obey their children.

Edward VIII (Duke of Windsor)

How many hopes and fears, how many ardent wishes and anxious apprehensions are twisted together in the threads that connect the parent with the child!

Samuel Griswold Goodrich

The most important thing a father can do for his children is to love their mother.

Theodore Martin Hesburgh

Parents wonder why the streams are bitter, when they themselves have poisoned the fountain.

John Locke

Children aren't happy with nothing to ignore,
And that's what parents were created for.

Ogden Nash

If parents would only realize how they bore their children!

George Bernard Shaw

The more people have studied different methods of bringing up children the more they have come to the conclusion that what good mothers and fathers instinctively feel like doing for their babies is usually best after all.

Benjamin McLane Spock

See also: **Ancestry, Birth, Family, Father, Mother**

PASSION

He only employs his passion who can make no use of his reason.

Cicero

What profits us, that we from heaven derive a soul immortal, and with looks erect survey the stars, if, like the brutal kind, we follow where passions lead the way?

Claudian

Our headstrong passions shut the door of our souls against God.

Confucius

An evil passion may give great physical and intellectual powers a terrible efficiency.

Charles William Eliot

Passion, though a bad regulator, is a powerful spring.

Ralph Waldo Emerson

The passionate are like men standing on their heads; they see all things the wrong way.

Plato

The ruling passion, be it what it will,
The ruling passion conquers reason still.

Alexander Pope

Men spend their lives in the service of their passions, instead of employing their passions in the service of their life.

Sir Richard Steele

Our passions are like convulsion fits, which, though they make us stronger for the time, leave us the weaker ever after.

Jonathan Swift

See also: **Anger, Desire, Emotion, Enthusiasm, Rage**

PAST

The past has little serious value save as a guide to what may come.

Brooks Adams

The true past departs not; no truth or goodness realized by man ever dies, or can die; but all is still here, and, recognized or not, lives and works through endless changes.

Thomas Carlyle

Study the past if you would divine the future.

Confucius

The past is never dead. It's not even past.

William Faulkner

O God! Put back Thy universe and give me yesterday.

Henry Arthur Jones

Some are so very studious of learning what was done by the ancients, that they know not how to live with the moderns.

William Penn

So sad, so fresh, the days that are no more.

Alfred, Lord Tennyson

We ought not to look back unless it is to derive useful lessons from past errors, and for the purpose of profiting by dear bought experience.

George Washington

See also: **Antiquity, Future, Present, Time**

PATIENCE

Patience is passion tamed.

Lyman Abbott

Patience is so like fortitude that she seems either her sister or her daughter.

Aristotle

Our patience will achieve more than our force.

Edmund Burke

To bear is to conquer our fate.

Thomas Campbell

Patience is power; with time and patience the mulberry leaf becomes silk,.

Chinese Proverb

Patient waiting is often the highest way of doing God's will.

Jeremy Collier

Beware the fury of a patient man.

John Dryden

It's easy finding reasons why other folks should be patient.

George Eliot (Mary Ann Evans)

He that can have patience, can have what he will.

Benjamin Franklin

They also serve who only stand and wait.

John Milton

Accustom yourself to that which you bear ill, and you will bear it well.

Seneca

See also: **Endurance, Perseverance**

PATRIOTISM

No man can be a patriot on an empty stomach.

William Cowper Brann

Bearing ourselves humbly before God, but conscious that we serve an unfolding purpose, we are ready to defend our native land.

Sir Winston Leonard Spencer Churchill

Patriotism is easy to understand in America; it means looking out for yourself by looking our for your country.

(John) Calvin Coolidge

Of the whole sum of human life no small part is that which consists of a man's relations to his country, and his feelings concerning it.

William Ewart Gladstone

I only regret that I have but one life to lose for my country.

Nathan Hale

Ask not what your country can do for you:
Ask what you can do for your country.

John Fitzgerald Kennedy

With a good conscience our only sure reward, with history the final judge of our deeds, let us go forth to lead the land we love, asking His blessing and His help, but knowing that here on earth God's work must truly be our own.

John Fitzgerald Kennedy

Patriotism is your conviction that this country is superior to all other countries because you were born in it.

George Bernard Shaw

You'll never have a quiet world till you knock the patriotism out of the human race.

George Bernard Shaw

For a man to love his country truly, he must also know how to love mankind, and this love must be the sustaining force in the search for world order.

Adlai Ewing Stevenson

Liberty and union, now and forever, one and inseparable.

Daniel Webster

See also: **Duty, Hero, Nation, War**

PEACE

Peace is positive, and it has to be waged with all our thought, energy, and courage and with the conviction that war is not inevitable.

Dean Gooderham Acheson

I am not very keen for doves or hawks. I think we need more owls.

George Aiken

Peace rules the day, where reason rules the mind.

Wilkie Collins

No world settlement that affords nations only a place on relief rolls will provide the basis for a just and durable peace.

William Orville Douglas

Peace cannot be kept by force. It can only be achieved by understanding.

Albert Einstein

I have said time and again there is no place on this earth to which I would not travel, there is no chore I would not undertake if I had any faintest hope that, by so doing, I would promote the general cause of world peace.

Dwight David Eisenhower

Nothing can bring you peace but yourself; nothing can bring you peace but the triumph of principles.

Ralph Waldo Emerson

The door of peace must be kept wide open for all who wish to avoid the scourge of war, but the door of agression must be closed and bolted if man is to survive.

Lyndon Baines Johnson

See also: **Aggression, Antagonism, Diplomacy, War**

PERFECTION

This is the very perfection of a man, to find out his own imperfection.

Augustine of Hippo

It is reasonable to have perfection in our eye that we may always advance toward it, though we know it can never be reached.

Samuel Johnson

He that seeks perfection on earth leaves nothing new for the saints to find in heaven; as long as men teach, there will be mistakes in divinity; and as long as they govern, errors in state.

Francis Osborn

Faultily faultless, icily regular, splendidly null, dead perfection; no more.

Alfred, Lord Tennyson

Perfection is attained by slow degrees; it requires the hand of time.

Voltaire (François Marie Arouet)

See also: **Excellence, Ideal**

PERSEVERANCE

The difference between perseverance and obstinacy is, that one often comes from a strong will, and the other from a strong won't.

Henry Ward Beecher

Every noble work is at first impossible.

Thomas Carlyle

The heights by great men reached and kept
    Were not attained by sudden flight,
But they, while their companions slept,
    Were toiling upward in the night.

Henry Wadsworth Longfellow

No rock so bard but that a little wave may beat admission in a thousand years.

Alfred, Lord Tennyson

Even in social life, it is persistency which attracts confidence more than talents and accomplishments.

Henry Benjamin Whipple

See also: **Endurance, Labor, Resolution, Work**

PESSIMISM

A pessimist is one who feels bad when he feels good for fear he'll feel worse when he feels better.

Anonymous

The optimist proclaims that we live in the best of all possible worlds; and the pessimist fears this is so.

James Branch Cabell

Away with pessimism! Let us work at whatsoever is pure, whatsoever is constructive, and not parade our failings and our sins.

Sir Wilfred Thomason Grenfell

My pessimism goes to the point of suspecting the sincerity of the pessimists.

Edmond Rostand

A pessimist is a man who thinks everybody as nasty as himself, and hates them for it.

George Bernard Shaw

See also: Despair

PHILOSOPHY

Philosophy: unintelligible answers to insoluble problems.

Henry Brooks Adams

Philosophy is the science which considers truth.

Aristotle

Philosophy, when superficially studied, excites doubt; when thoroughly explored, it dispels it.

Francis Bacon

To study philosophy is nothing but to prepare one's self to die.

Cicero

True philosophy invents nothing; it merely establishes and describes what is.

Victor Cousin

Philosophy consists largely of one philosopher arguing that all others are jackasses. He usually proves it, and I should add that he also usually proves that he is one himself.

Henry Louis Mencken

It is the bounty of nature that we live, but of philosophy, that we live well; which is, in truth, a greater benefit than life itself.

Seneca

Philosophy may teach us to bear with equanimity the misfortunes of our neighbors.

Oscar Wilde

See also: Logic, Reason

PITY

Pity makes the world soft to the weak and noble for the strong.

Sir Edwin Arnold

Of all the paths that lead to a woman's love, pity is the straightest.

Francis Beaumont and John Fletcher

Pity is best taught by fellowship in woe.

Samuel Taylor Coleridge

Let no one underestimate the need of pity. We live in a stony universe whose hard, brilliant forces rage fiercely.

Theodore Dreiser

It is through pity that we remain truly a man.

Anatole France

Pity is the feeling which arrests the mind in the presence of whatsoever is grave and constant in human sufferings and unites it with the human sufferer.

James Joyce

See also: **Compassion, Kindness, Mercy**

PLEASURE

The man of pleasure little knows the perfect joy he loses for the disappointing gratifications which he pursues.

Joseph Addison

Consider pleasures as they depart, not as they come.

Aristotle

In diving to the bottom of pleasures we bring up more gravel than pearls.

Honoré de Balzac

To make pleasures pleasant shorten them.

Charles Buxton

There is no sterner moralist than pleasure.

George Gordon Byron (Lord Byron)

Mental pleasures never cloy; unlike those of the body, they are increased by repetition, approved by reflection, and strengthened by enjoyment.

Charles Caleb Colton

Pleasure is very seldom found where it is sought. Our brightest blazes of gladness are commonly kindled by unexpected sparks.

Samuel Johnson

The greatest pleasure I know, is to do a good action by stealth, and have it found out by accident.

Charles Lamb

Enjoy present pleasures in such a way as not to injure future ones.

Seneca

All fits of pleasure are balanced by an equal degree of pain or languor; 'tis like spending this year, part of the next year's revenue.

Jonathan Swift

See also: **Amusement, Delight, Happiness, Joy**

POETRY

Poetry is the art of substantiating shadows, and of lending existence to nothing.

Edmund Burke

Writing free verse is like playing tennis with the net down.

Robert Lee Frost

Thoughts that breathe, and words that burn.

Thomas Gray

An artist that works in marble or colors has them all to himself and his tribe, but the man who moulds his thoughts in verse has to employ the materials vulgarized by everybody's use, and glorify them by his handling.

Oliver Wendell Holmes

When power leads man toward arrogance, poetry reminds him of his limitations. When power narrows the areas of man's concern, poetry reminds him of the richness and diversity of his existence. When power corrupts, poetry cleanses.

John Fitzgerald Kennedy

Poetry has been to me its own exceeding great reward: it has given me the habit of wishing to discover the good and beautiful in all that meets and surrounds me.

Samuel Taylor Coleridge

POLITICS

Knowledge of human nature is the beginning and the end of political education.

Henry Brooks Adams

This is the first Convention of a space age—where a candidate can promise the moon and mean it.

David Brinkly

The humblest in all the land, when clad in the armor of a righteous cause, is stronger than all the hosts of error.

William Jennings Bryan

Real politics are the possession and distribution of power.

Benjamin Disraeli

There is no gambling like politics.

Benjamin Disraeli

Politics is a profession; a serious, complicated and, in its true sense, a noble one.

Dwight David Eisenhower

The end of all political effort must be the well-being of the individual in a life of safety and freedom.

Dag Hammarskjold

Conferences at the top level are always courteous. Name-calling is left to the Foreign Ministers.

Averell W. Herriman

Politics is very much like taxes—everybody is against them, or everybody is for them as long as they don't apply to him.

Fiorello Henry La Guardia

He knows nothing; and he thinks he knows everything. That points clearly to a political career.

George Bernard Shaw

An independent is a person who wants to take the politics out of politics.

Adlai Ewing Stevenson

Polities I conceive to be nothing more than the science of the ordered progress of society along the lines of greatest usefulness and convenience to itself.

(Thomas) Woodrow Wilson

See also: Government

POOR: *See* POVERTY

POVERTY

Poverty is only contemptible when it is felt to be so. Doubtless the best way to make poverty respectable is to seem never to feel it as an evil.

Christian Nestell Bovee

Most of our realists and sociologists talk about a poor man as if he were an octopus or an alligator,

Gilbert Keith Chesterton

In a terrible crisis there is only one element more helpless than the poor, and that is the rich.

Clarence Seward Darrow

The cure for "Materialism" is to have enough for everybody and to spare. When people are sure of having what they need they cease to think about it.

Henry Ford

Poverty often deprives a man of all spirit and virtue; it is hard for an empty bag to stand upright.

Benjamin Franklin

To be poor, and seem to be poor, is a certain way never to rise.

Oliver Goldsmith

In America today we are nearer a final triumph over poverty than in any land. The poorhouse has vanished from amongst us.

Herbert Clark Hoover

See also: **Adversity, Crime, Riot, Want**

POWER

Nothing destroys authority so much as the unequal and untimely interchange of power, pressed too far and relaxed too much.

Francis Bacon

All human power is a compound of time and patience.

Honoré de Balzac

Power must always feel the check of power.

Louis Dembitz Brandeis

To know the pains of power, we must go to those who have it; to know its pleasures, we must go to those who are seeking it. The pains of power are real; its pleasures imaginary.

Charles Caleb Colton

We have more power than will; and it is often by way of excuse to ourselves that we fancy things are impossible.

Duc François de La Rochefoucauld

Even in war moral power is to physical as three parts out of four.

Napoleon I (Bonaparte)

Power acquired by guilt has seldom been directed to any good end or useful purpose.

Tacitus

There must be, not a balance of power, but a community of power; not organized rivalries, but an organized common peace.

(Thomas) Woodrow Wilson

See also: **Ability, Authority, Efficiency, Government, Influence, Strength**

PRAISE

Praise undeserved is satire in disguise.

Henry Broadhurst

Praise is a debt we owe to the virtues of others, and is due to our own from all whom malice has not made mutes, or envy struck dumb.

Sir Thomas Browne

We are all excited by the love of praise, and it is the noblest spirits that feel it most.

Cicero

The praises of others may be of use in teaching us, not what we are, but what we ought to be.

Augustus and Julius Hare

True praise is frequently the lot of the humble; false praise is always confined to the great.

Henry Home

Praise, like gold and diamonds, owes its value only to its scarcity. It becomes cheap as it becomes vulgar, and will no longer raise expectation or animate enterprise.

Samuel Johnson

When we disclaim praise, it is only showing our desire to be praised a second time.

Duc François de La Rochefoucauld

A man's accusations of himself are always believed, his praises never.

Michel Eyquem de Montaigne

Damn with faint praise.

Alexander Pope

His praise is lost who waits till all commend.

Alexander Pope

Think not those faithful who praise all your words and actions, but those who kindly reprove your faults.

Socrates

Whenever you commend, add your reasons for doing so; it is this which distinguishes the approbation of a man of sense from the flattery of sycophants and admiration of fools.

Sir Richard Steele

The more you speak of yourself, the more you are likely to lie.

Johann Georg von Zimmermann

See also: **Applause, Compliment, Flattery, Popularity**

PRAYER

People would be surprised to know how much I learned about prayer from playing poker.

Mary Hunter Austin

Prayer is a virtue that prevaileth against all temptations.

Bernard of Clairvaux

He who runs from God in the morning will scarcely find Him the rest of the day.

John Bunyan

In prayer it is better to have a heart without words, than words without a heart.

John Bunyan

Prayer is a binding necessity in the lives of men and nations.

Alexis Carrell

He prayeth best who loveth best.

Samuel Taylor Coleridge

Is not prayer a study of truth, a sally of the soul into the unfound infinite? No man ever prayed heartily without learning something.

Ralph Waldo Emerson

Certain thoughts are prayers. There are moments when, whatever be the attitude of the body, the soul is on its knees.

Victor Marie Hugo

I have been driven many times to my knees by the overwhelming conviction that I had nowhere else to go. My own wisdom, and that of all about me, seemed insufficient for the day.

Abraham Lincoln

The fewer words the better prayer.

Martin Luther

See also: **Worship**

PREACHING

I preached as never sure to preach
  again,
And as a dying man to dying men.
Richard Baxter

The world is dying for want, not of good
preaching, but of good hearing.
George Dana Boardman

And pulpit, drum ecclesiastic,
Was beat with fist, instead of a stick.
Samuel Butler

Let your sermon grow out of your text,
and aim only to develop and impress its
thought. Of a discourse that did not do
this it was once wittily said, "If the text
had the smallpox, the sermon would
never catch it."
Tryon Edwards

A strong and faithful pulpit is no mean
safeguard of a nation's life.
John Hall

A preacher should have the skill to teach
the unlearned simply, roundly, and
plainly; for teaching is of more importance than exhorting.
Martin Luther

Only the sinner has a right to preach.
Christopher Darlington Morley

My grand point in preaching is to break
the hard heart, and to heal the broken
one.
John Newton

To preach more than half an hour, a
man should be an angel himself or have
angels for hearers.
George Whitefield

See also: **Advice, Church, Instruction,
  Teaching**

PREJUDICE

The prejudices of ignorance are more
easily removed than the prejudices of
interest; the first are all blindly adopted,
the second willfully preferred.
George Bancroft

To divest one's self of some prejudices,
would be like taking off the skin to feel
the better.
Fulke Greville (First Baron Brooke)

Prejudice is never easy unless it can pass
itself off for reason.
William Hazlitt

The Negro says, "Now." Others say,
"Never." The voice of responsible
Americans . . . says "Together." There is
no other way. Until justice is blind to
color, until education is unaware of race,
until opportunity is unconcerned with
the color of men's skins, emancipation
will be a proclamation but not a fact.
Lyndon Baines Johnson

I hope that no American, considering
the really critical issues facing this
country, will waste his franchise and
throw away his vote by voting either for
me or against me solely on account of
my religious affiliation. It is not relevant.
John Fitzgerald Kennedy

Everyone is a prisoner of his own expe-
riences. No one can eliminate prejudices
—just recognize them.
Edward Roscoe Murrow

There is nothing stronger than human
prejudice. A crazy sentimentalism, like
that of Peter the Hermit, hurled half of
Europe upon Asia, and changed the
destinies of kingdoms.
Wendell Phillips

Prejudice is the reason of fools.
Voltaire (François Marie Arouet)

Prejudices are what rule the populace.
Voltaire (François Marie Arouet)

See also: **Fanaticism, Intolerance,
Opinion**

PRESENT

Duty and to-day are ours, results and futurity belong to God.
Horace Greeley

Abridge your hopes in proportion to the shortness of the span of human life; for while we converse, the hours, as if envious of our pleasure, fly away; enjoy therefore the present time, and trust not too much to what to-morrow may produce.
Horace

Trust no Future, howe'er pleasant!
  Let the dead Past bury its dead!
Act—act in the living Present!
  Heart within, and God o'erhead!
Henry Wadsworth Longfellow

Man, living, feeling man, is the easy sport of the over-mastering present.
Johann Christoph Friedrich von Schiller

See also: **Future, Past, Time**

PRETENSION

True glory strikes root, and even extends itself; all false pretensions fall as do flowers, nor can any feigned thing be lasting.
Cicero

We are only vulnerable and ridiculous through our pretensions.
Delphine de Girardin

Where there is much pretension, much has been borrowed; nature never pretends.
Johann Kaspar Lavater

Pretences go a great way with men that take fair words and magisterial looks for current payment.
Sir Roger L'Estrange

We had better appear what we are, than affect to appear what we are not.
Duc François de La Rochefoucauld

It is no disgrace not to be able to do everything; but to undertake or pretend to do what you are not made for, is not only shameful, but extremely troublesome and vexatious.
Plutarch

The only good in pretending is the fun we get out of fooling ourselves that we fool somebody.
Booth Tarkington

See also: **Ostentation**

PREVENTION

Preventives of evil are far better than remedies; cheaper and easier of application, and surer in result.
Tryon Edwards

Who would not give a trifle to prevent what he would give a thousand worlds to cure?
Edward Young

Laws act after crimes have been committed; prevention goes before them both.
Johann Georg von Zimmerman

See also: **Caution, Forethought**

PRIDE

When shall we learn to be proud? For only pride is creative.

Randolph Silliman Bourne

I think it humanly impossible for anyone to think of his own name as a word of little importance.

Frank Case

There is this paradox in pride—it makes some men ridiculous, but prevents others from becoming so.

Charles Caleb Colton

The proud are ever most provoked by pride.

William Cowper

Pride the first peer and president of hell.

Daniel Defoe

Pride breakfasted with plenty, dined with poverty, and supped with infamy.

Benjamin Franklin

Pride is increased by ignorance; those assume the most who know the least.

John Gay

There was one who thought himself above me, and he was above me until he had that thought.

Elbert Green Hubbard

The seat of pride is in the heart, and only there; and if it be not there, it is neither in the look, nor in the clothes.

Edward Hyde (Lord Clarendon)

Pride is a vice, which pride itself inclines every man to find in others, and to overlook in himself.

Samuel Johnson

Pride is seldom delicate; it will please itself with very mean advantages.

Samuel Johnson

Nature has given us pride to spare us the pain of being conscious of our imperfections.

Duc François de La Rochefoucauld

See also: **Arrogance, Vanity**

PROCRASTINATION

Everything comes to him who waits—among other things—death.

Francis Herbert Bradley

There is no fun in having nothing to do; the fun is having lots to do and not doing it.

Francis Herbert Bradley

Never do to-day what you can put off till tomorrow. Delay may give clearer light as to what is best to be done.

Aaron Burr

Indulge in procrastination, and in time you will come to this, that because a thing ought to be done, therefore you can't do it.

Charles Buxton

Delay not till to-morrow to be wise;
To-morrow's sun to thee may never rise.

William Congreve

Never put off till to-morrow that which you can do to-day.

Benjamin Franklin

Even if you're on the right track—
You'll get run over if you just sit there.

Arthur Godfrey

PROFANITY

The devil tempts men through their ambition, their cupidity or their appetite, until he comes to the profane swearer, whom he catches without any bait or reward.

Horace Mann

Nothing is a greater, or more fearful sacrilege than to prostitute the great name of God to the petulancy of an idle tongue.

Jeremy Taylor

The foolish and wicked practice of profane cursing and swearing is a vice so mean and low, that every person of sense and character detests and despises it.

George Washington

See also: **Oath**

PROGRESS

Intellectually, as well as politically, the direction of all true progress is toward greater freedom, and along an endless succession of ideas.

Christian Nestell Bovee

I have always considered that the substitution of the internal combustion engine for the horse marked a very gloomy milestone in the progress of mankind.

Sir Winston Leonard Spencer Churchill

If a man is not rising upward to be an angel, depend upon it, he is sinking downward to be a devil. He cannot stop at the beast.

Samuel Taylor Coleridge

Progress is the law of life; man is not man as yet.

Robert Browning

He that is good, will infallibly, become better, and be that is bad, will as certainly become worse; for vice, virtue, and time, are three things that never stand still.

Charles Caleb Colton

Progress is the activity of to-day and the assurance of to-morrow.

Ralph Waldo Emerson

I find the great thing in this world is not so much where we stand, as in what direction we are moving.

Oliver Wendell Holmes

The religion of inevitable progress— which is, in the last analysis, the hope and faith (in the teeth of all human experience) that one can get something for nothing.

Aldous Leonard Huxley

The mere absence of war is not peace. The mere absence of recession is not growth.

John Fitzgerald Kennedy

I look forward to a time when man shall progress upon something worthier and higher than his stomach.

Jack London

Let us labor for that larger comprehension of truth, and that more thorough repudiation of error, which shall make the history of mankind a series of ascending developments.

Horace Mann

See also: **Improvement, Reform, Science**

PROPERTY

Property is merely the art of democracy. It means that every man should have something that he can shape in his own image.

Gilbert Keith Chesterton

The accumulation of property is no guarantee of the development of character, but the development of character, or of any other good whatever, is impossible without property.

William Graham Sumner

Material blessings, when they pass beyond the category of need, are weirdly fruitful of headache.

Philip Wylie

See also: **Wealth**

PROSPERITY

Prosperity doth best discover vice, but adversity doth best discover virtue.

Francis Bacon

Watch lest prosperity destroy generosity.

Henry Ward Beecher

In prosperity prepare for a change; in adversity hope for one.

James Burgh

In prosperity, let us take great care to avoid pride, scorn, and arrogance.

Cicero

It is a frail mind that does not bear prosperity as well as adversity with moderation.

Cicero

Prosperity is only an instrument to be used, not a deity to be worshipped.

(John) Calvin Coolidge

The good things which belong to prosperity may be wished; but the good things which belong to adversity are to be admired.

Seneca

When God has once begun to tread upon the prosperous, He destroys them altogether. This is the end of the mighty.

Seneca

See also: **Fortune, Money, Property, Wealth**

PROVIDENCE

God hangs the greatest weights upon the smallest wires.

Francis Bacon

In the huge mass of evil as it rolls and swells, there is ever some good working toward deliverance and triumph.

Thomas Carlyle

The longer I live, the more convincing proofs I see of this truth, that God governs in the affairs of man; and if a sparrow cannot fall to the ground without his notice, is it probable that an empire can rise without his aid?

Benjamin Franklin

Who finds not Providence all good and wise,
Alike in what it gives and what it denies?

Alexander Pope

See also: **Economy, Forethought, Frugality, God, Prudence**

PRUDENCE

If the prudence of reserve and decorum dictates silence in some circumstances, in others prudence of a higher order, may justify us in speaking our thoughts.

Edmund Burke

It is by the goodness of God that in our country we have those three unspeakable precious things: freedom of speech, freedom of conscience, and the prudence never to practice either.

Samuel Langhorne Clemens (Mark Twain)

There is nothing more imprudent than excessive prudence.

Charles Caleb Colton

The one prudence in life is concentration; the one evil is dissipation.

Ralph Waldo Emerson

The prudence of the best heads is often defeated by the tenderness of the best of hearts.

Henry Fielding

There is no amount of praise which is not heaped on prudence; yet there is not the most insignificant event of which it can make us sure.

Duc François de La Rochefoucauld

See Also: Caution, Common Sense, Discretion, Intelligence, Wisdom

PSYCHOANALYSIS: See PSYCHOLOGY

PSYCHOLOGY

A wonderful discovery— psychoanalysis. Makes quite simple people feel they're complex.

Samuel Nathaniel Behrman

Anybody who is 25 or 30 years old has physical scars from all sorts of things, from tuberculosis to polio. It's the same with the mind.

Moses Ralph Kaufman

Every medical doctor needs to be also a doctor of the soul and . . . the parish minister needs to be a good psychologist as well as a good religionist.

Winfred Rhoades

See also: *Mind*

PUBLIC

The public is wiser than the wisest critic.

George Bancroft

If it has to choose who is to be crucified, the crowd will always save Barabbas.

Jean Cocteau

The public wishes itself to be managed like a woman; one must say nothing to it except what it likes to hear.

Johann Wolfgang von Goethe

The public, with its mob yearning to be instructed, edified and pulled by the nose, demands certainties; . . . but there are no certainties.

Henry Louis Mencken

In a free and republican government, you cannot restrain the voice of the multitide. Every man will speak as he thinks, or, more properly, without thinking, and consequently will judge of effects without attending to their causes.

George Washington

Very few public men but look upon the public as their debtors and their prey; so much for their pride and honesty.

Johann Georg von Zimmerman

See also: *Man, Mob, Nation, Society*

PUNCTUALITY

Appointments once made, become debts. If I have made an appointment with you, I owe you punctuality; I have no right to throw away your time, if I do my own.

Richard Cecil

I could never think well of a man's intellectual or moral character, if he was habitually unfaithful to his appointments.

Nathaniel Emmons

Want of punctuality is a want of virtue.
John Mitchell Mason

Nothing inspires confidence in a business man sooner than punctuality, nor is there any habit which sooner saps his reputation than that of being always behind time.

William Mathews

I have always been a quarter of an hour before my time, and it has made a man of me.

Horatio Nelson (Lord Nelson)

See also: **Haste**

PUNISHMENT

Punishment is justice for the unjust.
Augustine of Hippo

It is better that ten guilty persons escape than one innocent suffer.
Sir William Blackstone

God is on the side of virtue; for whoever dreads punishment suffers it, and whoever deserves it dreads it.

Charles Caleb Colton

The certainty of punishment, even more than its severity, is the preventive of crime.

Tryon Edwards

The work of eradicating crimes is not by making punishment familiar, but formidable.

Oliver Goldsmith

Jails and prisons are the complement of schools; so many less as you have of the latter, so many more you must have of the former.

Horace Mann

The object of punishment is the prevention of evil; it can never be made impulsive to good.

Horace Mann

This, it seems to me, is the most severe punishment—finding out you are wrong.
Walter Winchell

See also: **Crime, Discipline, Justice**

PURPOSE

The good man is the man who, no matter how morally unworthy he has been, is moving to become better.

John Dewey

The secret of success is constancy to purpose.

Benjamin Disraeli

Lack of something to feel important about is almost the greatest tragedy a man may have.

Arthur Ernest Morgan

Man's chief purpose . . . is the creation and preservation of values.

Lewis Mumford

A person is really alive only when he is moving forward to something more.

Winfred Rhoades

See also: **Aim, Ambition, Ideal, Objective, Resolution**

PURSUIT

Like one that on a lonesome road
    Doth walk in fear and dread,
And having once turned round walks on,
    And turns no more his head;
Because he knows a frightful fiend
    Doth close behind him tread.

Samuel Taylor Coleridge

The rapture of pursuing is the prize the vanquished gain.

Henry Wadsworth Longfellow

I take it to be a principal rule of life, not to be too much addicted to one thing.

Terence

See also: **Anticipation, Zeal**

QUARREL

So also those false alarms of strife
    Between the husband and the wife,
And little quarrels often prove
    To be but new recruits of love;
When those who're always kind of coy,
    In time must either tire or cloy.

Samuel Butler

Quarrels would not last long if the wrong was all on one side.

Duc François de La Rochefoucauld

When chickens quit quarrelling over their food they often find that there is enough for all of them. I wonder if it might not be the same with the human race.

Donald Robert Perry (Don) Marquis

See also: **Anger, Argument, Enemy**

QUESTION

Man will not live without answers to his questions.

Hans Joachim Morgenthau

No man really becomes a fool until he stops asking questions.

Charles Proteus Steinmetz

We must not expect simple answers to far-reaching questions. However far our gaze penetrates, there are always heights beyond which block our vision.

Alfred North Whitehead

See also: **Curiosity, Doubt**

QUIET

The good and the wise lead quiet lives.

Euripides

To have a quiet mind is to possess one's mind wholly; to have a calm spirit is to command one's self.

Hamilton Wright Mabie

The holy time is quiet as a Nun
Breathless with adoration.

William Wordsworth

See also: **Peace, Rest, Silence**

QUOTATION

When a thing has been said and well said, have no scruple: take it and copy it. Give references? Why should you? Either your readers know where you have taken the passage and the precaution is needless, or they do not know and you humiliate them.

Anatole France

Certain brief sentences are peerless in their ability to give one the feeling that nothing remains to be said.

Jean Rostand

Now we sit through Shakespeare in order to recognize the quotations.

Orson Welles

See also: Maxim

RAGE

Rage is essentially vulgar, and never more vulgar than when it proceeds from mortified pride, disappointed ambition, or thwarted wilfulness.

William Hart Coleridge

'Tis in my head; 'tis in my heart; 'tis everywhere; it rages like a madness, and I most wonder how my reason holds.

Thomas Otway

When transported by rage, it is best to observe its effects on those who deliver themselves up to the same passion.

Plutarch

See also: Anger, Emotion, Hate, Passion, Resentment

RAIN

We knew it would rain, for the poplars
    showed
The white of their leaves, the amber grain
Shrunk in the wind——and the lightning
    now
Is tangled in tremulous skeins of rain!

Thomas Bailey Aldrich

The thirsty earth soaks up the rain,
And drinks, and gapes, for drink again.

Abraham Cowley

Clouds dissolved the thirsty ground supply.

Wentworth Dillon (Earl of Roscommon)

Fall on me like a silent dew,
    Or like those maiden showers
Which, by the peep of day, doe strew
    A baptime o're the flowers.

Robert Herrick

The hooded clouds, like friars,
Tell their beads in drops of rain.

Henry Wadsworth Longfellow

The kind refresher of the summer heats.

Edward Thomas

See also: Nature

RANK

The rank is but the guinea's stamp,
    The man's the gowd for a'that.

Robert Burns

Every error of the mind is the more conspicuous, and culpable, in proportion to the rank of the person who commits it.

Juvenal

Rank is a great beautifier.

Edward G. Bulwer-Lytton (Baron Lytton)

Distinction of rank is necessary for the economy of the world, and was never called in question, but by barbarians and enthusiasts.

Nicholas Rowe

Rank and riches are chains of gold, but still chains.

Giovanni Ruffini

To be vain of one's rank or place, is to show that one is below it.

Stanislas I (Leszczynski)

I weigh the man, not his title; 'tis not the king's stamp can make the metal better.
William Wycherley

See also: **Birth**

READING

Reading is a basic tool in the living of a good life.
Mortimer Jerome Adler

It is well to read everything of something, and something of everything.
Henry Peter Brougham (Lord Brougham)

To read without reflecting, is like eating without digesting.
Edmund Burke

It was from my own early experience that I decided there was no use to which money could be applied so productive of good to boys and girls who have good within them and ability and ambition to develop it as the founding of a public library.
Andrew Carnegie

We should be as careful of the books we read, as of the company we keep. The dead very often have more power than the living.
Tryon Edwards

Reading, after a certain age, diverts the mind too much from its creative pursuits. Any man who reads too much and uses his own brain too little falls into lazy habits of thinking.
Albert Einstein

If one cannot enjoy reading a book over and over again, there is no use in reading it at all.
Oscar Wilde

See also: **Book, Learning, Newspaper**

REALITY

Facts are facts and will not disappear on account of your likes.
Jawaharlal Nehru

The non-recognition of realities naturally leads to artificial policies and programmes.
Jawaharlal Nehru

A theory must be tempered with reality.
Jawaharlal Nehru

The world of reality has its limits; the world of imagination is boundless. Not being able to enlarge the one, let us contract the other: for it is from their difference alone that all the evils arise which render us really unhappy.
Jean Jacques Rousseau

No matter how thin you slice it, it's still boloney.
Alfred Emanuel Smith

See also: **Philosophy, Truth**

REASON

If we would guide by the light of reason, we must let our minds be bold.
Louis Dembitz Brandeis

Wise men are instructed by reason; men of less understanding, by experience; the most ignorant, by necessity; and beasts by nature.
Cicero

The soundest argument will produce no more conviction in an empty head, than the most superficial declamation; a feather and a guinea fall with equal velocity in a vacuum.
Charles Caleb Colton

Reason of course, is weak, when measured against its never ending task. Weak indeed, compared with the follies and passions of mankind, which, we must admit, almost entirely control our human destinies, in great things and small.

Albert Einstein

Neither great poverty nor great riches will hear reason.

Henry Fielding

Most people reason dramatically, not quantitatively.

Oliver Wendell Holmes, Jr.

Irrationally held truths may be more harmful than reasoned errors.

Thomas Henry Huxley

Your giving a reason for it will not make it right. You may have a reason why two and two should make five, but they will still make but four.

Samuel Johnson

He is not a reasonable man who by chance stumbles upon reason, but he who derives it from knowledge, from discernment, and from taste.

Duc François de La Rochefoucauld

The three most important events of human life are equally devoid of reason—birth, marriage and death.

Austin O'Malley

Real life is, to most men, a long second-best, a perpetual compromise between the ideal and the possible; but the world of pure reason knows no compromise, no practical limitations, no barrier to the creative activity.

Bertrand Arthur William Russell

When a man has not a good reason for doing a thing, he has one good reason for letting it alone.

Sir Walter Scott

See also: **Common Sense, Intelligence, Judgment, Logic, Mind, Philosophy, Science, Wisdom**

REBELLION

Men seldom, or rather never for a length of time, and deliberately, rebel against anything that does not deserve rebelling against.

Thomas Carlyle

Rebellion against tyrants is obedience to God.

Benjamin Franklin

Any people anywhere being inclined and having the power, have the right to rise up and shake off the existing government, and form a new one that suits them better. This is a most valuable, a most sacred right—a right which we hope and believe is to liberate the world.

Abraham Lincoln

There is little hope of equity where rebellion reigns.

Sir Philip Sidney

See also: *Revolution*

REFLECTION

There is one art of which every man should be a master—the art of reflection. If you are not a thinking man, to what purpose are you a man at all?

Samuel Taylor Coleridge

The object of reflection is invariably the discovery of something satisfying to the mind which was not there at the beginning of the search.

Ernest Dimnet

They only babble who practise not reflection. I shall think; and thought is silence.

Richard Brinsley Sheridan

The advice of a scholar, whose piles of learning were set on fire by imagination, is never to be forgotten. Proportion an hour's reflection to an hour's reading, and so dispirit the book into the student.

Robert Eldridge Aris Willmott

REFORM

Public reformers had need first practice on their own hearts that which they propose to try on others.

Charles I

It has been the fate of all bold adventurers and reformers, to be esteemed insane.

George Barrell Cheever

Nothing so needs reforming as other people's habits.

Samuel Langhorne Clemens (Mark Twain)

We are reformers in spring and summer; in autumn and winter we stand by the old—reformers in the morning, conservatives at night. Reform is affirmative, conservatism is negative; conservatism goes for comfort, reform for truth.

Ralph Waldo Emerson

One vicious habit each year rooted out, in time might make the worst man good.

Benjamin Franklin

The lunatic fringe in all reform movements.

Theodore Roosevelt

There is a boldness, a spirit of daring, in religious reformers, not to be measured by the general rules which control men's purposes and actions.

Daniel Webster

See also: **Improvement, Progress, Repentance**

RELIGION

True religion and virtue give a cheerful and happy turn to the mind; admit of all true pleasures, and even procure for us the highest.

Joseph Addison

The true meaning of religion is thus not simply morality, but morality touched by emotion.

Matthew Arnold

If I did not feel . . . and hope that some day—perhaps millions of years hence—the Kingdom of God would overspread the whole world. . . then I would give my office over this morning to anyone who would take it.

Stanley Baldwin

One's religion is whatever he is most interested in, and yours is Success.

Sir James Matthew Barrie

Many would like religion as a sort of lightning rod to their houses, to ward off, by and by, the bolts of divine wrath.

Henry Ward Beecher

The tragedy is that with loss of faith in religion so many people have lost faith in the possibility of a unifying creed of any kind.

William Adams Brown

Nothing is so fatal to religion as indifference, which is, at least, half infidelity.
Edmund Burke

The noblest charities, the best fruits of learning, the richest discoveries, the best institutions of law and justice, every greatest thing the world has seen, represents, more or less directly, the fruitfulness and creativeness of religion.
Horace Bushnell

It is the test of a good religion whether you can joke about it.
Gilbert Keith Chesterton

Piety and holiness will propitiate the Gods.
Cicero

Religion should be the rule of life, not a casual incident in it.
Benjamin Disraeli

The soul of a civilization is its religion, and it dies with its faith.
Will (William James) Durant

I cannot believe that God plays dice with the cosmos!
Albert Einstein

All religions, arts and sciences are branches of the same tree.
Albert Einstein

If men are so wicked with religion, what would they be without it!
Benjamin Franklin

No sciences are better attested than the religion of the Bible.
Sir Isaac Newton

Religion is the best armor in the world, but the worst cloak.
John Newton

Religion is the fear and love of God; its demonstration is good works; and faith is the root of both, for without faith we cannot please God; nor can we fear and love what we do not believe.
William Penn

Day by day we should weigh what we have granted to the spirit of the world against what we have denied to the spirit of Jesus, in thought and especially in deed.
Albert Schweitzer

There is only one religion, though there are a hundred versions of it.
George Bernard Shaw

See also: **Church, Faith, Worship**

REMORSE

Remorse begets reform.
William Cowper

Not sharp revenge, nor hell itself can find
A fiercer torment than a guilty mind.
John Dryden

Remorse is the echo of a lost virtue.
Edward G. Bulwer-Lytton (Baron Lytton)

Remorse is beholding heaven and feeling hell.
Thomas Moore

Remorse is surgical in action; it cuts away foul tissues of the mind.
Christopher Darlington Morley

Remorse goes to sleep when we are in the enjoyment of prosperity, and makes itself felt in adversity.
Jean Jacques Rousseau

'Tis when the wound is stiffening with
the cold,
The warrior first feels pain—'tis when
the heat
And fiery fever of the soul is past,
The sinner feels remorse.

Sir Walter Scott

See also: **Grief, Guilt, Repentance,
Sorrow**

REPENTANCE

True repentance is to cease from sinning.

Ambrose of Milan

The best part of repentance is little sinning.

Arabian Proverb

Bad men are full of repentance.

Aristotle

Of all acts of man repentance is the most
divine. The greatest of all faults is to be
conscious of none.

Thomas Carlyle

Repentance, without amendment, is like
continually pumping without mending
the leak.

Lewis Weston Dillwyn

Great is the difference betwixt a man's
being frightened at, and humbled for his
sins.

Thomas Fuller

Our greatest glory consists not in never
falling, but in rising every time we may
fall.

Oliver Goldsmith

To do so no more is the truest repentance.

Martin Luther

The golden key that opens the palace of
eternity.

John Milton

Repentance is nothing else but a renun-
ciation of our will, and a controlling of
our fancies, which lead us which way
they please.

Michel Eyquem de Montaigne

The vain regret that steals above the
wreck of squandered hours.

John Greenleaf Whittier

See also: **Remorse, Sorrow**

REPETITION

Repetition may not entertain but it
teaches.

Frédéric Bastiat

Men get opinions as boys learn to spell,
By reiteration chiefly.

Elizabeth Barrett Browning

There is no absurdity so palpable but
that it may be firmly planted in the human head if you only begin to inculcate
it before the age of five, by constantly
repeating it with an air of great solem-
nity.

Arthur Schopenhauer

See also: **Loquacity**

REPUTATION

Reputation is sometimes as wide as the
horizon, when character is but the point
of a needle. Character is what one really
is; reputation what others believe him to
be.

Henry Ward Beecher

A man's reputation is not in his own keeping, but lies at the mercy of the profligacy of others. Calumny requires no proof.

William Hazlitt

Good will, like a good name, is got by many actions, and lost by one.

Francis Jeffrey (Lord Jeffrey)

A broken reputation is like a broken vase—it may be mended, but it always shows where the break was!

Henry Wheeler Shaw (Josh Billings)

The way to gain a good reputation, is, to endeavor to be what you desire to appear.

Socrates

Associate with men of good quality, if you esteem your own reputation; it is better to be alone than in bad company.

George Washington

See also: **Fame, Honor**

RESENTMENT

Resentment is, in every stage of the passion, painful, but it is not disagreeable, unless in excess.

Henry Home (Lord Kames)

Resentment is a union of sorrow with malignity; a combination of a passion which all endeavor to avoid with a passion which all concur to detest.

Samuel Johnson

Resentment seems to have been given us by nature for defence, and for defence only; it is the safeguard of justice, and the security of innocence.

Adam Smith

See also: **Anger, Hate, Rebellion**

RESOLUTION

Men die that might just as well live if they had resolved to live.

George Miller Beard

The block of granite which is an obstacle in the pathway of the weak, becomes a stepping-stone in the pathway of the strong.

Thomas Carlyle

There is nothing impossible in all the world except that the heart of man is wanting in resolution.

Confucius

A good intention clothes itself with power.

Ralph Waldo Emerson

He who is firm and resolute in will moulds the world to himself.

Johann Wolfgang von Goethe

You may be whatever you resolve to be. Determine to be something in the world, and you will be something. "I cannot," never accomplished anything; "I will try," has wrought wonders.

Joel Hawes

Either I will find a way, or I will make one.

Sir Philip Sidney

See also: **Courage, Firmness,
Perseverance, Purpose**

RESPECT

A man's real life is that accorded to him in the thoughts of other men by reason of respect or natural love.

Joseph Conrad

I must respect the opinions of others even if I disagree with them.

Herbert Henry Lehman

See also: *Courtesy, Manners*

RESPECTABILITY

To secure respect for law, we must make the law respectable.

Louis Dembitz Brandeis

The hat is the *ultimum moriens* of respectability.

Oliver Wendell Holmes

Respectable means rich, and decent means poor. I should die if I heard my family called decent.

Thomas Love Peacock

The more things a man is ashamed of, the more respectable he is.

George Bernard Shaw

See also: *Appearance*

RESPONSIBILITY

Every human being has a work to carry on within, duties to perform abroad, influences to exert, which are peculiarly his, and which no conscience but his own can teach.

William Ellery Channing

Responsibility is the thing people dread most of all. Yet it is the one thing in the world that develops us, gives us manhood or womanhood fibre.

Frank Crane

Responsibility walks hand in hand with capacity and power.

Josiah Gilbert Holland

Responsibility educates.

Wendell Phillips

The most important thought I ever had was that of my individual responsibility to God.

Daniel Webster

See also: *Duty, Integrity, Obligation*

REST

Absence of occupation is not rest;
A mind quite vacant is a mind distressed.

William Cowper

Too much rest itself becomes a pain.

Homer

Some seek bread; and some seek wealth and ease; and some seek fame, but all are seeking rest.

Frederick Langbridge

Alternate rest and labor long endure.

Ovid

Rest is the sweet sauce of labor.

Plutarch

When I rest I rust.

Fritz Thyssen

See also: *Peace, Quiet*

RESULT

Results! Why, man, I have gotten a lot of results. I know several thousand things that won't work.

Thomas Alva Edison

No action, whether foul or fair,
Is ever done, but it leaves somewhere
A record, written by fingers ghostly
As a blessing or a curse, and mostly
In the greater weakness or greater strength
Of the acts which follow it.

Henry Wadsworth Longfellow

Such souls
Whose sudden visitations daze the
  world,
Vanish like lightning; but they leave
  behind
A voice that in the distance far away
Wakens the slumbering ages.

Sir Henry Taylor

See also: **Beginning, Cause**

REVOLUTION

The surest way to prevent seditions is to
take away the matter of them; for if
there be fuel prepared, it is hard to tell
whence the spark shall come that shall
set it on fire.

Francis Bacon

Times and occasions and provocations
will teach their own lessons. But with or
without right, a revolution will be the
very last resource of the thinking and
the good.

Edmund Burke

The world is in a revolution which cannot be bought off with dollars . . . . A fire
is gathering for a mighty effort.

William Orville Douglas

Too long denial of guaranteed right is
sure to lead to revolution—bloody
revolution, where suffering must fall
upon the innocent as well as the guilty.

Ulysses Simpson Grant

All experience hath shown that mankind are more disposed to suffer, while
evils are sufferable, than to right themselves by abolishing the forms to which
they are accustomed.

Thomas Jefferson

Revolutions are like the most noxious
dungheaps, which bring into life the
noblest vegetables.

Napoleon I (Bonaparte)

See also: **Anarchy, Communism,
  Rebellion, Riot, Violence, War**

REWARD

He who wishes to secure the good of
others has already secured his own.

Confucius

Blessings ever wait on virtuous deeds,
And though a late, a sure reward
  succeeds.

William Congreve

It is the amends of a short and troublesome life, that doing good and suffering
ill entitles man to a longer and better.

William Penn

No man, who continues to add something to the material, intellectual, and
moral well being of the place in which
he lives, is left long without proper reward.

Booker Taliaferro Washington

RIDICULE

Cervantes smiled Spain's chivalry away.

George Gordon Byron (Lord Byron)

Scoff not at the natural defects of any
which are not in their power to amend.
It is cruel to beat a cripple with his own
crutches!

Thomas Fuller

Man learns more readily and remembers
more willingly what excites his ridicule
than what deserves esteem and respect.

Horace

Ridicule is the weapon most feared by enthusiasts of every description; from its predominance over such minds it often checks what is absurd, but fully as often smothers that which is noble.

Sir Walter Scott

Vices, when ridiculed
   First lose the horror they ought to raise,
Grow by degrees approved,
   And almost aim at praise.

William Whitehead

See also: **Absurdity, Criticism, Sarcasm**

RIGHTS

Many a person seems to think it isn't enough for the government to guarantee him the pursuit of happiness. He insists it also run interference for him.

Anonymous

The fears of one class of men are not the measure of the rights of another.

George Bancroft

How can you have states' rights when you keep running to Washington for money?

Bernard Mannes Baruch

Today, as rarely before, case after case comes to the Court which finds the individual battling to vindicate a claim under the Bill of Rights against the powers of government, federal and state.

William Joseph Brennan, Jr.

In our land, the citizen is the power, and every citizen should have his share.

Richard James Cushing

The fences have been broken down . . . The Bill of Rights—with the judicial gloss it has acquired—plainly is not adequate to protect the individual against the growing bureaucracy.

William Orville Douglas

"Freedom from fear" could be said to sum up the whole philosophy of human rights.

Dag Hammerskjold

We hold these truths to be self-evident that all men are created equal, that they are endowed by their Creator with certain unalienable Rights, that among these are Life, Liberty, and the pursuit of Happiness.

Thomas Jefferson

I do not say that all men are equal in their ability, character and motivation. I do say that every American should be given a fair chance to develop all the talents they may have.

John Fitzgerald Kennedy

In the cause of freedom, we have to battle for the rights of people with whom we do not agree; and whom, in many cases, we may not like. These people test the strength of the freedoms which protect all of us. If we do not defend their rights, we endanger our own.

Harry S Truman

See also: **Democracy, Justice**

RIOT

No nation, no matter how enlightened, can endure criminal violence. If we cannot control it we are admitting to the world and to ourselves that our laws are no more than a facade that crumbles when the winds of crisis rise.

Alan Bible

The poor suffer twice at the rioter's hands. First, his destructive fury scars their neighborhood; second, the atmosphere of accomodation and consent is changed to one of hostility and resentment.

Lyndon Baines Johnson

The summer of 1967 will be recorded as one of the most violent in the history of this Nation. This was a summer when racial unrest reached the point where violence was so common that it was news when it was quiet in our cities.

Walter F. Mondale

If we resort to lawlessness, the only thing we can hope for is civil war, untold bloodshed, and the end of our dreams.

Archie Lee Moore

One speaks of the possibility of violence with caution. Too often, to predict the possibility of violence is interpreted as an incitement to violence. But I infinitely prefer to be called an alarmist than to stand by, a silent witness to impending crisis.

Whitney Moore Young, Jr.

See also: **Poverty, Violence**

RISK

The policy of being too cautious is the greatest risk of all.

Jawaharlal Nehru

Everything is sweetened by risk.

Alexander Smith

See also: **Bravery, Fear**

RIVALRY

It is the privilege of posterity to set matters right between those antagonists who, by their rivalry for greatness, divided a whole age.

Joseph Addison

In ambition, as in love, the successful can afford to be indulgent toward their rivals. The prize our own, it is graceful to recognize the merit that vainly aspired to it,

Christian Nestell Bovee

Nothing is ever done beautifully which is done in rivalship; or nobly, which is done in pride.

John Ruskin

See also: **Jealousy**

ROMANCE

I despair of ever receiving the same degree of pleasure from the most exalted performances of genius which I felt in childhood from pieces which my present judgment regards as trifling and contemptible.

Edmund Burke

Romance has been elegantly defined as the offspring of fiction and love.

Benjamin Disraeli

Romance is the poetry of literature.

Albertine Adrienne de Saussure Necker

In this commonplace world every one is said to be romantic who either admires a finer thing or does one.

Alexander Pope

Lessons of wisdom have never such power over us as when they are wrought into the heart through the groundwork of a story which engages the passions.

Laurence Sterne

See also: **Fable, Love, Poetry, Reading**

RUMOR

Rumor was the messenger of defamation, and so swift, that none could be first to tell an evil tale.

Robert Pollok

When rumours increase, and when there is abundance of noise and clamor, believe the second report.

Alexander Pope

The flying rumours gather'd as they roll'd,
Scarce any tale was sooner heard than told;
And all who told it added something new,
And all who heard it made enlargements too.

Alexander Pope

He that easily believes rumors has the principle within him to augment rumors. It is strange to see the ravenous appetite with which some devourers of character and happiness fix upon the sides of the innocent and unfortunate.

Jane Porter

See also: **Babble, Gossip, Scandal, Slander**

SARCASM

Sarcasm is the language of the devil; for which reason I have long since as good as renounced it.

Thomas Carlyle

A graceful taunt is worth a thousand insults.

Louis Nizer

Sarcasm poisons reproof.

Edward Wigglesworth

See also: **Criticism, Humor, Ridicule**

SCANDAL

Scandal is the sport of its authors, the dread of fools, and the contempt of the wise.

William Benton Clulow

Great numbers of moderately good people think it fine to talk scandal; they regard it as a sort of evidence of their own goodness.

Frederick William Faber

Praise undeserved is scandal in disguise.

Alexander Pope

Believe that story false that ought not to be true.

Richard Brinsley Sheridan

Scandal is what one-half the world takes pleasure in inventing, and the other half in believing.

Horatio Smith (Paul Chatfield)

In scandal, as in robbery, the receiver is always as bad as the thief.

Philip Dormer Stanhope (Lord Chesterfield)

Scandal is but amusing ourselves with the faults, foibles, follies and reputations of our friends.

Royall Tyler

See also: *Gossip, Reputation, Rumor, Slander*

SCIENCE

The sciences are of sociable disposition, and flourish best in the neighborhood of each other; nor is there any branch of learning but may be helped and improved by assistance drawn from other arts.

Sir William Blackstone

The tendency of modern science is to reduce proof to absurdity by continually reducing absurdity to proof.

Samuel Butler

Modern science is standing on tiptoe, ready to open the doors of a golden age.

Sir Winston Leonard Spencer Churchill

It stands to the everlasting credit of science that by acting on the human mind it has overcome man's insecurity before himself and before nature.

Albert Einstein

Science surpasses the old miracles of mythology.

Ralph Waldo Emerson

New technology is needed to balance the costs and injustices of old technology.

Ralph Nader

Science is a collection of successful recipes.

Paul Ambroise Valéry

See also: *Communications Media, Knowledge, Logic, Reason, Technology, Truth*

SECRECY

There is a skeleton in every house.

Anonymous

Three may keep a secret, if two of them are dead.

Benjamin Franklin

To keep your secret is wisdom; but to expect others to keep it is folly.

Oliver Wendell Holmes

A man can keep the secret of another better than his own: a woman, on the contrary, keeps her own better than that of another.

Jean de La Bruyère

Trust him not with your secrets, who, when left alone in your room, turns over your papers.

Johann Kaspar Lavater

Secrecy is the chastity of friendship.

Jeremy Taylor

Conceal your domestic ills.

Thales

I usually get my stuff from people who promised somebody else that they would keep it a secret.

Walter Winchell

See also: *Mystery, Obscurity, Silence*

SELF-CONFIDENCE

He who places implicit confidence in his genius will find himself some day utterly defeated and deserted.

Benjamin Disraeli

The history of the world is full of men who rose to leadership, by sheer force of self-confidence, bravery and tenacity.

Mohandas Karamchand (Mahatma) Gandhi

There are admirable potentialities in every human being. Believe in your strength and your youth. Learn to repeat endlessly to yourself: "It all depends on me."

André Gide

The worst of poisons: to mistrust one's power.

Heinrich Heine

Self-confidence is of more importance in conversation than ability.

Duc François de La Rochefoucauld

See also: **Confidence**

SELF-CONTROL

No one who cannot master himself is worthy to rule, and only he can rule.

Johann Wolfgang von Goethe

Those who can command themselves command others.

William Hazlitt

No conflict is so severe as his who labors to subdue himself.

Thomas à Kempis

See also: **Reflection, Self-Knowledge**

SELF-IMPROVEMENT

There is no use whatever trying to help people who do not help themselves. You cannot push anyone up a ladder unless he be willing to climb himself.

Andrew Carnegie

Each year, one vicious habit rooted out in time ought to make the worst man good.

Benjamin Franklin

People seldom improve, when they have no other model but themselves to copy after.

Oliver Goldsmith

If we do not *better* our civilization, our way of life, and our democracy, there will be no use trying to "save" them by fighting; they will crumble away under the very feet of our armies.

Anne Spencer Morrow Lindbergh

The improvement of our way of life is more important than the spreading of it. If we make it satisfactory enough, it will spread automatically. If we do not, no strength of arms can permanently impose it.

Charles Augustus Lindbergh

If there is literally enough force in you to blow up the greatest city in the world, there is also literally enough power in you to overcome every obstacle in your life.

Norman Vincent Peale

See also: **Improvement, Progress, Reform**

SELF-INTEREST

Self-interest, that leprosy of the age, attacks us from infancy, and we are startled to observe little heads calculate before knowing how to reflect.

Delphine de Girardin

Self-interest speaks all kinds of languages, and plays all kinds of parts, even that of the disinterested.

Duc François de La Rochefoucauld

The modern trouble is in a low capacity to believe in precepts which restrict and restrain private interests and desires.

Walter Lippmann

The world is governed only by self-interest.

Johann Christoph Friedrich von Schiller

Self-interest is the enemy of all true affection.

Tacitus

SELFISHNESS

The selfish man suffers more from his selfishness than he from whom that selfishness withholds some important benefit.

Ralph Waldo Emerson

The man who lives by himself and for himself is apt to be corrupted by the company he keeps.

Charles Henry Parkhurst

He who lives only to benefit himself confers on the world a benefit when he dies.

Tertullian

A man is called selfish, not for pursuing his own good, but for neglecting his neighbor's.

Richard Whately

See also: **Avarice, Interest, Miser**

SELF-KNOWLEDGE

Resolve to be thyself: and know, that he Who finds himself, loses his misery.

Matthew Arnold

Other men's sins are before our eyes; our own are behind our back.

Seneca

The precept, "Know yourself," was not solely intended to obviate the pride of mankind; but likewise that we might understand our own worth.

Cicero

He that knows himself, knows others; and he that is ignorant of himself, could not write a very profound lecture on other men's heads.

Charles Caleb Colton

See also: **Intelligence, Knowledge, Reflection, Understanding, Wisdom**

SELF-RESPECT

The reverence of man's self, is, next to religion, the chiefest bridle of all vices.

Francis Bacon

All must respect those who respect themselves.

Benjamin Disraeli

Self-respect,—that corner-stone of all virtue.

Sir John Frederick William Herschel

Above all things, reverence yourself.

Pythagoras

To have a respect for ourselves guides our morals; and to have a deference for others governs our manners.

Laurence Sterne

Self-reverence, self-knowledge, self-control, these three alone lead life to sovereign power.

Alfred, Lord Tennyson

See also: **Conscience, Dignity, Pride**

SELF-SACRIFICE

No person . . . shall be compelled in any criminal case to be a witness against himself. [Amendment V].
Constitution of the United States

They will let you live only when you learn to die.
Theodor Herzl

Only he can understand what a farm is, what a country is, who shall have sacrificed part of himself to his farm or his county, sought to save it, struggled to make it beautiful.
Antoine de Saint-Exupéry

See also: Love

SENSUALITY

The body of a sensualist is the coffin of a dead soul.
Christian Nestell Bovee

Sensuality is the gave of the soul.
William Ellery Channing

A youth of sensuality and intemperance delivers over a worn-out body to old age.
Cicero

If sensuality were happiness, beasts were happier than men; but human felicity is lodged in the soul, not in the flesh.
Seneca

All sensuality is one, though it takes many forms, as all purity is one. It is the same whether a man eat, or drink, or cohabit, or sleep sensually. They are but one appetite, and we only need to see a person do any one of these things to know how great a sensualist he is.
Henry David Thoreau

See also: Vice

SENTIMENT

Nature has cast men in so soft a mould,
That but to hear a story, feigned for
pleasure,
Of some sad lover's death, moistens my
eyes,
And robs me of my manhood.
John Dryden

Cure the drunkard, heal the insane, mollify the homicide, civilize the Pawnee, but what lessons can be devised for the debaucher of sentiment?
Ralph Waldo Emerson

Sentiment is intellectualized emotion; emotion precipitated, as it were, in pretty crystals by the fancy.
James Russell Lowell

Sentiment has a kind of divine alchemy, rendering grief itself the source of tenderest thoughts and far-reaching desires, which the sufferer cherishes as sacred treasures.
Sir Thomas Noon Talfourd

See also: Assertion, Emotion, Opinion

SEX

The omnipresence process of sex, as it is woven into the whole texture of our man's or woman's body, is the pattern of all the process of our life.
(Henry) Havelock Ellis

Certainly no aspect of human biology in our current civilization stands in more need of scientific knowledge . . . than that of sex.
Alan Gregg

Sex has become one of the most discussed subjects of modern times. The Victorians pretended it did not exist; the moderns pretend that nothing else exists.

Fulton John Sheen

See also: **Men, Woman**

SILENCE

Silence never shows itself to so great an advantage as when it is made the reply to calumny and defamation.

Joseph Addison

As we must render an account of every idle word, so we must of our idle silence.

Ambrose of Milan

Silence is the virtue of fools.

Francis Bacon

He has observ'd the golden rule,
Till he's become the golden fool.

William Blake

This is such a serious world that we should never speak at all unless we have something to say.

Thomas Carlyle

I think the first virtue is to restrain the tongue; he approaches nearest to the gods who knows how to be silent, even though he is in the right.

Cato the Elder

If you don't say anything, you won't be called on to repeat it.

(John) Calvin Coolidge

Blessed is the man who, having nothing to say, abstains from giving wordy evidence of the fact.

George Eliot (Mary Ann Evans)

A judicious silence is always better than truth spoken without charity.

Francis of Sales

Fellows who have no tongues are often all eyes and ears.

Thomas Chandler Haliburton

If you keep your mouth shut you will never put your foot in it.

Austin O'Malley

See also: **Peace, Quiet, Secrecy**

SIMPLICITY

When thought is too weak to be simply expressed, it is a clear proof that it should be rejected.

Luc de Clapiers (Marquis de Vauvenargues)

Nothing is more simple than greatness; indeed, to be simple is to be great.

Ralph Waldo Emerson

Simplicity of character is the natural result of profound thought.

William Hazlitt

Simplicity, of all things, is the hardest to be copied.

Sir Richard Steele

Simplicity is making the journey of this life with just baggage enough.

Charles Dudley Warner

See also: **Brevity, Candor, Credulity, Ignorance, Innocence**

SIN

As sins proceed they ever multiply; and like figures in arithmetic, the last stands for more than all that went before it.

Sir Thomas Browne

One leak will sink a ship, and one sin will destroy a sinner.

John Bunyan

Whatever disunites man from God disunites man from man.

Edmund Burke

The deadliest sin were the consciousness of no sin.

Thomas Carlyle

A belief in a supernatural source of evil is not necessary; men alone are quite capable of every wickedness.

Joseph Conrad

Sins are like circles in the water when a stone is thrown into it; one produces another. When anger was in Cain's heart, murder was not far off.

Philip Henry

What is human sin but the abuse of human appetites, of human passions, of human faculties, in themselves all innocent?

Roswell Dwight Hitchcock

The recognition of sin is the beginning of salvation.

Martin Luther

Of Man's first disobedience, and the fruit
Of that forbidden tree whose mortal taste
Brought death into the world, and all our woe.

John Milton

If thou wouldst conquer thy weakness thou must never gratify it. No man is compelled to evil; only his consent makes it his. It is no sin to be tempted; it is to yield and be overcome.

William Penn

See also: **Error, Guilt, Offense, Vice, Wickedness, Wrong**

SKEPTICISM

Scepticism has never founded empires, established principles, or changed the world's heart. The great doers in history have always been men of faith.

Edwin Hubbel Chapin

Scepticism is slow suicide.

Ralph Waldo Emerson

Skeptics laugh in order not to weep.

Anatole France

The great trouble with the scepticism of the age is, that it is not thorough enough. It questions everything but its own foundations.

John Bannister Gibson

A skeptic who turns dogmatist has decided it is high time to take it easy.

Henry Stanley Haskins

I prefer credulity to skepticism and cynicism, for there is more promise in almost anything than in nothing at all.

Ralph Barton Perry

Every person who has mastered a profession is a sceptic concerning it.

George Bernard Shaw

The thorough sceptic is a dogmatist. He enjoys the delusion of complete futility.

Alfred North Whitehead

See also: **Agnosticism, Doubt, Unbelief**

SKILL: *See* ABILITY

SLANDER

Next to the slanderer, we detest the bearer of the slander to our ears.

Mary Catherwood

Who stabs my name would stab my person, too, did not the hangman's axe lie in the way.

John Crowne

The way to check slander is to despise it; attempt to overtake and refute it, and it will outrun you.

Alexandre Dumas (pére)

The slander of some people is as great a recommendation as the praise of others.

Henry Fielding

I hate the man who builds his name
On ruins of another's fame.

John Gay

There would not be so many open mouths if there were not so many open ears.

Joseph Hall

Slander is the revenge of a coward, and dissimulation his defence.

Samuel Johnson

Believe nothing against another, but on good authority; nor report what may hurt another, unless it be a greater hurt to some other to conceal it.

William Penn

A slander is like a hornet; if you cannot kill it dead the first blow, better not strike at it.

Henry Wheeler Shaw (Josh Billings)

The worthiest people are the most injured by slander, as it is the best fruit which the birds have been pecking at.

Jonathan Swift

See also: **Abuse, Babble, Gossip, Injury, Reputation Rumor, Scandal**

SMILE

A smile is the whisper of a laugh.

Anonymous

Wrinkles should merely indicate where smiles have been.

Samuel Langhorne Clemens (Mark Twain)

A woman has two smiles that an angel might envy—the smile that accepts a lover before words are uttered, and the smile that lights on the first-born babe, and assures it of a mother's love.

Thomas Chandler Haliburton

A face that cannot smile is never good.

Martial

Eternal smiles his emptiness betray, As shallow streams run dimpling all the way.

Alexander Pope

SOCIETY

The only worthwhile achievements of man are those which are socially useful.

Alfred Adler

The pressure of social influence about us is enormous, and no single arm can resist it.

Felix Adler

Our society distributes itself into Barbarians, Philistines, and Populace.

Matthew Arnold

No social system will bring us happiness, health, and prosperity unless it is inspired by something greater than materialism.

Clement Richard Atlee

Man was formed for society.

Sir William Blackstone

It is a community of purpose that constitutes society.

Benjamin Disraeli

We are a kind of chameleons, taking our hue—the hue or our moral character, from those who are about us.

John Locke

Clearly the ideal situation would be that in which society would increasingly respect the individual who would, in turn, increasingly respect society.

Jean Rostand

Other people are quite dreadful. The only possible society is oneself.

Oscar Wilde

To get into the best society nowadays, one has either to feed people, amuse people, or shock people.

Oscar Wilde

See also: **Man**

SOLITUDE

In Genesis it says that it is not good for a man to be alone, but sometimes it is a great relief.

John Barrymore

It would do the world good if every man in it would compel himself occasionally to be absolutely alone. Most of the world's progress has come out of such loneliness.

Bruce Barton

Conversation enriches the understanding, but solitude is the school of genius.

Edward Gibbon

An entire life of solitude contradicts the purpose of our being, since death itself is scarcely an idea of more terror.

Edmund Burke

In solitude, where we are least alone.

George Gordon Byron (Lord Byron)

The thoughtful Soul to Solitude retires.

Omar Khayyám

SORROW

Wherever souls are being tried and ripened, in whatever commonplace and homely way, there God is hewing out the pillars for His temple.

Phillips Brooks

Social sorrow loses half its pain.

Samuel Johnson

The world is so full of care and sorrow that it is a gracious debt we owe to one another to discover the bright crystals of delight hidden in somber circumstances and irksome tasks.

Helen Adams Keller

The mind profits by the wreck of every passion, and we may measure our road to wisdom by the sorrows we have undergone.

Edward G. Bulwer-Lytton (Baron Lytton)

Earth hath no sorrow that heaven cannot heal.

Thomas Moore

She would have made a splendid wife, for crying only made her eyes more bright and tender.

William Sydney Porter (O. Henry)

He that hath pity on another man's sorrow shall be free from it himself; and he that delighteth in, and scorneth the misery of another shall one time or other fall into it himself.

Sir Walter Raleigh

Light griefs do speak, while sorrow's tongue is bound.

Seneca

The deeper the sorrow the less tongue it has.

Talmud

Never morning wore to evening, but some heart did break.

Alfred, Lord Tennyson

Where there is sorrow, there is holy ground.

Oscar Wilde

See also: **Affliction, Grief, Suffering, Unhappiness**

SOUL

Whatever that be which thinks, which understands, which wills, which acts, it is something celestial and divine, and on that account must necessarily be eternal.

Cicero

A fiery soul, which, working out its
    way,
Fretted the pigmy body to decay,
And o'er-informed the tenement of clay.

John Dryden

The problem of restoring to the world original and eternal beauty is solved by the redemption of the soul

Ralph Waldo Emerson

Dust thou art, to dust returnest,
Was not spoken of the soul.

Henry Wadsworth Longfellow

The mind is never right but when it is at peace within itself; the soul is in heaven even while it is in the flesh, if it be purged of its natural corruptions, and taken up with divine thoughts and contemplations.

Seneca

See also: **Conscience, Emotion, Eternity, Heart, Immortality, Mind**

SPACE

A civilian-setting for the administration of space for the testing of missiles designed for of our nation that outer space be devoted to peaceful and scientific purposes.

Dwight David Eisenhower

I could have gone on flying through space forever.

Yuri Gagarin

The moon and other celestial bodies should be free for exploration and use by all countries. No country should be permitted to advance a claim of sovereignty.

Lyndon Baines Johnson

God has no intention of setting a limit to the efforts of man to conquer space.

Pius XII (Eugenio Pacelli)

For my confirmation, I didn't get a watch and my first pair of long pants, like most Lutheran boys. I got a telescope. My mother thought it would make the best gift.

Wernher Von Braun

See also: **Science**

SPEECH

Discretion of speech is more than eloquence; and to speak agreeably to him with whom we deal is more than to speak in good words, or in good order.

Francis Bacon

A superior man is modest in his speech but exceeds in his actions.

Confucius

As a vessel is known by the sound, whether it be cracked or not, so men are proved by their speeches whether they be wise or foolish

Demosthenes

Half the sorrows of women would be averted if they could repress the speech they know to be useless—nay, the speech they have resolved not to utter.

George Eliot (Mary Ann Evans)

We speak little if not egged on by vanity.

Duc François de La Rochefoucauld

I sometimes marvel at the extraordinary docility with which Americans submit to speeches.

Adlai Ewing Stevenson

STRENGTH

The strongest are those who renounce their own times and become a living part of those yet to come. The strongest, and the rarest.

Milovan Djilas

Strength is born in the deep silence of long-suffering hearts; not amidst joy.

Felicia Dorothea Browne Hemans

Strength, wanting judgment and policy to rule, overturneth itself.

Horace

Strength alone knows conflict; weakness is below even defeat, and is born vanquished.

Anne Sophie Swetchine

See also: **Endurance, Energy, Health, Power**

STUDY

I would live to study, and not study to live.

Francis Bacon

Studies teach not their own use; that is a wisdom without them and above them, won by observation.

Francis Bacon

There are more men ennobled by study than by nature.

Cicero

The understanding is more relieved by change of study than by total inactivity.

William Benton Clulow

The love of study, a passion which derives great vigor from enjoyment, supplies each day, each hour, with a perpetual round of independent and rational pleasure.

Edward Gibbon

Impatience of study is the mental disease of the present generation.

Samuel Johnson

There is no study that is not capable of delighting us after a little application to it.

Alexander Pope

The more we study the more we discover our ignorance.

Percy Bysshe Shelley

His studies were pursued but never effectually overtaken.

Herbert George Wells

See also: **Book, Education, Learning,
    Observation, Reading**

SUCCESS

If you wish success in life, make perseverance your bosom friend, experience your wise counselor, caution your elder brother, and hope your guardian genius.

Joseph Addison

The reason some men do not succeed is because their wishbone is where their backbone ought to be.

Anonymous

Not what men do worthily, but what they do successfully, is what history makes haste to record.

Henry Ward Beecher

The only infallible criterion of wisdom to vulgar judgments—success.

Edmund Burke

I believe the true road to preeminent success in any line is to make yourself master of that line.

Andrew Carnegie

Put all good eggs in one basket and then watch that basket.

Andrew Carnegie

All you need in this life is ignorance and confidence, and then Success is sure.

Samuel Langhorne Clemens (Mark Twain)

Success has a great tendency to conceal and throw a veil over the evil deeds of men.

Demosthenes

Success is counted sweetest by those who ne'er succeed.

Emily Elizabeth Dickinson

Success is the child of Audacity.

Benjamin Disraeli

Never one thing and seldom one person can make for a success. It takes a number of them merging into one perfect whole.

Marie Dressler

Nothing succeeds like success.

Alexandre Dumas (père)

Possessions, outward success, publicity, luxury—to me these have always been contemptible. I believe that a simple and unassuming manner of life is best for everyone, best both for the body and the mind.

Albert Einstein

Success is little more than a chemical compound of man with moment.

Philip Guedalla

We can do anything we want to do if we stick to it long enough.

Helen Adams Keller

The most important single ingredient in the formula of success is the knack of getting along with people.

Theodore Roosevelt

See also: **Fame, Power, Prosperity,
    Victory, Wealth**

SUFFERING

Night brings out stars, as sorrow shows us truths.

Gamaliel Bailey

God washes the eyes by tears until they can behold the invisible land where tears shall come no more.
Henry Ward Beecher

Suffering without understanding in this life is a heap worse than suffering when you have at least the grain of an idea what it's all for.
Mary Ellen Chase

The salvation of the world is in man's suffering.
William Faulkner

We need to suffer that we may learn to pity.
Letitia Elizabeth Landon

Know how sublime a thing it is to suffer and be strong.
Henry Wadsworth Longfellow

To love all mankind a cheerful state of being is required; but to see into mankind, into life, and still more into ourselves, suffering is requisite.
Jean Paul Richter

Humanity either makes, or breeds, or tolerates all its afflictions, great or small.
Herbert George Wells

See also: **Adversity, Grief, Misery, Pain**

SUPERIORITY

Almost every man you meet feels himself superior to you in some way; and a sure way to his heart is to let him realize that you recognize his importance.
Dale Carnegie

It is difficult to be convinced of one's superiority unless one can make the inferior suffer in some obvious way.
Max Radin

It is a great art to be superior to others without letting them know it.
Henry Wheeler Shaw (Josh Billings)

See also: **Excellence, Perfection**

SUPERSTITION

The master of superstition is the people, and in all superstition wise men follow fools.
Francis Bacon

Superstition is the religion of feeble minds.
Edmund Burke

Superstition is a senseless fear of God; religion the intelligent and pious worship of the deity.
Cicero

Superstitions are, for the most part, but the shadows of great truths.
Tryon Edwards

Superstition renders a man a fool, and scepticism makes him mad.
Henry Fielding

That the corruption of the best thing produces the worst, is grown into a maxim, and is commonly proved, among other instances, by the pernicious effects of superstition and enthusiasm, the corruptions of true religion.
David Hume

I think we cannot too strongly attack superstition, which is the disturber of society; nor too highly respect genuine religion, which is the support of it.
Jean Jacques Rousseau

Religion worships God, while superstition profanes that worship.
Seneca

See also: **Credulity, Fear, Ignorance**

SUSPICION

Ignorance is the mother of suspicion.
William Rounseville Alger

Suspicion is the poison of true friendship.
Augustine of Hippo

There is nothing makes a man suspect much more than to know little, and therefore men should remedy suspicion by procuring to know more, and not keep their suspicions in smother.
Francis Bacon

The less we know the more we suspect.
Henry Wheeler Shaw (Josh Billings)

There is no rule more invariable than that we are paid for our suspicions by finding what we suspect.
Henry David Thoreau

See also: **Distrust, Doubt**

SYMPATHY

Next to love, sympathy is the divinest passion of the human heart.
Edmund Burke

All sympathy not consistent with acknowledged virtue is but disguised selfishness.
Samuel Taylor Coleridge

To rejoice in another's prosperity, is to give content to your own lot; to mitigate another's grief, is to alleviate or dispel your own.
Tryon Edwards

More helpful than all wisdom or counsel is one draught of simple human pity that will not forsake us.
George Eliot (Mary Ann Evans)

Our sympathy is cold to the relation of distant misery.
Edward Gibbon

See also: **Compassion, Pity**

TACT

Tact consists in knowing how far we may go too far.
Jean Cocteau

Never join with your friend when he abuses his horse or his wife, unless the one is to be sold, and the other to be buried.
Charles Caleb Colton

Difficulties melt away under tact.
Benjamin Disraeli

A want of tact is worse than a want of virtue.
Benjamin Disraeli

See also: **Diplomacy, Discretion, Manners**

TASTE

I think I may define taste to be that faculty of the soul which discerns the beauties of an author with pleasure, and the imperfections with dislike.
Joseph Addison

Good taste is better than bad taste, but bad taste is better than no taste.
(Enoch) Arnold Bennett

Bad taste is a species of bad morals.
Christian Nestell Bovee

People care more about being thought to have taste than about being thought either good, clever, or amiable.
Samuel Butler

A truly elegant taste is generally accompanied with excellency of heart.
Henry Fielding

Taste may change, our inclinations never change.
Duc François de La Rochefoucauld

Talk what you will of taste, you will find two of a face as soon as two of a mind.
Alexander Pope

See also: **Appreciation, Artist, Judgment**

TAX

Neither will it be, that a people overlaid with taxes should ever become valiant and martial.
Francis Bacon

There is one difference between a tax collector and a taxidermist—the taxidermist leaves the hide.
Mortimer Maxwell Caplin

Taxes are the sinews of the state.
Cicero

Taxes are the price we pay for civilized society.
Oliver Wendell Holmes, Jr.

Thinking is one thing no one has ever been able to tax.
Charles Franklin Kettering

The income tax has made more liars out of the American people than gold has.
Will (William Penn Adair) Rogers

The thing generally raised on city land is taxes.
Charles Dudley Warner

See also: **Government, Money, Wealth**

TEACHER

A teacher affects eternity; he can never tell where his influence stops.
Henry Brooks Adams

The best teachers are those who make the fewest pretensions.
Mortimer Jerome Adler

I am indebted to my father for living, but to my teacher for living well.
Alexander III of Macedonia

A teacher who is not dogmatic is simply a teacher who is not teaching.
Gilbert Keith Chesterton

Educators should be chosen not merely for their special qualifications, but more for their personality and their character, because we teach more by what we are than by what we teach.
Will (William James) Durant

See also: **Education, Teaching**

TEACHING

The one exclusive sign of a thorough knowledge is the power of teaching.
Aristotle

If, in instructing a child, you are vexed with it for want of adroitness, try, if you have never tried before, to write with your left hand, and then remember that a child is all left hand.
John Frederick Boyes

A wisely chosen illustration is almost essential to fasten the truth upon the ordinary mind, and no teacher can afford to neglect this part of his preparation.
Howard Crosby

The most important method of education always has consisted of that in which the pupil was urged to actual performance.

Albert Einstein

The teacher who is attempting to teach without inspiring the pupil with a desire to learn is hammering on cold iron.

Horace Mann

Instruction in things moral is most necessary to the making of the highest type of citizenship.

Theodore Roosevelt

Everybody who is incapable of learning has taken to teaching.

Oscar Wilde

See also: *Education, Guidance, Instruction, Preaching, University*

TEMPER

Temper, if ungoverned, governs the whole man.

Anthony Ashley Cooper (Lord Shaftesbury)

Temperament is temper that is too old to spank.

Charlotte Greenwood

Good temper, like a sunny day, sheds a brightness over everything; it is the sweetener of toil and the soother of disquietude.

Washington Irving

A tart temper never mellows with age; and a sharp tongue is the only edged tool that grows keener with constant use.

Washington Irving

The happiness and misery of men depend no less on temper than fortune.

Duc François de La Rochefoucauld

A man who cannot command his temper should not think of being a man of business.

Philip Dormer Stanhope (Lord Chesterfield)

See also: *Anger, Emotion, Passion, Rage*

TEMPTATION

I see the devil's hook, and yet cannot help nibbling at his bait.

George William Bagby (Moses Adams)

Temptations without imply desires within; men ought not to say, "How powerfully the devil tempts," but "How strongly I am tempted."

Henry Ward Beecher

Temptations, when we meet them at first, are as the lion that roared upon Samson; but if we overcome them, the next time we see them we shall find a nest of honey within them.

John Bunyan

Most confidence has still most cause to doubt.

John Dryden

The last temptation is the greatest treason: To do the right deed for the wrong reason.

Thomas Stearns Eliot

THOUGHT

Learning without thought is labor lost; thought without learning is perilous.

Confucius

The rich are too indolent, the poor too weak, to bear the insupportable fatigue of thinking.

William Cowper

Nurture your mind with great thoughts; to believe in the heroic makes heroes.

Benjamin Disraeli

It is astonishing what an effort it seems to be for many people to put their brains definitely and systematically to work. They seem to insist on somebody else doing their thinking for them.

Thomas Alva Edison

Great men are they who see that spiritual is stronger than any material force—that thoughts rule the world.

Ralph Waldo Emerson

Thinking is the hardest work there is, which is the probable reason why so few engage in it.

Henry Ford

A thought is often original, though you have uttered it a hundred times. It has come to you over a new route, by a new and express train of association.

Oliver Wendell Holmes

Where all think alike, no one thinks very much.

Walter Lippmann

Living truth is that alone which has its origin in thinking. just as a tree bears year after year the same fruit and yet fruit which is each year new, so must all permanently valuable ideas be continually born again in thought.

Albert Schweitzer

Thinking is the most unhealthy thing in the world, and people die of it just as they die of any other disease. Fortunately, in England at any rate, thought is not catching.

Oscar Wilde

Thoughts that do often lie too deep for tears.

William Wordsworth

See also: **Idea, Logic, Reason, Reflection, Study**

THRIFT

Did wisely from expensive sins refrain,
And never broke the Sabbath, but for
  gain.

John Dryden

Penny saved is a penny got.

Henry Fielding

Thrift is the Philosopher's Stone.

Thomas Fuller

See also: **Bargain, Economy, Frugality**

TIME

Nothing lies on our hands with such uneasiness as time. Wretched and thoughtless creatures! In the only place where covetousness were a virtue we turn prodigals.

Joseph Addison

Time is so fleeting that if we do not remember God in our youth, age may find us incapable of thinking about him.

Hans Christian Andersen

He that will not apply new remedies must expect new evils; for time is the greatest innovator.

Francis Bacon

A man that is young in years may be old in hours, if he has lost no time.

Francis Bacon

To choose time is to save time.

Francis Bacon

The man who anticipates his century is always persecuted when living, and is always pilfered when dead.

Benjamin Disraeli

Time will teach more than all our thoughts.

Benjamin Disraeli

When you sit with a nice girl for two hours, you think it's only a minute. But when you sit on a hot stove for a minute, you think it's two hours. That's relativity.

Albert Einstein

TRADITION

Tradition is an important help to history, but its statements should be carefully scrutinized before we rely on them.

Joseph Addison

To a significant degree people express their traditions through their local organizations.

Saul David Antisky

I am well satisfied that if you let in but one little finger of tradition, you will have in the whole monster—horns and tail and all.

Thomas Arnold

What an enormous magnifier is tradition! How a thing grows in the human memory and in the human imagination, when love, worship, and all that lies in the human heart, is there to encourage it.

Thomas Carlyle

Tradition does not mean that the living are dead but that the dead are alive.

Gilbert Keith Chesterton

It takes an endless amount of history to make even a little tradition.

Henry James

See also: **Custom, Habit**

TRAGEDY

Tragedy warms the soul, elevates the heart and can and ought to create heroes. In this sense, perhaps, France owes a part of her great actions to Corneille.

Napoleon I (Bonaparte)

The tragedy is not that things are broken. The tragedy is that they are not mended again.

Alan Stewart Paton

The world is a comedy to those who think; a tragedy to those who feel.

Horace Walpole

See also: **Adversity, Literature**

TRAVEL

Men may change their climate, but they cannot change their nature. A man that goes out a fool cannot ride or sail himself into common sense.

Joseph Addison

Peregrinations charm our senses with such unspeakable and sweet variety, that some count him unhappy that never travelled—a kind of prisoner, and pity his case; that, from his cradle to his old age, he beholds the same, and still the same.

Richard Eugene Burton

Too often travel, instead of broadening the mind, merely lengthens the conversation.

Elizabeth Drew

If you travel you see people in variety. But if you stay home you see them in development.

Josef Washington Hall (Upton Close)

All travel has its advantages. If the traveller visits better countries, he may learn to improve his own; and if fortune carries him to worse, he may learn to enjoy his own.

Samuel Johnson

Usually speaking, the worst bred person in company is a young traveller just returned from abroad.

Jonathan Swift

Only that travelling is good which reveals to me the value of home, and enables me to enjoy it better.

Henry David Thoreau

See also: **Experience, Observation**

TREASON

A traitor is good fruit to hang from the boughs of the tree of liberty.

Henry Ward Beecher

There is no traitor like him whose domestic treason plants the poniard within the breast that trusted to his truth.

George Gordon Byron (Lord Byron)

Where trust is greatest, there treason is in its most horrid shape.

John Dryden

Caesar had his Brutus; Charles the First, his Cromwell; and George the Third— ["Treason!" cried the Speaker]—*may profit by their example, If this be treason, make the most of it.*

Patrick Henry

There is something peculiarly sinister and insidious in even a charge of disloyalty. Such a charge all too frequently places a stain on the reputation of an individual which is indelible and lasting, regardless of the complete innocence later proved.

John Lord O'Brian

See also: **Rebellion**

TRIFLES

There is nothing insignificant—nothing.

Samuel Taylor Coleridge

Little things affect little minds.

Benjamin Disraeli

It is in those acts which we call trivialities that the seeds of joy are forever wasted.

George Eliot (Mary Ann Evans)

The creation of a thousand forests is in one acorn.

Ralph Waldo Emerson

There is a kind of latent omniscience not only in every man, but in every particle.

Ralph Waldo Emerson

The million little things that drop into our hands, the small opportunities each day brings He leaves us free to use or abuse and goes unchanging along His silent way,

Helen Adams Keller

It is the little bits of things that fret and worry us; we can dodge an elephant, but we can't a fly.

Henry Wheeler Shaw (Josh Billings)

Small causes are sufficient to make a man uneasy when great ones are not in the way. For want of a block he will stumble at a straw.

Jonathan Swift

The power of duly appreciating little things belongs to a great mind; a narrow-minded man has it not, for to him they are great things.

Richard Whately

TRIVIA: *See* TRIFLES

TROUBLE

Never trouble trouble till trouble troubles you.

American Proverb

There are many troubles which you cannot cure by the Bible and the hymn book, but which you can cure by a good perspiration and a breath of fresh air.

Henry Ward Beecher

Adversity, if a man is set down to it by degrees, is more supportable with equanimity by most people than any great prosperity arrived at in a single lifetime.

Samuel Butler

Trouble creates a capacity to handle it.

Oliver Wendell Holmes, Jr.

There is nothing so consoling as to find that one's neighbor's troubles are at least as great as one's own.

George Moore

There are people who always anticipate trouble, and in that way they manage to enjoy many sorrows that never really happen to them.

Henry Wheeler Shaw (Josh Billings)

See also: **Adversity, Tragedy**

TRUST

A trustee is held to something stricter than the morals of the market place. Not honesty alone, but the punctilio of an honor the most sensitive, is then the standard of behavior.

Benjamin Nathan Cardozo

We must not let go manifest truths because we cannot answer all questions about them.

Jeremy Collier

The trust which we put in ourselves causes us to feel trust in others.

Duc François de La Rochefoucauld

If thou be subject to any great vanity or ill, then therein trust no man; for every man's folly ought to be his greatest secret.

Sir Walter Raleigh

How calmly may we commit ourselves to the hands of Him who bears up the world..

Jean Paul Richter

I think that we may safely trust a good deal more than we do. We may waive just so much care of ourselves as we honestly bestow elsewhere.

Henry David Thoreau

See also: **Confidence, Duty, Expectation, Faith, Hope**

TRUTH

Truth is not only violated by falsehood; it may be equally outraged by silence.
Henri Frédéric Amiel

If it is the truth what does it matter who says it.
Anonymous

There are three parts in truth: first, the inquiry, which is the wooing of it; secondly, the knowledge of it, which is the presence of it, and thirdly, the belief, which is the enjoyment of it
Francis Bacon

I am not struck so much by the diversity of testimony as by the many-sidedness of truth.
Stanley Baldwin

Some men love truth so much that they seem in continual fear lest she should catch cold on over-exposure.
Samuel Butler

It is strange but true; for truth is always strange, stranger than fiction.
George Gordon Byron (Lord Byron)

I have always found that the honest truth of our own mind has a certain attraction for every other mind that loves truth honestly.
Thomas Carlyle

Men occasionally stumble over the truth, but most of them pick themselves up and hurry off as if nothing had happened.
Sir Winston Leonard Spencer Churchill

Most writers regard truth as their most valuable possession, and therefore are most economical in its use.
Samuel Langhorne Clemens (Mark Twain)

Truth is stranger than fiction, but it is because Fiction as obliged to stick to possibilities; Truth isn't.
Samuel Langhorne Clemens(Mark Twain)

When you have eliminated the impossible, whatever remains, *however improbable*, must be the truth.
Sir Arthur Conan Doyle

If you are out to describe the truth, leave elegance to the tailor.
Albert Einstein

The greatest homage we can pay to truth is to use it.
Ralph Waldo Emerson

No truth so sublime but it may be seen to be trivial to-morrow in the light of new thoughts.
Ralph Waldo Emerson

Seven years of silent inquiry are needful for a man to learn the truth, but fourteen in order to learn how to make it known to his fellowmen.
Plato

Truth is so great a perfection, that if God would render himself visible to men, he would choose light for his body and truth for his soul.
Pythagoras

The old faiths light their candles all about, but burly Truth comes by and blows them out.
Lizette Woodworth Reese

Great men tell the truth and are never believed. Lesser men are always believed, but seldom have the brains or the courage to tell the truth.
Kenneth Roberts

The deepest truths are the simplest and the most common.
Frederick William Robertson

Most of the change we think we see in
life
Is due to truths being in and out of
favour.
Edwin Arlington Robinson

I cannot get along either with those who
shun the blunt truth or those who make
their peace with it too easily.
Jean Rostand

I should hesitate to deprive any being of
the illusion he lives by; but humanity as
a whole interests me only insofar as it
can stand up to truth.
Jean Rostand

It is after truth has been discovered that
we become aware of the simpler approach by which we might have reached
it.
Jean Rostand

One cannot bring a given set of truths to
light without obscuring others. Every
discovery covers up.
Jean Rostand

The only thing one cannot embellish
without causing its death is truth.
Jean Rostand

Truth is always served by great minds,
even if they fight it.
Jean Rostand

Philosophy should be piecemeal and
provisional like science; final truth belongs to heaven, not to this world.
Bertrand Arthur William Russell

Truth is a jewel which should not be
painted over; but it may be set to advantage and shown in a good light
George Santayana

A truth that is merely acquired from
others only clings to us as a limb added
to the body, or as a false tooth, or a wax
nose. A truth we have acquired by our
own mental exertions, is like our natural
limbs, which really belong to us. This is
exactly the difference between an original thinker and the mere learned man.
Arthur Schopenhauer

One must never, when dealing with
primitives, hold out hopes of recovery to
the patient and his relatives, if the case
is really hopeless . . . . One must tell the
truth without reservation. They wish to
know it and they can endure it, for
death is to them something natural.
They are not afraid of it but face it
calmly.
Albert Schweitzer

It is the special privilege of truth always
to grow on candid minds.
Frederick Henry Scrivener

My way of joking is to tell the truth. It's
the funniest joke in the world.
George Bernard Shaw

Men must love the truth before they
thoroughly believe it.
Robert South

Perfect truth is possible only with
knowledge, and in knowledge the whole
essence of the thing operates on the soul
and is joined essentially to it.
Baruch (Benedict) Spinoza

When a man has no design but to speak
plain truth, he may say a great deal in a
very narrow compass.
Sir Richard Steele

The most striking contradiction of our civilization is the fundamental reverence for truth which we profess and the thorough-going disregard for it which we practice.

Vilhjalmur Stefansson

But men do not seek the truth. It is truth that pursues men who run away and will not look around.

(Joseph) Lincoln Steffens

As Thales measured the pyramids from their shadows, so we may measure the height and antiquity of the truth, by the extent of its corruptions.

Edward Stillingfleet

When two truths seem directly opposed to each other, we must not question either, but remember there is a third—God—who reserves to himself the right to harmonize them.

Anne Sophie Swetchine

Some modern zealots appear to have no better knowledge of truth, nor better manner of judging it, than by counting noses.

Jonathan Swift

Fear is not in the habit of speaking truth; when perfect sincerity is expected, perfect freedom must be allowed; nor has any one who is apt to be angry when he hears the truth, any cause to wonder that he does not hear it.

Tacitus

Truth is established by investigation and delay; falsehood prospers by precipitancy.

Tacitus

To all appearances, fiction is the native dialect of mankind, and the truth an esoteric language as yet but imperfectly learned and little loved.

Carl Van Doren

He who seeks truth should be of no country.

Voltaire (François Marie Arouet)

Seize upon truth, wherever it is found, amongst your friends, amongst your foes, on Christian or on heathen ground; the flower's divine where'er it grows.

Isaac Watts

Truth is always congruous and agrees with itself; every truth in the universe agrees with all others.

Daniel Webster

Every one wishes to have truth on his side but it is not every one that sincerely wishes to be on the side of truth,

Richard Whately

There are no whole truths; all truths are half-truths. It is trying to treat them as whole truths that plays the devil.

Alfred North Whitehead

See also: **Accuracy, Ambiguity, Confession, Honesty, Integrity, Knowledge, Science**

TWILIGHT

Parting day
Dies like the dolphin, whom each pang imbues
With a new colour as it gasps away,
The last till loveliest, till—'tis gone—and all is gray.

George Gordon Byron (Lord Byron)

From that high mount of God whence
    light and shade
Spring both, the face of brightest heaven
    had changed
To grateful twilight.
                John Milton

When twilight dews are falling soft
Upon the rosy sea, love,
I watch the star, whose beam so oft
Has lighted me to thee, love.
              Thomas Moore

Twilight, ascending slowly from the
    east,
Entwined in duskier wreaths her
    braided locks
O'er the fair front and radiant eyes of
    day;
Night followed, clad with stars.
           Percy Bysshe Shelley

TYRANNY

A king ruleth as he ought; a tyrant as he
lists; a king to the profit of all, a tyrant
only to please a few.
              Aristotle

I can see why so many movements
against injustice became such absolute
tyrannies.
       Samuel Nathaniel Behrman

Every wanton and causeless restraint of
the will of the subject, whether practised
by a monarch, a nobility, or a popular
assembly, is a degree of tyranny.
        Sir William Blackstone

Free governments have committed more
flagrant acts of tyranny than the most
perfectly despotic governments we have
ever known.
           Edmund Burke

We should know by now that where
weakness and dependence are not trans-
formed into strength and self-reliance,
we can expect only chaos, and then tyranny, to follow.
       John Fitzgerald Kennedy

Where law ends, tyranny begins.
      William Pitt (Lord Chatham)

TYRANT

Degeneracy follows every autocratic
system of violence, for violence inevita-
bly attracts moral inferiors. Time has
proved that illustrious tyrants are suc-
ceeded by scoundrels.
           Albert Einstein

Of all the evils that infest a state, a tyrant is the greatest; his sole will commands the laws, and lords it over them.
           Euripides

Rebellion to tyrants is obedience to God.
        Benjamin Franklin

Necessity is the argument of tyrants; it
is the creed of slaves.
           William Pitt

Tyrants have always some slight shade
of virtue; they support the laws before
destroying them.
   Voltaire (François Marie Arouet)

UGLINESS

I cannot tell by what logic we call a toad,
a bear, or an elephant ugly; they being
created in those outward shapes and
figures which best express the actions of
their inward forms; and having passed
that general visitation of God, who saw
that all that He had made was good.
         Sir Thomas Browne

Ugliness is a point of view; an ulcer is wonderful to a pathologist.

Austin O'Malley

I doubt if there is anything in the world uglier than a midwestern city.

Frank Lloyd Wright

She is most splendidly, gallantly ugly.

William Wycherley

See also: **Beauty**

UNBELIEF

In all unbelief there are these two things: a good opinion of one's self, and a bad opinion of God.

Horatius Bonar

There is but one thing without honor, smitten with eternal barrenness, inability to do or to be, and that is unbelief. He who believes nothing, who believes only the shows of things, is not in relation with nature and fact at all.

Thomas Carlyle

Unbelief, in distinction from disbelief, is a confession of ignorance where honest inquiry might easily find that just so much light is necessary, and no more. Whatever is beyond, brings darkness and confusion.

Anthony Ashley Cooper (Lord Shaftesbury)

How deeply rooted must unbelief be in our hearts, when we are surprised to find our prayers answered, instead of feeling sure that they will be so, if they are only offered up in faith, and in accordance with the will of God!

Augustus and Julius Hare

Disbelief in futurity loosens in a great measure the ties of morality, and may be for that reason pernicious to the peace of civil society.

David Hume

Take my word for it, it is not prudent to trust yourself to any man who does not believe in a God or in a future after death.

Sir Robert Peel

I would rather dwell in the dim fog of superstition than in air rarified to nothing by the air-pump of unbelief, in which the panting breast expires, vainly and convulsively gasping for breath.

Jean Paul Richter

Charles II, hearing Vossius, a free-thinker, repeating some incredible stories of the Chinese, turned to those about him and said, "This learned divine is a very strange man; he believes everything but the Bible."

Samuel Smiles

See also: **Agnosticism, Atheism, Credulity, Distrust, Doubt, Incredulity, Skepticism**

UNDERSTANDING

It is by no means necessary to understand things to speak confidently about them.

Pierre Augustin Caron de Beaumarchais

Nine-tenths of the serious controversies which arise in life result from misunderstanding.

Louis Dembitz Brandeis

There exists a passion for comprehension, just as there exists a passion for music. Without this passion there would be neither mathematics nor rational science.

Albert Einstein

There is a great difference between knowing a thing and understanding it. You can know a lot about something and not really understand it.

Charles Franklin Kettering

Understanding is a two-way street.

Anna Eleanor Roosevelt

It is difficult to get a man to understand something when his salary depends upon his not understanding it.

Upton Sinclair

I know of no evil so great as the abuse of the understanding, and yet there is no one vice more common.

Sir Richard Steele

See also: **Intelligence, Wisdom**

UNHAPPINESS

Man's unhappiness comes of his greatness; it is because there is an infinite in him, which, with all his cunning, he cannot quite bury under the finite.

Thomas Carlyle

A perverse temper, and a discontented, fretful disposition, wherever they prevail, render any state of life unhappy.

Cicero

It is better not to be than to be unhappy.

John Dryden

The most unhappy of all men is he who believes himself to be so.

David Hume

Men who are unhappy, like men who sleep badly, are always proud of the fact.

Bertrand Arthur William Russell

See also: **Affliction, Pain, Sorrow, Suffering**

UNITED NATIONS

We are a nation of differences, and the values and principles that protect those differences are the sources of a unity far more lasting and stronger than any contrived harmony could be.

Lyndon Baines Johnson

We prefer world law, in the age of self-determination, to world war in the age of mass extermination.

John Fitzgerald Kennedy

This organization is created to prevent you from going to hell. It isn't created to take you to heaven.

Henry Cabot Lodge

The whole basis of the United Nations is the right of all nations—great or small—to have weight, to have a vote, to be attended to, to be a part of the twentieth century.

Adlai Ewing Stevenson

UNITY

Men's hearts ought not to be set against one another, but set with one another, and all against evil only.

Thomas Carlyle

What science calls the unity and uniformity of nature, truth calls the fidelity of God.

James Martineau

The number two hath by the heathen, been accounted accurst, because it was the first departure from unity.

Joseph Trapp

We were two and had but one heart between us.

François Villon

See also: **Love, Marriage, Peace**

UNIVERSITY

Today the great university in a metropolis must have a special and urgent concern for the future of the city and the future of those in our cities who lack full equality of opportunity.

McGeorge Bundy

A university should be a place of light, of liberty, and of learning.

Benjamin Disraeli

I suspect that when a university becomes very closely oriented to the current needs of government it takes on some of the atmosphere of a place of business while losing that of a place of learning.

James William Fulbright

A university . . . by its very name professes to teach universal knowledge.

John Henry Newman

The task of a university is the creation of the future, so far as rational thought and civilized modes of appreciation can affect the issue.

Alfred North Whitehead

See also: **Education, Knowledge**

VANITY

Vain-glorious men are the scorn of the wise, the admiration of fools, the idols of parasites, and the slaves of their own vaunts.

Francis Bacon

When a man has no longer any conception of excellence above his own, his voyage is done; he is dead; dead in the trespasses and sins of blear-eyed vanity.

Henry Ward Beecher

If you cannot inspire a woman with love of you, fill her above the brim with love of herself, all that runs over will be yours.

Charles Caleb Colton

Vanity plays lurid tricks with our memory.

Joseph Conrad

Feminine vanity, that divine gift which makes women charming.

Benjamin Disraeli

The vainest woman is never thoroughly conscious of her beauty till she is loved by the man who sets her own passion vibrating in return.

George Eliot (Mary Ann Evans)

Of all our infirmities, vanity is the dearest to us; a man will starve his other vices to keep that alive.

Benjamin Franklin

To be a man's own fool is bad enough, but the vain man is everybody's.

William Penn

Every man has just as much vanity as he wants understanding.

Alexander Pope

Take away from mankind their vanity and their ambition, and there would be but few claiming to be heroes or patriots.

Seneca

Vanity makes men ridiculous, pride odious, and ambition terrible.

Sir Richard Steele

The strongest passions allow us some rest, but vanity keeps us perpetually in motion. What a dust do I raise! says the fly upon a coach-wheel. And at what a rate do I drive! says the fly upon the horse's back.

Jonathan Swift

Vanity is so intimately associated with our spiritual identity that whatever hurts it, above all if it came from it, is more painful in the memory than serious sin.

William Butler Yeats

VARIETY

Variety's the very spice of life,
That gives it all its flavour.

William Cowper

Variety is the mother of enjoyment.

Benjamin Disraeli

Variety of mere nothings gives more pleasure than uniformity of something.

Jean Paul Richter

I take it to be a principal rule of life, not to be too much addicted to any one thing.

Terence

See also: *Change, Liberal, Novelty,*
Originality

VICE

The willing contemplation of vice is vice.

Arabian Proverb

Vice—that digs her own voluptuous tomb.

George Gordon Byron (Lord Byron)

The vicious obey their passions as slaves do their masters.

Diogenes

One big vice in a man is apt to keep out a great many smaller ones.

(Francis) Bret Harte

When our vices have left us we flatter ourselves that we have left them.

Duc François de La Rochefoucauld

But when to mischief mortals bend their will,
How soon they find fit instruments of ill!

Alexander Pope

Vices are contagious, and there is no trusting the well and sick together.

Seneca

VICTORY

Anybody can win, unless there happens to be a second entry.

George Ade

Victories that are easy are cheap. Those only are worth having which come as the result of hard fighting.

Henry Ward Beecher

To the victors belong the spoils.

William Learned Marcy

Who overcomes by force hath overcome but half his foe.

John Milton

Victory or Westminster Abbey.
> *Viscount Horatio Nelson*

We have met the enemy and they are ours.
> *Oliver Hazard Perry*

In victory the hero seeks the glory, not the prey.
> Sir *Philip Sidney*

I do not think that winning is the most important thing. I think winning is the only thing.
> *William (Bill) Veeck*

The smile of God is victory.
> *John Greenleaf Whittier*

See also: **Prosperity, Success, Wealth**

VIOLENCE

The nation recoils with horror over the second assassination in the Kennedy family. What an astounding commentary upon violence in the land.
> *Everett McKinley Dirksen*

I am your anointed Queen. I will never be by violence constrained to do anything. I thank God I am endued with such qualities that if I were turned out of the Realm in my petticoat I were able to live in any place in Christome.
> *Elizabeth I*

It is organized violence on top which creates individual violence at the bottom.
> *Emma Goldman*

The violence done us by others is often less painful than that which we do to ourselves.
> *Duc François de La Rochefoucauld*

Nothing good ever comes of violence.
> *Martin Luther*

See also: **Riot, War**

VIRTUE

Virtue is like a rich stone, best plain set.
> *Francis Bacon*

If you can be well without health, you may be happy without virtue.
> *Edmund Burke*

No state of virtue is complete save as it is won by a conflict with evil, and fortified by the struggles of a resolute and even bitter experience.
> *Horace Bushnell*

Virtue is not to be considered in the light of mere innocence, or abstaining from harm; but as the exertion of our faculties in doing good.
> *Joseph Butler*

Virtue knows that it is impossible to get on without compromise, and tunes herself, as it were, a trifle sharp to allow for an inevitable fall in playing.
> *Samuel Butler*

To be innocent is to be not guilty; but to be virtuous is to overcome our evil feelings and intentions.
> *William Penn*

Virtue consists, not in abstaining from vice, but in not desiring it.
> *George Bernard Shaw*

VISION

Visions of glory, spare my aching sight! Ye unborn ages, crowd not on my soul.
> *Thomas Gray*

Do I sleep? do I dream?
Do I wonder and doubt?
Are things what they seem?
Or is visions about?

(Francis) Bret Harte

Was it a vision, or a waking dream?
Fled is that music: —do I wake or sleep?

John Keats

It is a dream, sweet child! a waking
    dream,
A blissful certainty, a vision bright,
Of that rare happiness, which even on
    earth
Heaven gives to those it loves.

Henry Wadsworth Longfellow

See also: **Dream, Eye, Ideal, Imagination**

VOCATION

A good vocation is simply a firm and
constant will whereby one is called to
serve God in whatsoever manner and
place Almighty God beckons him.

Francis of Sales

The most important thing in life is the
choice of calling: it is left to chance.

Blaise Pascal

The test of a vocation is the love of the
drudgery it involves.

Logan Pearsall Smith

VOICE

The devil hath not in all his quiver's
    choice
An arrow for the heart like a sweet
    voice.

George Gordon Byron (Lord Byron)

The tones of human voices are mightier
than strings or brass to move the soul.

Friedrich Klopstock

The sweetest of all sounds is that of the
voice of the woman we love.

Jean de La Bruyère

A voice so thrilling ne'er was heard
In spring-time from the cuckoo bird,
Breaking the silence of the seas
Among the farthest Hebrides.

Henry Wadsworth Longfellow

How sweetly sounds the voice of a good
woman! When it speaks it ravishes all
senses.

Philip Massinger

There is no index of character so sure as
the voice.

Tancred

See also: **Speech**

VOTING

A vote is not an object of art. It is the sacred and most important instrument of
democracy and of freedom.

Abe Fortas

Bad officials are elected by good citizens
who do not vote.

George Jean Nathan

A straw vote only shows which way the
hot air blows.

William Sydney Porter (O. Henry)

See also: **Democracy, Politics**

VULGARITY

There are no people who are quite so
vulgar as the over-refined ones.

Samuel Langhorne Clemens (Mark Twain)

To endeavor to work upon the vulgar
with fine sense is like attempting to hew
blocks with a razor.

Alexander Pope

By vulgarity I mean that vice of civilization which makes man ashamed of himself and his next of kin, and pretend to be somebody else.

Solomon Schechter

Vulgarity is more obvious in satin than in homespun.

Nathaniel Parker Willis

See also: **Mob**

WANT

If any one say that he has seen a just man in want of bread, I answer that it was in some place where there was no other just man.

Clement I (Clemens Romanus)

It is not from nature, but from education and habits, that our wants are chiefly derived.

Henry Fielding

To men pressed by their wants all change is ever welcome.

Ben (Benjamin) Jonson

The fewer our wants, the nearer we resemble the gods.

Socrates

The stoical scheme of supplying our wants by lopping off our desires, is like cutting off our feet when we want shoes.

Jonathan Swift

Choose rather to want less, than to have more.

Thomas à Kempis

See also: **Adversity, Desire, Necessity, Poverty, Wish**

WAR

War is the science of destruction.

John Stevens Cabot Abbott

No one can guarantee success in war, but only deserve it.

Sir Winston Leonard Spencer Churchill

This [victory in Egypt] is not the end. It is not even the beginning of the end. But it is, perhaps, the end of the beginning.

Sir Winston Leonard Spencer Churchill

War is the desperate, vital problem of our time.

Thomas Alva Edison

The bomb has been made more effective .... Unless another war is prevented it is likely to bring destruction on a scale never before held possible and even now hardly conceived, and ... little civilization would survive it.

Albert Einstein

The man who enjoys marching in line and file to the strains of music falls below my contempt; he received his great brain by mistake—the spinal cord would have been amply sufficient.

Albert Einstein

As never before, the essence of war is fire, famine and pestilence. They contribute to its outbreak; they are among its weapons; they become its consequences.

Dwight David Eisenhower

When people speak to you about a preventive war, you tell them to go and fight it. After my experience, I have come to hate war. War settles nothing.

Dwight David Eisenhower

There never was a good war, or a bad peace.

Benjamin Franklin

When wars do come, they fall upon the many, the producing class, who are the sufferers.

Ulysses Simpson Grant

Never think that war, no matter how necessary, nor how justified, is not a crime. Ask the infantry and ask the dead.

Ernest Hemingway

Older men declare war. But it is youth that must fight and die. And it is youth who must inherit the tribulation, the sorrow, and the triumphs that are the aftermath of war.

Herbert Clark Hoover

War is an instrument entirely inefficient toward redressing wrong; and multiplies, instead of indemnifying losses.

Thomas Jefferson

Mankind must put an end to war or war will put an end to mankind.

John Fitzgerald Kennedy

War, which society draws upon itself, is but organized barbarism, an inheritance of the savage state, however disguised or ornamented.

Napoleon III (Louis Napoleon)

There is only one virtue, pugnacity; only one vice, pacifism. That is an essential condition of war.

George Bernard Shaw

They made a speech, and played a trumpet and dressed me in a uniform and then they killed me.

Irwin Shaw

Heroic men can die upon the battlefield in vain, because of what occurs after a war, as well as because of what happens during a war.

Harold Edward Stassen

The human race is a family. Men are brothers. All wars are civil wars. All killing is fratricidal—as the poet Owen put it, "I am the enemy you killed, my friend."

Adlai Ewing Stevenson

The difficulty about arguing is that when you get before an audience everybody is in favor of peace . . . . But when it comes to an election the issue as to international peace does not play any part at all.

William Howard Taft

To be prepared for war is one of the most effectual ways of preserving peace.

George Washington

The imponderables and the unforeseen cannot be ignored in formulating foreign policy. That is why a preventive war should always be regarded as an act of criminal folly.

Sumner Welles

Militarism and warfare are childish things, if they are not more horrible than anything childish can be. They must become things of the past.

Herbert George Wells

As long as war is regarded as wicked it will always have its fascinations. When it is looked upon as vulgar, it will cease to be popular.

Oscar Wilde

WATER

Water, taken in moderation, cannot hurt anybody.

Samuel Langhorne Clemens (Mark Twain)

Deep waters noiseless are; and this
know,
That chiding streams betray small depth
below.

Robert Herrick

Water is the only drink for a wise man.
Henry David Thoreau

See also: **Nature, Water Pollution**

WATER POLLUTION

Among these treasures of our land is
water—fast becoming our most valuable, most prized, most critical resource.
A blessing where properly used—but it
can bring devastation and ruin when left
uncontrolled.

Dwight David Eisenhower

It should be clear by now that we are in
a race with disaster. Either the world's
water needs will be met, or the inevitable result will be mass starvation, mass
epidemic and mass poverty greater than
anything we know today.

Lyndon Baines Johnson

We in Government have begun to recognize the critical work which must be
done at all levels—Local, State and Federal—in ending the pollution of our
waters.

Robert Francis Kennedy

See also: **Health, Water**

WEAKNESS

The weakest soul, within itself unblest,
Leans for all pleasure on another's
breast.

Oliver Goldsmith

In all our weaknesses we have one element of strength if we recognize it.
Here, as in other things, knowledge of
danger is often the best means of safety.

Edward Payson Roe

Men are in general so tricky, so envious,
and so cruel, that when we find one who
is only weak, we are happy.

Voltaire (François Marie Arouet)

We all have weaknesses. But I have fig-
ured that others have put up with mine
so tolerably that I would be much less
than fair not to make a reasonable discount for theirs.

William Allen White

See also: **Cowardice**

WEALTH

The wealth of man is the number of
things which he loves and blesses,
which he is loved and blessed by.

Thomas Carlyle

Surplus wealth is a sacred trust which
its possessor is bound to administer in
his lifetime for the good of the community.

Andrew Carnegie

The real wealth, not only of America,
but of the world, is in the resources of
the ground we stand on, and in the resources of the human mind.

Norman Cousins

The concentration of wealth is made inevitable by the natural inequality of
men.

Will (William James) Durant

It is no longer a distinction to be rich .... People do not care for money as they once did .... What we accumulate by way of useless surplus does us no honor.

Henry Ford

Wealth is not his that has it, but his that enjoys it.

Benjamin Franklin

When I caution you against becoming a miser, I do not therefore advise you to become a prodigal or a spendthrift.

Horace

Excess of wealth is cause of covetousness.

Christopher Marlowe

He is richest who is content with the least, for content is the wealth of nature.

Socrates

See also: **Money, Success**

WICKEDNESS

There is a method in man's wickedness; it grows up by degrees.

Francis Beaumont and John Fletcher

There is wickedness in the intention of wickedness, even though it be not perpetrated in the act.

Cicero

To see and listen to the wicked is already the beginning of wickedness.

Confucius

The happiness of the wicked passes away like a torrent.

Jean Baptiste Racine

It is a statistical fact that the wicked work harder to reach hell than the righteous do to enter heaven.

Henry Wheeler Shaw (Josh Billings)

The sure way to wickedness is always through wickedness.

Seneca

See also: **Crime, Dishonesty, Fraud, Sin, Vice, Wrong**

WIFE

Wives are young men's mistresses, companions for middle age, and old men's nurses.

Francis Bacon

The graveyards are full of women whose houses were so spotless you could eat off the floor. Remember the second wife always has a maid.

Heloise Cruse

Here lies my wife; here let her lie! Now she's at rest, and so am I.

John Dryden

There is one thing more exasperating than a wife who can cook and won't, and that's the wife who can't cook and will.

Robert Lee Frost

For a wife take the daughter of a good mother.

Thomas Fuller

I chose my wife, as she did her wedding-gown, for qualities that would wear well.

Oliver Goldsmith

Heaven will not be heaven to me if I do not meet my wife there.

Andrew Jackson

The sum of all that makes a just man happy consists in the well choosing of his wife.

Philip Massinger

A good wife is like the ivy which beautifies the building to which it clings, twining its tendrils more lovingly as time converts the ancient edifice into a ruin.

Samuel Johnson

Teacher, tender comrade, wife,
A fellow-farer true through life.

Robert Louis Stevenson

An ideal wife is any woman who has an ideal husband.

Booth Tarkington

See also: **Love, Marriage, Mother, Woman**

WILL

Then . . . is our will truly free, when it serves neither vice nor sin.

Augustine of Hippo

Great souls have wills; feeble ones have only wishes.

Chinese Proverb

The general of a large army may be defeated, but you cannot defeat the determined mind of a peasant.

Confucius

If we make God's will our law, then God's promise shall be our support and comfort, and we shall find every burden light, every duty a joy.

Tryon Edwards

There is nothing good or evil save in the will.

Epictetus

To deny the freedom of the will is to make morality impossible.

James Anthony Froude

It is the will that makes the action good or bad.

Robert Herrick

People do not lack strength; they lack will.

Victor Marie Hugo

Will is character in action.

William McDougall

No action will be considered blameless, unless the will was so, for by the will the act was dictated.

Seneca

See also: **Aim, Enthusiasm, Firmness, Purpose, Resolution, Wish**

WISDOM

When a man is made up wholly of the dove, without the least grain of the serpent in his composition, he becomes ridiculous in many circumstances of life, and very often discredits his best actions.

Joseph Addison

It is better to speak wisdom foolishly like the saints than to speak folly wisely like the deans.

Gilbert Keith Chesterton

Common-sense in an uncommon degree is what the world calls wisdom.

Samuel Taylor Coleridge

Among mortals second thoughts are wisest.

Euripides

Some are weather-wise, some are otherwise.

Benjamin Franklin

The wise man is he who knows the relative value of things.

William Ralph Inge

The art of being wise is the art of knowing what to overlook.

William James

Very few men are wise by their own counsel, or learned by their own teaching; for he that was only taught by himself had a fool to his master.

Ben (Benjamin) Jonson

Our wisdom is not less at the mercy of fortune than our goods.

Duc François de La Rochefoucauld

To know that which before us lies in daily life is the prime wisdom.

John Milton

Speed is good when wisdom leads the way.

Edward Roscoe Murrow

What is it to be wise? 'Tis but to know how little can be known—to see all other's faults and feel our own.

Alexander Pope

Nine-tenths of wisdom consists in being wise in time.

Theodore Roosevelt

Life is full of perils, but the wise man ignores those that are inevitable.

Bertrand Arthur William Russell

The Delphic oracle said I was the wisest of all the Greeks. It is because that I alone, of all the Greeks, know that I know nothing.

Socrates

The dog has seldom been successful in pulling Man up to its level of sagacity, but Man has frequently dragged the dog down to his.

James Grover Thurber

Wisdom is ofttimes nearer when we stoop than when we soar.

William Wordsworth

See also: *Common Sense, Intelligence, Judgment, Knowledge, Learning, Prudence, Understanding, Wit*

WISH

Every wish is like a prayer with God.

Elizabeth Barrett Browning

A man will sometimes devote all his life to the development of one part of his body—the wishbone.

Robert Lee Frost

Happy the man who early learns the wide chasm that lies between his wishes and his powers!

Johann Wolfgang von Goethe

If wishes were horses beggars might ride.

English Proverb

Many of us spend half our time wishing for things we could have if we didn't spend half our time wishing.

Alexander Woollcott

See also: *Ambition, Desire, Hope, Want, Will*

WIT

Wit should be used as a shield for defence rather than as a sword to wound others.

Thomas Fuller

Wit is a form of lightning calculation; humour the exploitation of disproportion.

Russell Green

Wit is the salt of conversation, not the food.

William Hazlitt

He who has provoked the shaft of wit, cannot complain that he smarts from it.

Samuel Johnson

A man of wit would often be at a loss were it not for the company of fools.

Duc François de La Rochefoucauld

Impropriety is the soul of wit.

(William) Somerset Maugham

The impromptu reply is precisely the touchstone of the man of wit.

Molière (Jean Baptiste Poquelin)

Wit is the only wall
Between us and the dark.

Mark Van Doren

See also: **Humor, Jesting, Levity,
Ridicule, Sarcasm, Wisdom**

WOMAN

Find a man anywhere who has saved any considerable amount of money and he is likely to tell you that some woman made him do it.

James Randolph Adams

There is nothing enduring in life for a woman except what she builds in a man's heart.

Dame Judith Anderson

The errors of women spring, almost always, from their faith in the good, or their confidence in the true.

Honoré de Balzac

The way to fight a woman is with your hat. Grab it and run.

John Barrymore

A Frenchwoman, when double-crossed, will kill her rival; the Italian woman would rather kill her deceitful lover; the Englishwoman simply breaks off relations—but they all will console themselves with another man.

Charles Boyer

Alas! the love of women! it is known To be a lovely and a fearful thing!

George Gordon Byron (Lord Byron)

A female friend, amiable, clever, and devoted, is a possession more valuable than parks and palaces; and without such a muse, few men can succeed in life, none can be content.

Benjamin Disraeli

Woman's honor is nice as ermine, will not bear a soil

John Dryden

The emancipation of women, despite the biological problems which it entails, indicates a certain growing gentility in the once-murderous male.

Will (William James) Durant

A woman's lot is made for her by the love she accepts.

George Eliot (Mary Ann Evans)

There is no reason why we should not some day have a female chief of staff or even a commander in chief.

Lyndon Baines Johnson

A woman's guess is much more accurate than a man's certainty.

Rudyard Kipling

The thing needed . . . to raise women (and to raise men too) is these friendships without love between men and women. And if between married men and married women, all the better.

Florence Nightingale

A beautiful young lady is an accident of nature. A beautiful old lady is a work of art.

Louis Nizer

There is no such thing as romance in our day, women have become too brilliant; nothing spoils a romance so much as a sense of humor in the woman

Oscar Wilde

See also: **Laughter, Wife**

WONDER

It was through the feeling of wonder that men now and at first began to philosophize.

Aristotle

The man who cannot wonder, who does not habitually wonder and worship, is but a pair of spectacles behind which there is no eye.

Thomas Carlyle

He who can no longer pause to wonder and stand rapt in awe, is as good as dead; his eyes are closed.

Albert Einstein

All wonder is the effect of novelty on ignorance.

Samuel Johnson

As knowledge increases, wonder deepens.

Charles Morgan

See also: **Curiosity, Mystery**

WORD

Words are merely the vehicle on which thoughts ride; and when the vehicle creaks too loudly in the wheels it distracts attention from the cargo.

James Randolph Adams

Men suppose their reason has command over their words; still it happens that words in return exercise authority on reason.

Francis Bacon

Words are the clothes that thoughts wear—only the clothes.

Samuel Butler

Eating words has never given me indigestion.

Sir Winston Leonard Spencer Churchill

Short words are best and the old words when short are best of all.

Sir Winston Leonard Spencer Churchill

The difference between the right word and the almost right word is the difference between lightning and the lightning bug.

Samuel Langhorne Clemens (Mark Twain)

With words we govern men.

Benjamin Disraeli

Although words exist for the most part for the transmission of ideas, there are some which produce such violent disturbance in our feelings that the role they play in transmission of ideas is lost in the background.

Albert Einstein

No man has a prosperity so high or firm, but that two or three words can dishearten it; and there is no calamity which right words will not begin to redress.

Ralph Waldo Emerson

Words are like leaves; and where they
    most abound,
Much fruit of sense beneath is rarely
    found.

Alexander Pope

Such as your words are, such will your affections be esteemed; and such will your deeds be as your affections; and such your life as your deeds.

Socrates

See also: **Language, Loquacity, Name, Speech, Writing**

WORK

Nothing is really work unless you would rather be doing something else.
Sir James Matthew Barrie

Find your place and hold it: find your work and do it. And put everything you've got into it.
Edward William Bok

If you do your work with complete faithfulness, . . . you are making as genuine a contribution to the substance of the universal good as is the most brilliant worker whom the world contains.
Phillips Brooks

We have too many people who live without working, and we have altogether too many who work without living.
Charles Reynolds Brown

Blessed is the man that has found his work. One monster there is in the world, the idle man.
Thomas Carlyle

Concentration is my motto—first honesty, then industry, then concentration.
Andrew Carnegie

As a cure for worrying, work is better than whiskey.
Thomas Alva Edison

I never did anything worth doing by accident, nor did any of my inventions come by accident.
Thomas Alva Edison

He who would really benefit mankind must reach them through their work.
Henry Ford

I don't pity any man who does hard work worth doing. I admire him. I pity the creature who doesn't work, at whichever end of the social scale he may regard himself as being.
Theodore Roosevelt

A man can be freed from the necessity of work only by the fact that he or his fathers before him have worked to a good purpose.
Theodore Roosevelt

A day's work is a day's work, neither more nor less, and the man who does it needs a day's sustenance, a night's repose, and due leisure, whether he be painter or plough-man.
George Bernard Shaw

A man should inure himself to voluntary labor, and not give up to indulgence and pleasure, as they beget no good constitution of body nor knowledge of mind.
Socrates

See also: **Business, Capitalism, Diligence, Effort, Employment, Labor, Perseverance**

WORLD

The world is God's workshop for making men.
Henry Ward Beecher

The world will, in the end, follow only those who have despised as well as served it.

Samuel Butler

There are many that despise half the world; but if there be any that despise the whole of it, it is because the other half despises them.

Charles Caleb Colton

What is meant by a "knowledge of the world" is simply an acquaintance with the infirmities of men.

Charles John Huffam Dickens

"The world," is a conventional phrase, which being interpreted, signifies all the rascality in it.

Charles John Huffam Dickens

All the world's ends, arrangements, changes, disappointments, hopes, and fears, are without meaning, if not seen and estimated by eternity!

Tryon Edwards

This is the way the world ends
Not with a bang but with a whimper.

Thomas Stearns Eliot

I would rather live in a world where my life is surrounded by mystery than live in a world so small that my mind could comprehend it.

Harry Emerson Fosdick

We all, whether we know it or not, are fighting to make the kind of a world that we should like.

Oliver Wendell Holmes Jr.

He who imagines he can do without the world deceives himself much; but he who fancies the world cannot do without him is still more mistaken.

Duc François de La Rochefoucauld

See also: **Earth, Life, Man, Nature, Society**

WORRY

Don't tell me that worry doesn't do any good. I know better. The things I worry about don't happen.

Anonymous

There are two days about which nobody should ever worry, and these are yesterday and tomorrow.

Robert Jones Burdette

Anxiety destroys our figure.

Benjamin Disraeli

Care is a god, invisible but omnipotent. It steals the bloom from the cheek and lightness from the pulse; it takes away the appetite, and turns the hair grey.

Benjamin Disraeli

It's a funny thing that when a man hasn't got anything on earth to worry about, he goes off and gets married.

Robert Lee Frost

The reason why worry kills more people than work is that more people worry than work.

Robert Lee Frost

It is better to try to bear the ills we have, than anticipate those which may befall us.

Duc François de La Rochefoucauld

Worry is a thin stream of fear trickling through the mind. If encouraged, it cuts a channel into which all other thoughts are drained.

Arthur Somers Roche

See also: **Anxiety, Fear Trouble**

WORSHIP

What greater calamity can fall upon a nation than the loss of worship.

Thomas Carlyle

Ritual will always mean throwing away something; destroying our corn or wine upon the altar of our gods.

Gilbert Keith Chesterton

We should worship as though the Deity were present. If my mind is not engaged in my worship, it is as though I worshipped not.

Confucius

It is only when men begin to worship that they begin to grow.

(John) Calvin Coolidge

See also: **Christianity, Church, Esteem, Praise, Prayer, Religion**

WORTH

I am not sure that God always knows who are His great men; He is so very careless of what happens to them while they live.

Mary Hunter Austin

For anything worth having one must pay the price; and the price is always work, patience, love, self-sacrifice.

John Burroughs

Worth begets in base minds, envy; in great souls, emulation.

Henry Fielding

Where quality is the thing sought after, the thing of supreme quality is cheap, whatever the price one has to pay for it.

William James

One of the most important truths in the world is that there is worth enough in any rascal to cost the spilling of the Precious Blood.

Austin O'Malley

See also: **Excellence, Expense, Merit, Perfection, Virtue**

WRITING

My task which I am trying to achieve is, by the power of the written word, to make you hear, to make you feel—it is, before all, to make you *see*. That, and no more, and it is everything.

Joseph Conrad

You don't write because you want to say something; you write because you've got something to say.

Francis Scott Key Fitzgerald

A writer's problem does not change. He himself changes and the world he lives in changes but his problem remains the same. It is always how to write truly and, having found what is true, to project it in such a way that it becomes a part of the experience of the person who reads it.

Ernest Hemingway

Everything which I have created as a poet has had its origin in a frame of mind and a situation in life; I never wrote because I had, as they say, found a good subject.

Henrik Ibsen

Welcome, O life! I go to encounter for the millionth time the reality of experience and to forge in the smithy of my soul the uncreated conscience of my race.

James Joyce

In Hollywood the woods are full of people, that learned to write, but evidently can't read. If they could read their stuff, they'd stop writing.

Will (William Penn Adair) Rogers

See also: *Ballad, Book, Fable, History, Journalism, Literature, Poetry, Romance, Tragedy, Word*

WRONG

The essence of immorality is the tendency to make an exception of one's self.

Jane Addams

It is better to suffer wrong than to do it, and happier to be sometimes cheated than not to trust.

Samuel Johnson

A man should never be ashamed to own he has been in the wrong, which is but saying in other words that he is wiser to-day than he was yesterday.

Alexander Pope

See also: *Crime, Cruelty, Dishonesty, Error, Evil, Fraud, Injustice, Sin, Vice, Wickedness*

YESTERDAY

There are two days in the week about which and upon which I never worry. Two carefree days, kept sacredly free from fear and apprehension. One of these days is Yesterday .... And the other ... is Tomorrow.

Robert Jones Burdette

But where are the snows of yesteryear?

François Villon

Whose yesterdays look backward with a smile.

Edward Young

See also: *Antiquity, Future, Past, Present*

YOUTH

Young men are fitter to invent than to judge, fitter for execution than for counsel, and fitter for new projects than for settled business.

Francis Bacon

Frustrations and denials which seem to youth cruel and unfair often are important equipment for life.

Bruce Barton

Youth is to all the glad season of life, but often only by what it hopes, not by what it attains or escapes.

Thomas Carlyle

It is a truth but too well known, that rashness attends youth, as prudence does old age.

Cicero

Almost everything that is great has been done by youth.

Benjamin Disraeli

Over the trackless past, somewhere, lie the lost days of our tropic youth.

(Francis) Bret Harte

It is not possible for civilization to flow backwards while there is youth in the world.

Helen Adams Keller

Youth has steadily gained on the enemy ... through it alone shall salvation come.

Helen Adams Keller

Youth had been a habit of hers so long that she could not part with it.

Rudyard Kipling

Youth, when thought is speech and speech is truth.

Sir Walter Scott

Youth is a wonderful thing; what a crime to waste it on children.

George Bernard Shaw

In youth we run into difficulties, in old age difficulties run into us.

Henry Wheeler Shaw (Josh Billings)

For God's sake give me the young man who has brains enough to make a fool of himself.

Robert Louis Balfour Stevenson

See also: Age, Ambition, Energy, Hope,
Ideal, Innocence, Love, Romance

ZEAL

Whether zeal or moderation be the point we aim at, let us keep fire out of the one, and frost out of the other.

Joseph Addison

Nothing hath wrought more prejudice to religion, or brought more disparagement upon truth, than boisterous and unseasonable zeal.

Washington Barrow

When we see an eager assailant of wrongs, a special reformer, we feel like asking him, What right have you, sir, to your one virtue? Is virtue piecemeal?

Ralph Waldo Emerson

Zealots have an idol, to which they consecrate themselves high-priests, and deem it holy work to offer sacrifices of whatever is most precious.

Nathaniel Hawthorne

Zeal without knowledge is like expedition to a man in the dark.

John Newton

To be furious in religion is to be irreligiously religious.

William Penn

For virtue's self may too much zeal be had;
The worst of madness is a saint run mad.

Alexander Pope

Zeal for the public good is the characteristic of a man of honor and a gentleman, and must take place of pleasures, profits, and all other private gratifications. Whoever wants this motive, is an open enemy, or an inglorious neuter to mankind, in proportion to the misapplied advantages with which nature and fortune have blessed him.

Sir Richard Steele

Violent zeal even for truth has a hundred to one odds to be either petulancy, ambition, or pride.

Jonathan Swift

All true zeal for God is a zeal also for love, mercy, and goodness.

Robert Ellis Thompson

See also: Ambition, Enthusiasm,
Fanaticism, Intolerance,
Prejudice

SUBJECT INDEX

Subject Index

Subject Index

Subject Index

Subject Index

Subject Index